CURRENT ISSUES AND TRENDS IN SPECIAL EDUCATION: RESEARCH, TECHNOLOGY, AND TEACHER PREPARATION

ADVANCES IN SPECIAL EDUCATION

Series Editor: Anthony F. Rotatori

Recent Volumes:

Volume 11: Issues, Practices and Concerns in Special Education – Edited by Anthony F. Rotatori, John O. Schwenn and Sandra Burkhardt

Volume 12: Multicultural Education for Learners with Exceptionalities – Edited by Festus E. Obiakor, John O. Schwenn and Anthony F. Rotatori

Volume 13: Intervention Techniques for Individuals with Exceptionalities in Inclusive Settings – Edited by Festus E. Obiakor, Sandra Burkhardt, Anthony F. Rotatori and Tim Wahlberg

Volume 14: Autistic Spectrum Disorders: Educational and Clinical Interventions – Edited by Tim Wahlberg, Festus E. Obiakor, Sandra Burkhardt and Anthony F. Rotatori

Volume 15: Effective Education for Learners with Exceptionalities – Edited by Anthony F. Rotatori, Festus E. Obiakor and Cheryl A. Utley

Volume 16: Current Perspectives on Learning Disabilities – Edited by Sandra Burkhardt, Festus E. Obiakor and Anthony F. Rotatori

Volume 17: Current Perspectives in Special Education Administration – Edited by Festus E. Obiakor, Anthony F. Rotatori and Sandra Burkhardt

Volume 18: Autism and Developmental Disabilities: Current Practices and Issues – Edited by Anthony F. Rotatori, Festus E. Obiakor and Sandra Burkhardt

Volume 19: Current Issues and Trends in Special Education: Identification, Assessment and Instruction – Edited by Festus E. Obiakor, Jeffrey P. Bakken and Anthony F. Rotatori

ADVANCES IN SPECIAL EDUCATION VOLUME 20

CURRENT ISSUES AND TRENDS IN SPECIAL EDUCATION: RESEARCH, TECHNOLOGY, AND TEACHER PREPARATION

EDITED BY

FESTUS E. OBIAKOR
University of Wisconsin-Milwaukee, Milwaukee, WI, USA

JEFFREY P. BAKKEN
Illinois State University, Normal, IL, USA

ANTHONY F. ROTATORI
Saint Xavier University, Chicago, IL, USA

United Kingdom – North America – Japan
India – Malaysia – China

Emerald Group Publishing Limited
Howard House, Wagon Lane, Bingley BD16 1WA, UK

First edition 2010

Copyright © 2010 Emerald Group Publishing Limited

Reprints and permission service
Contact: booksandseries@emeraldinsight.com

No part of this book may be reproduced, stored in a retrieval system, transmitted in any form or by any means electronic, mechanical, photocopying, recording or otherwise without either the prior written permission of the publisher or a license permitting restricted copying issued in the UK by The Copyright Licensing Agency and in the USA by The Copyright Clearance Center. No responsibility is accepted for the accuracy of information contained in the text, illustrations or advertisements. The opinions expressed in these chapters are not necessarily those of the Editor or the publisher.

British Library Cataloguing in Publication Data
A catalogue record for this book is available from the British Library

ISBN: 978-1-84950-954-1
ISSN: 0270-4013 (Series)

Awarded in recognition of
Emerald's production
department's adherence to
quality systems and processes
when preparing scholarly
journals for print

INVESTOR IN PEOPLE

CONTENTS

LIST OF CONTRIBUTORS — ix

PREFACE — xi

PART I: RESEARCH IN EDUCATION

CHAPTER 1   QUANTITATIVE RESEARCH IN EDUCATION: IMPACT ON EVIDENCE-BASED INSTRUCTION
Frederick J. Brigham — 3

CHAPTER 2   QUALITATIVE RESEARCH IN EDUCATION: OTHER METHODS OF SEEKING KNOWLEDGE
Julia B. Stoner — 19

PART II: LANGUAGE, COMMUNICATION, AND EDUCATION

CHAPTER 3   BILINGUALISM AND EDUCATION: EDUCATING AT-RISK LEARNERS
Fabiola P. Ehlers-Zavala — 43

CHAPTER 4   MASTERING ENGLISH TO ENHANCE EDUCATION
Dike Okoro — 59

PART III: TECHNOLOGY AND STUDENTS WITH DISABILITIES

CHAPTER 5   USING ASSISTIVE TECHNOLOGY TO SUPPORT THE INSTRUCTIONAL PROCESS OF STUDENTS WITH DISABILITIES
Howard P. Parette, Jr. and George R. Peterson-Karlan   *73*

CHAPTER 6   TECHNOLOGY AND STUDENTS WITH DISABILITIES: DOES IT SOLVE ALL THE PROBLEMS
Emily C. Bouck   *91*

PART IV: MULTICULTURAL EDUCATION

CHAPTER 7   MULTICULTURAL EDUCATION: A NECESSARY TOOL FOR GENERAL AND SPECIAL EDUCATION
Satasha L. Green   *107*

CHAPTER 8   MULTICULTURAL EDUCATION: NOT A GENERAL AND SPECIAL EDUCATION PANACEA
Festus E. Obiakor   *123*

PART V: TRANSITION

CHAPTER 9   TRANSITION PLANNING, PREPARATION, AND IMPLEMENTATION: COLLABORATION AND CONSULTATION AT WORK
Kagendo Mutua and James Siders   *145*

CHAPTER 10   TRANSITION: WHY IT DOES NOT WORK
Michelle J. McCollin and Festus E. Obiakor   *163*

PART VI: HOW PREPARED ARE TEACHERS?

CHAPTER 11   INCREASING PROFESSIONALISM
THROUGH TEACHER PREPARATION
Elizabeth Drame   *177*

CHAPTER 12   TEACHING IS NOT A PROFESSION:
HOW GENERAL AND SPECIAL EDUCATION
TEACHER EDUCATION HAVE FAILED
Barbara J. Dray and Cathy Newman Thomas   *187*

LIST OF CONTRIBUTORS

Emily C. Bouck	Department of Educational Studies, Purdue University, West Lafayette, IN, USA
Frederick J. Brigham	Department of Human Development, George Mason University, Fairfax, VA, USA
Elizabeth Drame	Department of Exceptional Education, University of Wisconsin–Milwaukee, Milwaukee, WI, USA
Barbara J. Dray	Department of Education and Human Development, University of Colorado Denver, Denver, CO, USA
Fabiola P. Ehlers-Zavala	Department of English, Colorado State University, Fort Collins, CO, USA
Satasha L. Green	Exceptional Education Department State University of New York College at Buffalo, Buffalo, NY, USA
Michelle J. McCollin	Department of Special Education, Slippery Rock University, Slippery Rock, PA, USA
Kagendo Mutua	Department of Special Education and Multiple Abilities, University of Alabama, Tuscaloosa, AL, USA
Festus E. Obiakor	Department of Exceptional Education, University of Wisconsin–Milwaukee, Milwaukee, WI, USA
Dike Okoro	Department of English/World Literature, Olive Harvey College, Chicago, IL, USA

Howard P. Parette, Jr.	Department of Special Education, Illinois State University, Normal, IL, USA
George R. Peterson-Karlan	Department of Special Education, Illinois State University, Normal, IL, USA
James Siders	Department of Special Education and Multiple Abilities, University of Alabama, Tuscaloosa, AL, USA
Julia B. Stoner	Department of Special Education, Illinois State University, Normal, IL, USA
Cathy Newman Thomas	Department of Special Education, University of Missouri, Columbia, MO, USA

PREFACE

Current Issues and Trends in Special Education is divided into two volumes, namely, *Volume 19: Identification, Assessment and Instruction* and *Volume 20: Research, Technology, and Teacher Preparation*. The field of special education constantly changes as a result of legislation, new instructional formats and current research investigations. It can be difficult for general and special educators, school counselors and psychologists, administrators, and practicing clinicians to keep up with these changes and be current in all areas relating to special education. The special education literature knowledge base should reflect these changes; however, there is no current resource that effectively and comprehensively does this. The purpose of *Current Issues and Trends in Special Education* is to fulfill this void.

Volumes 19 and 20 address the top issues and trends in special education by providing chapters written by active researchers and practitioners in their respective areas. Volume 19 first delineates traditional topics such as identification, assessment, and labeling by reviewing historical aspects and then discussing current concerns. Then this volume addresses newer innovations and issues related to placement and inclusion, scientifically supported and unsupported interventions, instructional methods such as response to intervention and positive behavioral supports, and programming students with challenging conditions such as attention-deficit hyperactivity and autism spectrum disorders. Volume 20 addresses issues that impact all teachers, such as preparation of teachers; multicultural considerations for instruction; the use of assistive technology with special needs students; transition planning, preparation, and implementation; language, communication, and education; and quantitative and qualitative research endeavors.

The layout of *Current Issues and Trends in Special Education* follows the special education process, namely, identification, placement, instruction, and transitional programming. This process allows readers to progress through the chapters in a sequential manner that builds and enhances their knowledge base. Volumes 19 and 20 provide the reader with a comprehensive resource for general and special educators. As such, individual chapters from each volume can be read separately in any order as each chapter has the breath and depth to stand on its own.

Festus E. Obiakor
Jeffrey P. Bakken
Anthony F. Rotatori
Editors

PART I
RESEARCH IN EDUCATION

CHAPTER 1

QUANTITATIVE RESEARCH IN EDUCATION: IMPACT ON EVIDENCE-BASED INSTRUCTION

Frederick J. Brigham

Quantitative research techniques are very well suited to the specific purposes for which they were developed. The development of quantitative research techniques and tools of analysis has encouraged the expression of the kinds of questions that yield to the logic of counting and measuring, the core of quantitative research, rather than logic of describing and searching for meaning, and the core of qualitative research (admittedly oversimplifications of each research tradition). It is clear, however, that current calls for increased rigor in educational research such as is found in the *No Child Left Behind Act of 2001* (NCLB, 2008) clearly point toward models derived from biological, medical, and physical sciences (Kelly, 2006). The models used in biological, medical, and physical sciences are predominantly quantitative. Although this chapter addresses the impact of quantitative research on evidence-based practice (EBP), it makes no suppositions that this form of inquiry is in any absolute sense superior to others.

This chapter traces the impact of quantitative research ideas on EBP. It briefly outlines the basic assumptions of quantitative research and the kind of questions that it serves best to answer. In addition, a summary definition of what is meant by EBP and its development in the field of special education as well as in related fields, primarily in the area of medicine, is delineated. This delineation is followed by an examination of the way that thinking in quantitative research reflects current ideas about EBP. The chapter concludes with a discussion of responsible practice in the absence of complete and certain knowledge.

QUANTITATIVE RESEARCH

Group and Single-Subject Approaches

Quantitative research is based on epistemic beliefs that can be traced back to David Hume. Hume and others who followed in his wake suggested that we can never directly observe cause and effect. Rather we perceive what is called "constant conjunction" or the regularities of relationships among events. Through observing these regularities, we can develop generalizable laws that, once established, describe predictable patterns that can be replicated with reliability. This form of reasoning involves studying groups of individuals and is often called nomothetic and is contrasted with idiographic research that focuses on the uniqueness of the individual. It is clear that large-scale experiments with random assignment to treatment are based on nomothetic models, as are quasi-experimental studies where intact groups of people (e.g., students in a particular classroom) are assigned to treatments.

The term "single-subject research" (SSR) suggests an idiographic approach. Many idiographic approaches to research are nonquantitative (e.g., case studies) and produce outcomes that are not intended to generalize beyond the individuals included in the study. However, current trends in SSR suggest that generalization beyond the participants of a given study is possible and desirable – a nomothetic proposition. Additionally, SSR is characterized by the use of quantitative measures (e.g., frequencies and response latencies) (Tawney & Gast, 1984). Statistical approaches such as randomization trials (Todman & Dugard, 2001) and other tools that are more commonly associated with group studies are also appropriate for SSR (Kazdin, 1982). More importantly SSR relies on a logic that is similar to that found in group designs relative to demonstrating that an effect is caused by a specified intervention in such a way that alternative explanations are extremely implausible. Therefore, the present treatment of quantitative research will include both group/quasi-experimental research and SSR. The general discussion that follows applies to both kinds of research.

In broad strokes, the research enterprise can be broken into four interrelated parts: design, implementation, analysis, and interpretation/application.

Each part serves a different function and all the parts combine to answer questions such as: What do you know? How do you know it? and How trustworthy is your knowledge? Quantitative research uses numbers in asking and answering these questions, but there is much more to quantitative research than numbers. Each of the parts of the research endeavor shows up in determinations regarding EBP, so that a brief summary of each of these parts will help to demonstrate the impact of quantitative research on EBP.

Design

An experiment is "a study in which an intervention is deliberately introduced to observe its effects" (Shadish, Cook, & Campbell, 2002, p. 12). Experimental designs are employed to produce data that allow warranted conclusions to be drawn at the conclusion of the study (Schoenfeld, 2006). Conclusions are most warranted when the design rules out likely sources of design validity issues. There are two kinds of design validity issues, internal design validity issues, which are concerned with the extent to which the intervention caused the observed effects, and external design validity issues, which are concerned with the populations, settings, and so forth on which the effect noted in the experiment can be generalized (Thompson, 2006). The importance of clear and high-quality design is quite prominent in discussions of EBP. It is a necessary but insufficient component of EBP.

Implementation

This element is usually subsumed under discussions of internal validity; however, fidelity of treatment implementation in research has a major influence on judgments of EBP, so that it deserves its own section in this discussion. Implementation of a study refers to the extent that the experimenters delivered each treatment under consideration with *fidelity*. Another word for fidelity is integrity. When interventions or treatments are implemented with fidelity or integrity, we mean that they are clearly described and records are maintained to indicate the extent to which the experimenters mirrored the descriptions in their work. Also fidelity can include concepts such as duration of the intervention, setting variables, and so forth (Fletcher, Francis, Morris, & Lyon, 2005; Van Acker, Yell, & Bradley, 2004). Like design, fidelity of implementation data is necessary but insufficient for determination that a given interventions reflects EBP.

Analysis

All forms of scientific endeavor that work to predict and control use numbers to describe the phenomenon or phenomena at hand (Krathwohl, 2004). Quantitative research uses numbers for three basic purposes, naming and counting, ranking, and placing on a scale (*ibid.*). These purposes form the basis for the systems of measurement that we use in education and other areas of social science. At its core, measurement consists of rules for assigning numbers to objects in such a way as to represent quantities of attributes (Nunnally & Bernstein, 1994). Statistical methodology is the hallmark of quantitative research in the social sciences.

In very general terms, the influences on the score or measurement that are different from the influences of the intervention that we are attempting to measure are classified as error.[1] The basic model for measurement in quantitative research may be expressed in this way: "the true score arises from an observed score plus error" (National Research Council, 2001, p. 120).

If the true score and the observed score were the same value, all measurement tasks would be quite simple. However, the admission that error is present in all measures, particularly those of abstract phenomena, leads us to employ statistical tools for verifying our findings. In very simple form, statistical tests answer the question: what are the chances that our conclusions are based simply on chance (error) and not on the reliable and true observation of the phenomena we think we are measuring (Abelson, 1995). Thus, the analysis of quantitative data at a basic level seeks to protect against accepting random events as observable patterns. That is the traditional $p \leq .05$ statement in research reports. It should be noted that there is nothing magical about .05 as the benchmark for acceptance of a finding as nonrandom. Several authors (e.g., Abelson, 1995; Creswell, 2008; Thompson, 2006) have argued for a more sophisticated approach to statistical reasoning. The custom in most educational research, however, appears to be acceptance of .05 as the gate for acceptability of outcomes in statistical analyses.

There are numerous ways of approaching data analysis and few absolute rules for which tool to use (Kavale & Forness, 1995). Nevertheless, clear and properly executed data analysis is a fundamental part of EBP. Studies in which the data are incorrectly analyzed or collected in such a manner that any analysis at all would yield only spurious results are pointless and misleading. Such studies cannot inform EBP, hence the emphasis of proper data analysis.

Interpretation and Application

No single study can fully answer any of the important questions in educational research and EBP. That an outcome is not likely to have happened by chance is not the same thing as saying that it is important or that a given teaching technique is powerful (i.e., something with impact). For measures of impact, researchers turn to measures of practical importance (Thompson, 2006). To address the need for a measure of practical importance, quantitative researchers developed a statistic called an "effect size" (Lipsey & Wilson, 2001). There are several effect size statistics available, but their discussion is beyond the scope of the present chapter. Each effect size statistic, however, places differences between groups on a standardized metric enabling interpretation of outcome results to be made in a consistent manner across different studies. Effect sizes can be classified as small, medium, or large, and various classification schemes have been developed for this purpose. Thompson (2006) pointed out that strict adherence to an arbitrary scale for interpreting effects sizes is a less than desirable practice for making education decisions. Nevertheless, the concept of practical importance as manifested by effect sizes has a substantial role to play in determination of EBP. Effect sizes are primarily associated with group designs. For SSR, impact is often determined by visual inspection of graphed data. Also, SSR outcomes can be statistically aggregated in a manner similar to effect sizes called the *percent of nonoverlapping data* statistic (Scruggs, Mastropieri, & Casto, 1987).

Summary

Although there is no chance of a perfect study ever being conducted (Hunter & Schmidt, 2004), well-designed studies that are carried out with high degrees of fidelity and analyzed appropriately can provide indications of the extent to which an effect is systematic and a nonrandom event. Additional decisions about the practical importance of the effect are added in the form of effect size calculations. Studies with high-quality design and implementation characteristics add to determination of EBP when they produce statistically significant results that are of tangible practical importance. But what is EBP and how does it relate to this model of research?

EVIDENCE-BASED PRACTICE

The first problem in defining EBP is that there is no official body that sanctions the use of the term "evidence-based practice." Thus, anyone is free to call anything they wish an EBP. As the term EBP became fashionable, the names of many textbooks appearing on publisher's catalogs and displays at conferences changed to include the phrase EBP in their titles. Few of these texts actually spent much or any time discussing what they meant by EBP and how they screened the information in their texts as meeting the EBP standards.

The history of special education is filled with well-intentioned people who made the best effort they could in understanding and treating a problem in human development or education and got it wrong. Some erroneous ideas have been discarded from the field because they have been replaced by other, more effective approaches. For example, Bruno Bettelheim claimed to have found the cause (refrigerator mothers) and a cure for autism. Throughout the late 1960s and early 1970s, Bettelheim was quite prominent on talk shows such as *The Dick Cavett Show* (the Oprah of his day). After a great deal of expense, effort, and disappointment, his claims were found to be fraudulent. Worse than simple fraud, Bettelheim's claims about the cause autism induced guilt and shame for many parents that were simply undeserved (Offit, 2008).

It is easy to look back at the tragic events surrounding that practice (which at the time was considered to be the best available) with a degree of smug self-assurance that we would never make a similar mistake given our more developed understanding of education, cognition, and behavior, yet the smugness is unjustified. Despite numerous studies that refute the ideas of "modality-based training" (the idea that visual learners should be taught visually, auditory learners taught though the auditory channel, and kinesthetic learners taught kinesthetically[2]), most university students and educators (estimates are up to 90%) believe that matching instruction to modality strengths is a highly beneficial enterprise (Willingham, 2009). Despite the consensual opinion that modality-based instruction works, the evidence – science – does not support interventions based on this idea (Jacobson, Foxx, & Mulick, 2005). Many teachers continue to report using this contraindicated in their work with students with disabilities (Burns & Ysseldyke, 2009). In the face of evidence to the contrary, educators regularly protest that they have seen it work with their own eyes. Such claims are the reason that we need to conduct and aggregate research to determine EBP. Modality-based instruction is far from the only fraudulent or unfounded practice in special education. A more complete description of fads and frauds in current practice can be found in Jacobson et al. (2005).

The Run-Up to EBP

Best Practices

It is hard to believe that special educators have only recently acquired the desire to engage in EBP. Over the history of special education research and advocacy, there seems to be a trajectory from "I really, really believe..." through a vague claim of "research shows..." The foregoing discussion of problems in interpretation and implementation of educational research demonstrates that belief and vague claims are insufficient to guide our endeavor. In an effort to overcome the disparate claims made under the "research shows" banner, special educators developed the idea of "best practices." One example of best practice analysis is found in the *Current Practice Alert* series jointly sponsored by the Council for Exceptional Children's Division for Learning Disabilities and the Division for Research ("Current Practice Alerts," n.d.).

The current practice alerts series are practitioner-friendly summaries of individual topics related to education of students with learning disabilities, emotional and behavioral disorders, and similar conditions. The series was founded in 1999 and continues to date. The analysis of the topics considered in the Alerts series clearly reflects the influence of quantitative research. Topics such as reliability, validity, and effect sizes are a major part of many of the analyses provided. The series is an excellent resource for practitioners and teacher-trainers; however, it does not explicitly represent EBP in the meaning that EBP currently holds.

"Scientifically Proven"

With the arrival of the *No Child Left Behind* act of 2001, the term "scientifically proven" became prominent in discussion of how to judge practices in education. Through the U.S. Department of Education, NCLB compels educators to employ practices that have been proven to work. The "What Works Clearinghouse" (WWC, U.S. Department of Education, n.d.) provides a series of guides that rate the Institute of Education Sciences (IES) on various topics.

When the IES began rating educational practices, the only type of evidence that was accepted as adequate was data from large-scale studies using random assignment to treatments (Odom et al., 2005). This standard is clearly aligned with the quantitative research traditions in biological, medical, and physical sciences; however, other forms of research may be as useful in determining EBP in special education. Furthermore, the highly restrictive approach applied by IES yielded few practices that could be determined to meet the criteria for EBP. This was not because the practices did not yield significant findings with tangible effects, but because the studies were conducted with smaller numbers of students in applied settings where random assignment to treatment was not feasible. Dissatisfaction with the restrictiveness of IES evaluation of educational practices has resulted in some authors referring to WWC as the "Nothing Works Clearinghouse" (Viadero & Huff, 2006, p. 8).

The WWC is not directly aimed at services for students with disabilities. It is likely that many things found on these sites will help to improve schools and improving schools is likely to help many students with disabilities. The extent to which improving the general education curriculum will benefit students with disabilities enough to resolve the problems they face is a dubious proposition.

Expanding the Questions

The National Academy of Sciences (NAS) examined the state of educational research with an eye toward improving its quality. The NAS made several critical recommendations. First, it proposed that there were at least three general types of questions: (a) descriptions of what is happening; (b) questions about cause and effect; and (c) questions about how the process or mechanism under consideration is happening (National Research Council (U.S.), Committee on Scientific Principles for Education Research, Shavelson, & Towne, 2002). Furthermore, the NAS effort stated that each of the three types of questions was scientific and that the different types of questions would require different types of methodologies to answer them (Odom et al., 2005). This observation opened the door for IES and other agencies to consider methodologies other than large-scale random assignment studies in establishing EBP. Questions about what is happening and questions about how things work are likely to yield to a number of research methods including those outside of the qualitative realm. Nevertheless, questions about cause and effect remain the purview of quantitative research for most scientists in education (Brigham, 2009). The concern that is expressed in NCLB and the WWC about how to reliably and systematically improve student achievement leads most questions about EBP back to quantitative methods.

EBP Efforts in Special Education

The Council for Exceptional Children's Division for Research launched an initiative to develop quality indicators (QIs) that could be used to evaluate research in special education. QIs were described for group experimental studies (Gersten et al., 2005); SSR designs (Horner et al., 2005); correlational designs (Thompson, Diamond, McWilliam, Snyder, & Snyder, 2005); and for qualitative studies (Brantlinger, Jimenez, Klingner, Pugach, & Richardson, 2005). Each of these papers listed and described the features that would be present in high-quality research and whose omission would suggest that the research was of substandard quality. Gersten et al. also provided recommendations for determining EBP in experimental and quasi-experimental research as did Horner et al. for SSR. The recommendations include examinations of the number of studies, the number of participants and adequacy of their description, clearly identified fidelity of treatment implementation procedures, as well as indications of treatment magnitude. Group/quasi-experimental studies and SSR had somewhat different recommendations, but the recommendations all related to the essential concern for internal and external validity that characterizes both forms of research.

Cook, Tankersley, and Landrum (2009) noted that only experimental and single-subject designs could currently be used in considerations of EBP because they were the only domains with clear standards for EBP. They suggested that the decision to move these two forms of research forward was probably because they were uniquely suited to provide experimental control. The influence of quantitative research designs is clearly evident in that statement. In fact, nomothetic researchers suggest that without establishing clear experimental control, it is impossible to say what, if anything the outcomes of any form of research mean (but, see Maxwell, 2004 for an alternative explanation).

Application of the Proposed Standards for EBP in Special Education

As a trial for the proposed standards of EBP, teams of educational researchers evaluated five different educational techniques and reported their judgment of the techniques relative to EBP. The techniques included repeated reading for students with LD (Chard, Ketterlin-Geller, Baker, Doabler, & Apichatabutra, 2009); cognitive strategy instruction in mathematics (Montague & Dietz, 2009); function-based interventions for secondary students with emotional or behavioral disorders (E/BD) (Lane, Kalberg, & Shepcaro, 2009); self-regulated strategy development for teaching writing (Baker, Chard, Ketterlin-Geller, Apichatabutra, & Doabler, 2009); and using time delay to teach literacy skills to students with severe developmental disabilities (Browder, Ahlgrim-Delzell, Spooner, Mims, & Baker, 2009).

It should be noted that all the interventions elected for this application effort posses sufficient impact to qualify as a "best practice." In other words, the research is consistently positive enough that the impact of the intervention can be expected to be strong and positive. Thus, the determination that the intervention is an EBP is not identical to the determination that the intervention is likely to produce positive outcomes. Although only interventions that produce positive outcomes can be determined to be EBPs, positive outcomes are not enough. The EBP determination is also an assessment of the *quality* of the research base supporting the intervention.

The evaluation of five topics in special education research led to mixed results. Browder et al. (2009) determined the research base in support of time delay procedures for literacy instruction with individuals who have severe developmental disabilities to be adequate for EBP status. Baker et al. (2009) found the research in support of self-regulated strategy development to be sufficient for making it an EBP as well. In each of the other examinations, the research evidence for function-based interventions for students with EBD (Lane et al., 2009), for cognitive strategy instruction in mathematical problem solving (Montague & Dietz, 2009), and for repeated reading interventions for students with LD (Chard et al., 2009) failed to meet the methodological criteria to qualify as EBP. Two things are clear from these efforts. One is that research in special education is in continuing need of improvement. More studies on clearly defined topic conducted with the high degree of rigor set forth in the standards for EBP are clearly needed, and, as conditions in society continue to change, the questions addressed will require occasional revisiting to ensure that previously established knowledge still applies in the same way it had in the past.

The second is that the standards themselves may need adjustment. Further efforts will be needed to determine the optimal mix of research rigor and promoting better intervention practices in a timely manner. We can be so cautious that we never get anything done (Neiman, 2009).

Summary

The influence of quantitative research procedures in the current efforts of determining EBP is quite clear. EBP determination is a statement regarding both the adequacy of the research base and the impact of the intervention under consideration. It makes sense that the EBP determinations should be heavily influenced by quantitative research. Quantitative research in education is more developed than other forms of research. Additionally, the metrics involved in quantitative research lend themselves to scale and rubric-making so that evaluations of the research base can be carried out in a relatively straightforward manner. So long as the evaluation of this kind of research data remains more developed, it is likely that quantitative ideas will continue to influence determination of EBP more heavily than will other kinds of research.

RESPONSIBLE PRACTICE IN THE ABSENCE OF COMPLETE KNOWLEDGE

Efforts to determine EBP for special educators are clearly warranted and also exceptionally difficult to carry out. One of the major problems is finding sufficient numbers of well-planned and executed studies to populate our decision procedure. Despite the difficulty in establishing EBP according to the stringent standards that the seriousness of our enterprise warrants, we can make some tentative steps toward using techniques that are likely to attain EBP status at some point in the future.

One way of judging probable EBPs is by examining the meta-analytic literature to find studies that are associated with the largest effect sizes. Lloyd, Forness, and Kavale (1998) summarized the findings of 18 meta-analyses of techniques in the special education data base. Findings were ranked as possessing strong, medium, or weak effect sizes, and teachers were encouraged to employ those with strong effect sizes and avoid those with weak effect sizes. Despite the age of this paper, the results remain important. The research in each of the areas included in the report remains roughly on the same trajectory (i.e., treatments associated with strong effects in 1998 continue to yield strong effects in subsequent research). Ironically, summative assessment, the hallmark of the NCLB legislation that started much of the EBP efforts in education would not be considered an EBP according to current understandings of EBP (Brigham, Tochterman, & Brigham, 2000).

Teachers and program administrators could probably evaluate the quality of their programs by the number of examples of each category of finding they employ or avoid. Avoiding weak treatments and pursuing strong treatments should be the hallmark of high-quality programs and excellence in professional practice. Nevertheless, there is insufficient research to guide every decision that educators must make. Brigham, Gustashaw, and Brigham (2004) noted that, in the absence of complete knowledge, educators must still make decisions about what to do in their schools and classrooms.

Brigham et al. (2004) suggested that professionals were responsible to carry out the extant research, monitor the professional literature (an admittedly daunting task) for new developments and to incorporate them into practice in a timely manner, and to "fill in the gaps" according to sound educational principles. Educators, however, seem to have difficulty discerning the differences between well-established principles and fads and philosophical statements. A firm understanding of the principles of behavioral and cognitive psychology seems to be a good place to start.

Willingham (2009) provided a general summary of the larger ideas of cognitive psychology that could be useful in screening treatments to fill in the gaps. Suggestions that are in line with the principles that Willingham describes are more likely to be in line with EBPs than are ideas that are outside of the findings of cognitive psychology. Similarly, Kauffman and Brigham (2009) provided a general overview of application of behavioral principles to working with children and youths who present behavior management issues. Suggestions that are in line with the principles outlined by Kauffman and Brigham are likely to be in line with EBP. Also, the Current Practice Alert series ("Current Practice Alerts," n.d.) produced by the Council for Exceptional Children's Division for Learning Disabilities and the Division for Research provide a great deal of guidance for practitioners who wish to align their own efforts with EBP.

Clinical judgment will remain a part of professional practice in special education just as it does in medicine and other areas of professional practice where EBP is a guiding force. Clinical judgment is based on the union of strong preparation, deep understanding of the principles of the discipline and experience. When educators act in accordance with the principles of their discipline and employ techniques that are in line with the most effective approaches available, they are probably engaging in activities that are likely to be EBPs.

Although EBPs are not yet in place for special education on a wide scale, there clearly is much about professional practice that can be improved so that the arrival of EBP recommendations will not be so jarring to many of our practitioners. Engaging in powerful treatments that are based on sound theoretical principles from cognitive and behavioral psychology and that yield reliable outcomes remains a major and still largely unrealized step in the right direction. We have much that we can do to improve our profession while awaiting the results of EBP determinations.

NOTES

1. There are more complex models of analysis (e.g., structural equation modeling) that allow researchers to include many of the elements that are classified as error components in the simpler models to generate and evaluate complex theories and to examine the extent to which these variables mediate or influence the target variable. Discussion of these models is beyond the scope of this chapter. Additionally, the ideas of internal and external validity apply to these more complex models as well as to the simpler approach employed here to illustrate the concept.
2. Kinesthesia is the sense that detects bodily position, weight, or movement of the muscles, tendons, and joints, and according to some, the body's position in space. How this sense conveys the meaning of abstract concepts is inconceivable. Practitioners have stated that having students stand up when they hear an example of justice and sit down when they hear an example of injustice is a way of involving kinesthesia in learning abstract concepts. A more parsimonious explanation is that the activity encouraged the students to pay attention and prevented their minds from wandering too far during the lesson.

REFERENCES

Abelson, R. P. (1995). *Statistics as principled argument*. Hillsdale, NJ: Lawrence Erlbaum Associates, Publishers.

Baker, S. K., Chard, D. J., Ketterlin-Geller, L. R., Apichatabutra, C., & Doabler, C. (2009). Teaching writing to at-risk students: The quality of evidence for self-regulated strategy development. *Exceptional Children, 75*(3), 303.

Brantlinger, E., Jimenez, R., Klingner, J., Pugach, M., & Richardson, V. (2005). Qualitative studies in special education. *Exceptional Children, 71*(2), 195–207.

Brigham, F. J. (2009). Evidence-based practices in special education: State of the art, progress of the science. Paper presented at the anual meeting of the Massachucetts Association of Approved Private Schools, Marlborough, MA.

Brigham, F. J., Gustashaw, W. E., III., & Brigham, M. S. P. (2004). Scientific practice and the tradition of advocacy in special education. *Journal of Learning Disabilities, 37*(3), 200–206.

Brigham, F. J., Tochterman, S., & Brigham, M. S. P. (2000). Students with emotional and behavioral disorders and their teachers in test-linked systems of accountability. *Assessment for Effective Intervention, 26*(1), 19–27.

Browder, D., Ahlgrim-Delzell, L., Spooner, F., Mims, P. J., & Baker, J. N. (2009). Using time delay to teach literacy to students with severe developmental disabilities. *Exceptional Children, 75*(3), 343.

Burns, M. K., & Ysseldyke, J. E. (2009). Reported prevalence of evidence-based instructional practices in special education. *Journal of Special Education, 43*(1), 3–11.

Chard, D. J., Ketterlin-Geller, L. R., Baker, S. K., Doabler, C., & Apichatabutra, C. (2009). Repeated reading interventions for students with learning disabilities: Status of the evidence. *Exceptional Children, 75*(3), 263.

Cook, B. G., Tankersley, M., & Landrum, T. J. (2009). Determining evidence-based practices in special education. *Exceptional Children, 75*(3), 365.

Creswell, J. W. (2008). *Educational research: Planning, conducting, and evaluating quantitative and qualitative research* (3rd ed.). Upper Saddle River, NJ: Pearson/Merrill Prentice Hall.

Current Practice Alerts (n.d.). from http://www.cecdr.org/subpage.cfm?id = DEA7864A-C09F-1D6F-F9008ABF5B1B71B1

Fletcher, J. M., Francis, D. J., Morris, R. D., & Lyon, G. R. (2005). Evidence-based assessment of learning disabilities in children and adolescents. *Journal of Clinical Child & Adolescent Psychology, 34*(3), 506–522.

Gersten, R., Fuchs, L. S., Compton, D., Coyne, M., Greenwood, C., & Innocenti, M. S. (2005). Quality indicators for group experimental and quasi-experimental research in special education. *Exceptional Children, 71*(2), 149–164.

Horner, R. H., Carr, E. G., Halle, J., McGee, G., Odom, S., & Wolery, M. (2005). The use of single-subject research to identify evidence-based practice in special education. *Exceptional Children, 71*(2), 165–179.

Hunter, J. E., & Schmidt, F. L. (2004). *Methods of meta-analysis: Correcting error and bias in research findings* (2nd ed.). Thousand Oaks, CA: Sage Publications.

Jacobson, J. W., Foxx, R. M., & Mulick, J. A. (2005). *Controversial therapies for developmental disabilities: Fad, fashion, and science in professional practice.* Mahwah, NJ: Lawrence Erlbaum Associates, Publishers.

Kauffman, J. M., & Brigham, F. J. (2009). *Working with troubled children.* Verona, WI: Full Court Press.

Kavale, K. A., & Forness, S. R. (1995). *The nature of learning disabilities: Critical elements of diagnosis and classification.* Mahwah, NJ: Lawrence Erlbaum Associates, Publishers.

Kazdin, A. E. (1982). *Single-case research designs: Methods for clinical and applied settings.* New York: Oxford University Press.

Kelly, G. J. (2006). Epistemology and educational research. In: J. L. Green, G. Camilli & P. B. Elmore (Eds), *Handbook of complementary methods in education research* (pp. 33–55). Mahwah, NJ: Lawrence Erlbaum Associates, Publishers.

Krathwohl, D. R. (2004). *Methods of educational and social science research: An integrated approach* (2nd ed.). Long Grove, IL: Waveland Press.

Lane, K. L., Kalberg, J. R., & Shepcaro, J. C. (2009). An examination of the evidence base for function-based interventions for students with emotional and/or behavioral disorders attending middle and high schools. *Exceptional Children, 75*(3), 321.

Lipsey, M. W., & Wilson, D. B. (2001). *Practical meta-analysis.* Thousand Oaks, CA: Sage Publications.

Lloyd, J. W., Forness, S. R., & Kavale, K. A. (1998). Some methods are more effective than others. *Intervention in School and Clinic, 33*(4), 195–200.

Maxwell, J. A. (2004). Causal explanation, qualitative research, and scientific inquiry in education. *Educational Researcher, 33*(2), 3–11.

Montague, M., & Dietz, S. (2009). Evaluating the evidence base for cognitive strategy instruction and mathematical problem solving. *Exceptional Children, 75*(3), 285.

National Research Council. (2001). *Knowing what students know: The science and design of educational assessment.* Washington, DC: National Academy Press.

National Research Council (U.S.). Committee on Scientific Principles for Education Research, Shavelson, R. J., & Towne, L. (2002). *Scientific research in education.* Washington, DC: National Academy Press.

Neiman, S. (2009). *Moral clarity: A guide for grown-up idealists* (Rev. ed.). Princeton, NJ: Princeton University Press.

No Child Left Behind Act of 2001 § 20 U.S.C. § 6319. (2008).
Nunnally, J. C., & Bernstein, I. H. (1994). *Psychometric theory* (3rd ed.). New York: McGraw-Hill.
Odom, S. L., Brantlinger, E., Gersten, R., Horner, R. H., Thompson, B., & Harris, K. R. (2005). Research in special education: Scientific methods and evidence-based practices. *Exceptional Children, 71*(2), 137–148.
Offit, P. A. (2008). *Autism's false prophets: Bad science, risky medicine, and the search for a cure.* New York: Columbia University Press.
Schoenfeld, A. H. (2006). Design experiments. In: J. L. Green, G. Camilli & P. B. Elmore (Eds), *Handbook of complementary methods in education research* (3rd ed., pp. 193–205). Mahwah, NJ: Lawrence Erlbaum Associates, Publishers.
Scruggs, T. E., Mastropieri, M. A., & Casto, G. (1987). The quantitative synthesis of single-subject research: Methodology and validation. *Remedial & Special Education, 8*(2), 24–33.
Shadish, W. R., Cook, T. D., & Campbell, D. T. (2002). *Experimental and quasi-experimental designs for generalized causal inference.* Boston: Houghton Mifflin.
Tawney, J. W., & Gast, D. L. (1984). *Single subject research in special education.* Columbus, OH: C.E. Merrill Publishing Company.
Thompson, B. (2006). *Foundations of behavioral statistics: An insight-based approach.* New York: Guilford Press.
Thompson, B., Diamond, K. E., McWilliam, R., Snyder, P., & Snyder, S. W. (2005). Evaluating the quality of evidence from correlational research for evidence-based practice. *Exceptional Children, 71*(2), 181–194.
Todman, J. B., & Dugard, P. (2001). *Single-case and small-n experimental designs: A practical guide to randomization tests.* Mahwah, NJ: Lawrence Erlbaum Associates, Publishers.
U.S. Department of Education. (n.d.). Doing what works, from http://dww.ed.gov/index.cfm
Van Acker, R., Yell, M. L., & Bradley, R. (2004). Experimental research designs in the study of children and youth with emotional and behavioral disorders. In: R. B. Rutherford, M. M. Quinn & S. R. Mathur (Eds), *Handbook of research in emotional and behavioral disorders* (pp. 546–566). New York: Guilford Press.
Viadero, D., & Huff, D. J. (2006). "One stop" research shop seen as slow to yield views that educators can use. *Education Week, 26*(5), 8–9.
Willingham, D. T. (2009). *Why don't students like school? A cognitive scientist answers questions about how the mind works and what it means for your classroom.* San Francisco: Jossey-Bass.

CHAPTER 2

QUALITATIVE RESEARCH IN EDUCATION: OTHER METHODS OF SEEKING KNOWLEDGE

Julia B. Stoner

Qualitative research has been used in the field of education for decades and has made significant contributions to the specific area of special education (Brantlinger, Jimenez, Klingner, Pugach, & Richardson, 2005; McDuffie & Scruggs, 2008; Scruggs, Mastropieri, & McDuffie, 2007). To understand the current and future value of qualitative research in the field of special education, it is necessary to have a foundational understanding of the nature and conceptual framework of qualitative methodology. This chapter is organized to provide a basic description of qualitative research and a discussion of the essential components for providing quality in qualitative research studies. Several research studies in the field of special education that have used qualitative methodology are summarized and their contributions are highlighted.

CHOOSING QUALITATIVE RESEARCH

Research begins with a question that begs to be answered. The research question must be well articulated and specific. Once the research question is established, the methodology is chosen. Thus, it is the research question that determines the methodology. In the field of special education, many methodologies have been used to answer research questions. For example, Stoner et al. (2006c) used a single subject design to determine the effectiveness of the Picture Exchange Communication System (PECS) for adults with intellectual disabilities. Quasi-experimental methodology may be the appropriate methodology for determining the effectiveness of intervention with a group of students. The effectiveness of two math curricula for students at risk was conducted by Woodward and Brown (2006) using quasi-experimental research. If the research question centers on attitudes or opinions of a large group of individuals, then quantitative research may be used. Brown, Welsh, Haegle Hill, and Cipko (2008) reported on preservice teacher attitudes about teaching students with learning disabilities (LD). However, if one wants to broaden and enhance understanding and to fully and deeply comprehend the perspectives of individuals, then qualitative methodology would be used. For example, through the use of qualitative methodology, two studies (Bailey, Parette, Stoner, Angell, & Carroll, 2006a; Bailey, Stoner, Parette, & Angell, 2006b) described the perspectives of members of individual education plan (IEP) teams and perspectives of family members regarding augmentative and alternative communication (AAC) use in public schools. The findings of these studies (a) offered in-depth understanding of the process of obtaining AAC devices, (b) identified barriers and facilitators to AAC device use, and (c) provided strategies for effective use of AAC devices.

Approximately 30 years ago, qualitative methodology in education emerged as a means to study and focus on participants themselves (Creswell, 2008). Many researchers (i.e., Lincoln & Guba, 1985) called for an alternative to quantitative approaches, which often employed artificial, experimental environments that were dissimilar to participants' lived experiences. Essentially, the rationale for the use of qualitative methodology in the field of education was multifaceted and included (a) comprehensive understanding of participants' unique experiences (Strauss & Corbin, 1998), (b) describing the setting in which their experiences occurred (Creswell, 2008), and (c) investigating the meanings participants attributed to their experiences (Strauss & Corbin, 1998). So what exactly does the term "qualitative research" mean? Several terms, such as "naturalistic, inquiry, ethnography, case studies, and field studies," are synonymously used with qualitative research (Brantlinger et al., 2005, p. 196). The underlying theme, regardless of the terminology used, is that qualitative methods seek to understand a phenomenon that individuals have experienced. According to Brantlinger et al. (2005), qualitative research is "a systematic approach to understanding qualities, or the essential nature of a phenomenon, within a particular context (p. 196)." This definition dominates the premise of this chapter.

TYPES OF QUALITATIVE RESEARCH

There are several types of qualitative research. The types include case study (both single case studies and collective case studies), grounded theory, ethnography, action research, narrative research, phenomenology, discourse analysis, conversational analysis, and ethnographic content analysis (for a complete description of the various types of qualitative research, see Brantlinger et al., 2005). However, the case study, grounded theory, and ethnography have been the types that have been used the most in the field of special education (McDuffie & Scruggs, 2008). Following are brief descriptions of each of these three types of qualitative research; however, it should be noted that these descriptions do not provide guidance on how to *conduct* these types of studies.

Case Studies

Case studies involve the investigation of a case, which can be defined as an entity or an object of study (Stake, 1995) that is bounded, or separated for research in terms of "time, place, or some physical boundaries" (Creswell, 2008, p. 476). It is important to understand that cases can be individuals, programs, events, schools, classrooms, or groups. Once cases are clearly defined, the researcher investigates them in-depth, typically using multiple data collection methods, such as interviews, field observations, and documentation (Stake, 2000). Butera (2005) used a case study and collected data through interviews, observations, and document (e.g., IEP) reviews to describe team collaboration with a 4-year-old child in West Virginia. Collective case studies (a) involve multiple cases, (b) can occur over many sites, and (c) use many individuals. The conceptual framework for case studies is that by gathering in-depth information about a case, the researcher will achieve an in-depth understanding of the case, whether that case is an individual, group, classroom, or school. Using a collective case study approach, Purcell, Horn, and Palmer (2007) investigated inclusion of students with disabilities in five preschool programs and gathered data through interviews and focus groups.

Grounded Theory

Grounded theory is an approach that allows the researcher to develop or discover a theory based on the study of a phenomenon and was originally articulated by Strauss and Corbin (1998). These researchers developed a procedure that conformed to "basic scientific tenets and principles" (Shank, 2006) while allowing enough flexibility for the researcher to develop a theory that explained a process, action, or interaction among participants that was grounded in the data. When using grounded theory, the researcher purposefully (a) chooses participants who have experienced the phenomenon being studied, (b) analyzes the data (i.e., interviews, documents, and records), and (c) approaches the phenomenon under study without preconceived notions. This conceptual framework allows voices of participants to emerge, requires that the researcher identify major themes or concepts from participant data, and provides an avenue to develop a theory from participant perspectives. One approach to conducting a grounded theory study is continually returning to the data and comparing experiences of participants, investigating similarities and differences, and focusing on the interrelationships among emerging themes (Charmaz, 2000). A grounded theory approach was used by Bays and Crockett (2007) to investigate instructional leadership for special education in elementary schools.

Ethnographic Studies

Ethnographies are in-depth analysis of social groups. Data is typically gathered through observations, interviews, and documents. Ethnography that "literally means writing about groups of people" (Creswell, 2008, p. 435) focuses on a group's culture. The researcher becomes immersed in the group to understand its inner workings, structure, and functioning (McDuffie & Scruggs, 2008). This type of research focuses on building a record of the behavior and beliefs of a group over time (see Creswell, 2008). Ethnographies require that the researcher participate, either as an observer or active participant, over a considerable length of time with the group under study (Shank, 2006). The conceptual framework of ethnographies is that immersion into the culture of the group will allow the researcher to view the world from the group's perspective, and that view will provide understanding of the group's behavior and beliefs. For example, Harry, Klingner, and Hart (2005) published an ethnographic study of African American students in special education in a culturally diverse urban school district.

Overall, the basic objective of all three types of qualitative research described above is to *understand*. Understanding must be comprehensive, deep, and accurately portray participant's perspectives so that their voices can be heard. The qualitative researcher has a strong obligation to allow voices of participants to be heard clearly. To accomplish this, the thorough researcher strives to (a) collect enough data to adequately represent participants' views, (b) analyze the data systematically, (c) confirm that participants were truthful, (d) and report the findings clearly.

COLLECTING DATA IN QUALITATIVE RESEARCH

So how does the researcher gain the perspective of the participants? Choosing participants is the first step. Researchers must choose participants who have experienced the phenomenon that is being studied. Qualitative researchers typically use purposeful sampling, which simply means choosing participants who have directly experienced the phenomenon in question. The researcher aims to choose participants from whom rich, detailed information can be gathered (Creswell, 2008). In qualitative research, data is the substance from which the researcher gains understanding of the phenomenon under study. Data can be obtained from various forms that may include interviews, documents, open-ended questions on questionnaires, field observations, conversations among participants, or even pictorial documents. A thorough qualitative study will use many forms of data, not only for analysis but also for confirmation of the findings. Data collection requires a substantial amount of time because it is usually collected over a prolonged period (Shank, 2006). Interviews, observations, and documents are the most common type of data collected. These are explained in the following sections.

Interviews

Interviews can be unstructured or semi-structured and typically involve asking broad questions. For example, when investigating trust between parents of children with disabilities and education professionals, Angell, Stoner, and Shelden (2009) began interviews with the request, "Tell me about your relationship with education professionals." This allowed participants to guide the researchers and explain their perspective of the phenomenon under study while providing an opportunity for the researchers to probe emerging issues with follow-up questions, such as "You spoke of trouble in the third grade, can you explain that to me?" Several interviews with each participant may occur until the researcher determines that no new information is forthcoming. When this occurs, we contend that the researcher has reached saturation of the data (Creswell, 2008). Completing several interviews with one participant allows for probing of issues and offers the opportunity to clarify any information that was previously provided. Interviews can be conducted individually or within focus groups. Individual interviews allow more comprehensive questioning and probing whereas focus groups are more efficient in gaining multiple views in a shorter period of time. Interviewing effectively requires the ability to listen, remember important responses, and probe for other information related to the phenomenon under investigation. Interviewing has been described as one of the most powerful ways to understand another person's perspective (Fontana & Frey, 2000). Yet, from this complex and intimate interaction, the interviewer bears a heavy responsibility. The interview must be conducted with respect and nonjudgment of whatever viewpoint the participant shares. The researcher must be respectful and trustworthy because participants are allowing the researcher to essentially enter their lives and trust that the information they provide will be valued. If the interview is done well, this can be a benefit to the participant. In an address to the American Sociological Society, Barbara Heyl (1997), the president at the time, stated that "there is a positive impact on the person who is being listened to attentively" (p. 1) when discussing participation in qualitative studies. The participant has a chance to tell his/her story. During this process, he/she can deepen legitimacy of views, as well as get the chance to help others who are experiencing or will be experiencing the phenomenon in question. Thus, when conducted ethically and thoroughly, the interview can connect the researcher with the participant and yield an in-depth understanding that is the basic premise of qualitative research.

Observations

Observations are another form of data and can take many forms. Some observations are unstructured with the researcher attempting to disrupt the environment as little as possible. O'Brian, Stoner, Appel, and Gresens (2007) used observations of conferences between cooperating teachers and preservice teachers to gain a more comprehensive view of the relationship and its effect on preservice teachers. Other observations may require the researcher to participate within the environment or group activity to gain the participant perspective. Or, observations may begin with the researcher as an observer, distant from the group or setting, and the researcher may become a participant of the group after a certain period of time. Regardless of the form, the primary purpose of observations is to gain information firsthand. Field notes, which are text recorded by the researcher, are frequently taken either during or immediately following the observation. Observations, like interviews, are completed to gain a more comprehensive understanding of the phenomenon under study.

Documents

Documents are considered a form of data in qualitative research. These are "public or private records that qualitative researchers obtain about a site or participants in a study" (Creswell, 2008, p. 219). Documents can include personal records such as IEPs, medical reports, personal letters, or reports from consultants. Documents can also be public such as minutes of a school board meeting, newspaper articles, or posts on a LISTSERV. The advantage of using documents is that they are typically readily available, eliminate transcription time and costs, and may be written by the participants themselves. However, documents may be incomplete and do not allow the researcher to probe for any information needed to clarify what is presented.

ANALYZING DATA IN QUALITATIVE RESEARCH

Once data is collected, analysis begins. Data analysis is a recursive process, meaning that the researcher is coding data, identifying themes or categories, and returning to the data. Returning to the data allows the researcher to reinvestigate the data that may lead to merging, expanding, deleting, or refining of the themes or categories. Line-by-line coding is a process where each line or complete thought of the participant's interview transcript is coded. Interview transcripts, field notes, or documents can be coded using this procedure. For an example of line-by-line coding, see Table 1.

Table 1. Example of Line-by-Line Coding.

Transcription	Line-by-Line Coding	Categories
Well let me put it this way, when you are young, and when Pete was little	inexperienced	
and he was not as good as he is now.	getting services, child progress	
And I always worry, I mean I am not the expert,	worry	
as far as what is available to Pete.	available services	IEP
And I hope that they are	trust	
(referring to the teachers and staff).	recognition of costs	
And the school has budgets and all this other stuff.	recognition of budget	
And you just feel like finances are the bottom line.	finances bottom line	
Not Pete's needs. So you have to sit down.		
And you do not want to walk away feeling	obligation fighting for services	
like you never accomplished		
what you wanted to accomplish.	worry	
Because you love Pete.	love of child	advocacy
And that is why I feel like that.	frustration	
I mean you can never do enough.	helplessness	
And that I guess, that is why I hate them (referring to IEP meetings).		

Once all data is coded, it is grouped into emerging themes or categories. These categories are not firmly set but undergo refinement by merging, expanding, deleting, or refining. It is beyond the scope of this chapter to specifically discuss qualitative data analysis, but numerous resources on coding data are available. The type of qualitative research that was used (e.g., case study, grounded theory, and ethnography) determines how the themes are presented. In a case study or ethnography, the data may be descriptive and relationships among the themes may or may not be discussed. In grounded theory, relationships among the themes build the theory. Occasionally, these

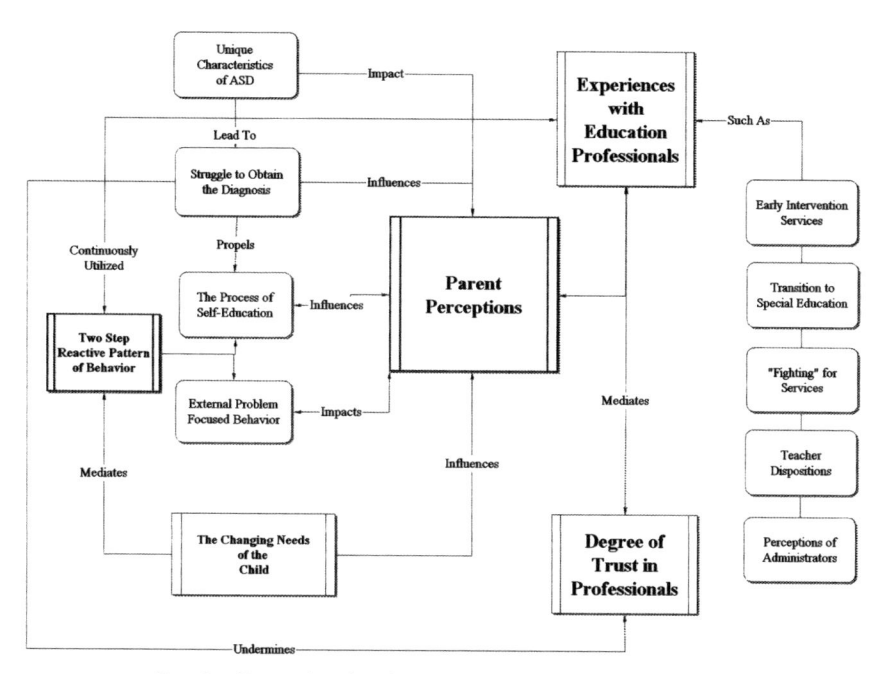

Fig. 1. Example of a Concept Map (Stoner et al., 2005).

relationships are depicted in the form of a graphic representation or concept map to guide the reader in understanding the theory that has emerged and was grounded in the participant perspectives. Two studies that included concept maps were Blaska (1998) and Stoner et al. (2005). See Fig. 1 for an example of a concept map.

Data analysis completed by multiple researchers is known as multiple coding. Barbour (2001) contended that multiple coding requires the "cross checking of coding strategies and interpretation of data by independent researchers (p. 1114)." Once the coding has been completed, researchers meet and discuss the emerging categories and merge, refine, expand, or delete major categories or themes. The value of using multiple researchers is that it offers an opportunity to filter the data through multiple viewpoints, and this process encourages thoroughness in both the analysis and the method description (Barbour, 2001). One of the most important tasks of the qualitative researcher is to clearly and specifically convey the process by which the study was completed. This is done in a transparent manner so that the reader has confidence that the study is thorough and systematic.

OBTAINING CONFIRMABILITY IN QUALITATIVE RESEARCH

One of the necessities of qualitative research is to assure confirmability of the data. Confirmability means that the researcher has determined the accuracy or credibility of the findings through specific strategies. Several qualitative researchers have suggested alternative words such as authenticity, credibility, dependability, trustworthiness, validation, verification, and transferability (e.g., Bogden & Biklen, 1998; Creswell, 2008; Leedy & Ormrod, 2001). Regardless of the terminology used, qualitative researchers must be concerned with testing and confirming their findings (Miles & Huberman, 1994). Common approaches to confirmability are triangulation, respondent validation, strong data collection methods, and member checking. For example, consider a recent study that investigated eight parents (four married couples or cases), of children with autism spectrum disorder (ASD) regarding their perspectives on their relationships with education professionals (Stoner et al., 2005). All of the approaches listed earlier were utilized to achieve confirmability.

Triangulation

Triangulation is the process of corroborating evidence from different individuals, different types of data, and different methods of data collection (Creswell, 2008). In the Stoner et al. (2005) study, each case consisted of a mother and father, who were interviewed separately. Confirmability was achieved when the mother and the father provided the researcher with the same information during individual interviews. During data analysis, corroborative accounts were noted and compared between spouses. Additionally, incidences that occurred across the four cases added further confirmability to the findings. Differences or discrepancies between married participants or between cases were probed with follow-up interview questions. Confirmability may also be gathered from different types of data. In the Stoner et al. (2005) study, all families provided the researcher with documentation. The documentation consisted of their children's IEPs, modifications of school work, and evaluations, such as speech and language evaluations. Communication notebooks, used by all participants, which traveled between home and school, were reviewed for confirming evidence. Data was gathered from other available documents, such as parent-made materials used in the classroom and preparation notes for IEP meetings.

The researchers reviewed the documents by describing the documents into an audiotape. This description of the documents was then transcribed and reviewed for corroboration with the data gathered from the interviews of the participants. For example, a participant spoke of her use of a visual strategy for the morning routine. The visual strategy was presented to the researcher, who described the visual strategy, including layout and pictures, into the tape recorder. This document added confirmation to the participant's statement that she used visual strategies with her child.

Respondent Validation

Respondent validation is a process in which the researcher asks the participants to check the accuracy of the study in the areas of descriptions, themes, and interpretations (Creswell, 2008). Once the data is analyzed and the study completed, the researcher meets with all the participants and explains the findings of the study, using a concept map as a visual representation of the findings. Confirmation is achieved when all participants are given the opportunity to add any additional information and validate the accuracy of the findings.

Strong Data Collection Methods

Adhering to rigorous data collection strategies can strengthen the data and thus add to the confirmation of the findings (Miles & Huberman, 1994). These strategies include (a) data is collected after repeated contact, (b) data is seen, (c) behavior is observed, (d) data is collected in informal settings, and (e) the respondent is alone with the researcher. All of these procedures were followed in the Stoner et al. (2005) study; specifically, (a) the data was collected after the participants knew the researcher from a pilot study and parent support group meetings; (b) the researcher saw documentation (e.g., IEPs, communication notebooks) that comprised the data; (c) the researcher observed the behavior between the parents and the child, (d) interviews occurred in the home or a setting chosen by the parent, all considered informal settings; and (e) interviews were conducted when the respondent was alone with the researcher.

Member Checking

Member checking is utilized to add further confirmability to the findings. Member checking is the process of providing participants the opportunity to review the material (Janesick, 2000). In the Stoner et al. (2005) study, member checking was completed by providing all participants with a transcript of their personal quotes that were used in the final report. All participants confirmed the quotes and granted approval for the use of all quotes.

WRITING THE REPORT IN QUALITATIVE RESEARCH

Once the themes and their relationships have been determined, the researcher writes the report. One of the difficulties with qualitative research is that the findings can be complex, intricate, numerous, and substantial. The researcher is required to make difficult decisions as to what to report given the limited amount of space in peer-reviewed journals. Frequently, there is more than one report generated from a single qualitative study (i.e., Stoner & Angell, 2006; Stoner, Angell, House, & Bock, 2007; Stoner et al., 2005).

At times, qualitative researchers will guide the reader by using a graphic representation of their findings, known as a concept map. The concept map is intended to provide a means for the researcher to represent the understanding of the study's topic (Kinchin & Hay, 2000). Concept mapping allows the researcher to clearly articulate the major findings of a study, present the interrelationships between the major findings, and represent the findings in the form of a graphic map. An example of the concept map used by Stoner et al. (2005) is presented in Fig. 1.

HEARING THE VOICES IN QUALITATIVE RESEARCH

Qualitative research that is thorough and systematic is labor-intensive and requires substantial commitment and time. However, it is well worth the effort. Qualitative research can shed light on issues that no one but those experiencing the phenomenon can know. Understanding other perspectives and responding effectively to individual needs is the base of special education. Qualitative research can strengthen that base and inform education professionals and direct policy makers.

Who are the participants in special education and why would the field benefit from hearing those voices? Participants in special education are numerous and include individuals with disabilities, teachers (both general and special educators), parents of children with disabilities, school administrators, paraprofessionals, related service personnel such as speech and language pathologists (SLPs), occupational therapists (OTs), physical therapists (PTs), job coaches, vocational rehabilitation counselors, teacher educators, and preservice teachers. This list is not exhaustive by any means, but it does serve to exemplify the multifaceted perspectives that can contribute to the understanding of certain phenomenon and issues within the field of special education. The following section highlights qualitative research studies that investigated a phenomenon by listening to the voices of those who have lived the experience. The selection of peer-reviewed journal articles was arbitrary, and the articles were chosen to exemplify the range of qualitative methodology and topics.

Listening to Individuals with Disabilities

Individuals with disabilities often do not have a voice in their education, and choices are made for them by well-meaning adults. It can be difficult to obtain the voices of some individuals with communication and significant cognitive impairments; yet, there are many individuals with disabilities who can speak for themselves and articulate what they desire. Qualitative research focusing on the voices of individuals with disabilities is limited. Far more common are qualitative research articles that describe the voices of educators and parents, both of whom are important and have a valid stake in the field of special education. Yet, we can learn from those individuals with disabilities, because they are the ones who are living the experience. The following two articles are briefly summarized to provide a clear picture of the value of listening to the voices of individuals with disabilities.

Research that has focused on individuals with disabilities has encompassed a wide variety of issues from educational programming to achieving self-determination (Klassen, 2007). Klassen and Lynch (2007) conducted focus group interviews with 28 Grades 8 and 9 students with LD and 7 interviews with their teachers about perspectives of the students' self-efficacy. This study was unusual because the authors had previously published two other articles related to the topic of self-determination, and this study was the third in the series. The first author initially conducted an extensive review of the literature (Klassen, 2002) and then completed a quantitative study that compared the self-efficacy beliefs of children with LD to their performance (Klassen & Lynch, 2007). The results of these two studies indicated that "adolescents with LD miscalibrate their performance in some contexts" (Klassen & Lynch, 2007, p. 496). In other words, the authors found that students with LD had a tendency to overestimate their academic performance. Clearly, they wanted to gain a more comprehensive understanding of why this occurred and conducted a qualitative study to gain "student and teacher perceptions about this miscalibration" (p. 496). Klassen and Lynch found disparate views among students and teachers which were (a) students viewed themselves as accurate in calibrating self-efficacy and performance whereas teachers viewed the students as overconfident, (b) students desired praise to boost their confidence whereas teachers indicated opportunities for successful experiences were more beneficial, and (c) students identified academic difficulties as controllable and due to their effort whereas teachers felt the difficulties were due to uncontrollable deficits.

Klassen and Lynch (2007) provided several implications for practice from their results, namely, (a) teacher interventions may not be valued by adolescents with LD because they do not have the metacognitive skills to understand the value of these interventions, (b) students desired discreet assistance and preferred that the whole class have the assistance instead of being singled out, and (c) teachers need to be sensitive to adolescents' sensitivity to support. Importantly, Klassen and Lynch provided guidelines to support adolescents with LD in inclusive settings, based on voices of adolescents themselves.

Stoner, Angell, House, and Goins (2006a) conducted semi-structured interviews with 12 adults with physical disabilities to ascertain their perspective on self-determination. Using a grounded theory approach, the interviews were coded line-by-line, themes were developed, and confirmability was achieved through triangulation, respondent validation, and member checking. The major findings of this study were depicted in a concept map and included (a) identification of facilitators of self-determination, (b) identification of barriers to self-determination, and (c) the process of developing an action plan for overcoming barriers and facilitating self-determination. Facilitators of self-determination were intrinsic factors, such as perseverance, family support, opportunities to experience self-determination, and setting goals. Barriers included intrinsic factors, such as shyness, their physical disability, attitudinal barriers of others, financial factors, and physical accessibility in the environment. To overcome identified barriers, participants described their individual strategies. The researchers then developed an action plan, based on the data analysis, that included intrinsic characteristics, such as finding an appropriate avenue for communication, focusing on the goal, and developing action strategies.

Stoner et al.'s (2006a) study offered several recommendations to foster self-determination in individuals with physical disabilities. These included (a) incorporating self-determination goals in IEPs, (b) involving the individual student in the IEP and transition process, (c) providing opportunities to practice self-determination, (d) assisting with goal setting, (e) evaluating and identifying required support to meet the goal, and (f) setting an action plan to achieve the goal. Furthermore, if the goal was not met, the researchers recommended assisting the student with a reevaluation to ascertain the difficulties and provide a plan to overcome them. The value of this study was that individuals with significant physical disabilities were allowed to contribute to recommendations on incorporating self-determination into special education programs.

Listening to the Voices of Parents of Children with Disabilities

Qualitative research has investigated parents of children with disabilities on numerous and varied topics such as relationships and trust with education professionals (Angell et al., 2009; Stoner et al., 2005), conflict with educational systems (Lake & Billingsley, 2000), perspectives on the implementation of alternative and augmentative communication systems (Bailey et al., 2006a, 2006b), perspectives of dysphagia intervention in the schools (Angell, Bailey, & Stoner, 2008; Stoner, Bailey, Angell, Robbins, & Polewski, 2006b), and perspectives of parenting a child with disabilities (Blaska, 1998). Blaska's study is discussed below as an example of the value of understanding parent perspectives.

Blaska (1998) investigated the concept of cyclical grieving during interviews with parents of adult children with disabilities. The ages of the children with disabilities ranged from 21 to 39 years and represented a wide range of disabilities (e.g., Down syndrome, cerebral palsy, ASD, and intellectual disabilities) and severity. Blaska detailed the cyclical grieving process and provided a visual representation to illustrate the conceptual model. The concept map consisted of three concentric circles, with each circle representing a different aspect of emotions of parents interviewed. The inner circle represented shattered dreams experienced by parents when they were initially informed their child had a disability. Blaska contended the grief expressed during this time was functional because it allowed parents to move on and refocus on the child they had instead of the child they expected. The second circle represented the emotions parents felt and experienced intermittently since the diagnosis. These emotions were not experienced in any specific order but may have appeared and reappeared either separately or simultaneously throughout their life. The outer circle depicted four life cycles of a family: "a family with young children, a family with adolescents, a family launching children, and a family later in life" (Blaska, 1998, p. 4). The cyclical grieving model emphasizes that during the life cycle of a family, there are many events that may trigger the reoccurrence of emotions involved in the grieving process. All parents could recall, in detail, the time of the initial diagnosis and the emotions they experienced. Parents also reported that events could trigger a reoccurrence of these emotions. The emotions would reappear and then disappear for varying lengths of time as the child aged. The events triggering the reoccurrence of these emotions were unique to each participant and were not necessarily significant events. Blaska (1998) concluded the study by discussing implications for professionals. Professionals need to understand the emotions that families undergo and become sensitive to the changing needs of the family. This is especially significant for special educators who may interact with families during times of typical transitions, such as first words, walking, toilet training, getting a driver's license, or leaving for college. Educators who are sensitive and recognize that parents may repeatedly experience the grief cycle can offer support and strengthen their collaboration in educating the child with the disability. This qualitative study enhances the understanding of the parental perspective. Blaska contended that through listening to the voices of parents, and acknowledging and respecting their emotions, a stronger family–professional relationship can be forged. And most importantly, the ultimate beneficiary of strong family–professional relationships is the student with disabilities.

Listening to the Voices of Special Educators

The field of special education is constantly changing and special educators are immersed in these changes. Gaining the perspectives of those who are teaching in the field is vital to identify, assess, and understand the issues in the field. Qualitative research that has involved educators has focused on numerous topics such as inclusion, co-teaching, and relationships with paraprofessionals, parents, administration, and students. The two studies reviewed below focus on the perspectives of teachers regarding co-teaching and inclusion.

Mastropieri et al. (2005) used qualitative methodology to compare four case studies that had been completed separately. The 2005 report compared the four case studies on the process of collaboration and co-teaching in middle school and high school. The first case involved two teams of educators who co-taught in upper elementary school and middle school science classes. The second case was a team that co-taught in a middle school social studies class. The third case was a co-teaching team in a high school world history class. The fourth case was a team that co-taught in high school chemistry class. Teachers were interviewed, observed, and data was analyzed to provide a description of each of the cases. Findings from the Mastropieri et al. study offered several insights from educators who experienced the phenomenon of co-teaching. By listening to their voices, the voices of teachers who were actually doing the co-teaching, the researchers found numerous factors that affected the success of co-teaching. One of the surprising findings was that the academic content itself, whether it was social studies or chemistry, did not appear to affect the success of co-teaching. However, if the special educator had mastered the academic content, the co-teaching experience was described as having a more equal teaching balance between the special and the general educators. If the special educator did not have a strong knowledge of the content, their role became one of assistant to the general educator. Another substantial finding of the case studies was that if the school was involved in high-stakes testing, the pace of instruction increased and there was less time for review or activities that reinforced content. When high-stakes testing was a priority, the special educator was again relegated to more of an assistant role rather than a co-teacher. Teacher compatibility emerged as a primary factor in the effectiveness of co-teaching. When teachers worked well together, students with disabilities were more likely to be fully included and treated like other students. When there was conflict between the teachers, the "inclusive experience of students with disabilities was more challenging" (Mastropieri et al., 2005, p. 268). The authors stated that the best co-teaching cases were built on mutual respect and trust, with each teacher valuing the other's expertise. Findings from this qualitative study are informative and could certainly be used to form effective co-teaching teams. If administrators understand the need to pair teachers who are compatible, who have knowledge in the content area, and who have the opportunity and time to provide supplemental activities to the content, co-teaching can benefit all stakeholders, students, and teachers, in the classroom. By listening to the voices of teachers who were experiencing co-teaching, insights were gained and could lead to policies within schools regarding effective co-teaching opportunities.

A qualitative study by Antia and Kreimeyer (2001) investigated teacher perspectives in inclusive settings on the use of interpreters for students who were deaf or hard of hearing. The case studied was at a school and involved 10 education professionals (i.e., three general educators, two special educators, three interpreters, one principal, and one special education coordinator) and were interviewed over the course of 3 years. In addition to the interview data, the researchers videotaped and observed in the classroom. The major findings of this study centered on the responsibility of the interpreters, the differing perspectives of the interpreters' role in the classroom, issues regarding full-time or part-time employment, and the change in the role of the interpreter over the length of the study. Findings indicated that interpreters assumed various roles within the classroom, with the primary role to provide "access to classroom communication through translation" (Antia & Kreimeyer, 2001, p. 363). Tutoring, facilitating peer communication, and informing both the general and the special educators of student progress were among the various roles interpreters were observed to perform. One of the interesting findings of this study was that general educators in the classroom preferred the interpreters to assume more roles and encourage a full participation model of interpreting. Conversely, special educators and administrators preferred the interpreters to assume a more mechanical model of interpreting and were actually concerned about the full participation model because they were concerned about the dependency of the student on the interpreter. Two of the interpreters, who were employed as interpreter/aides, viewed themselves as part of the classroom team. The third interpreter, who was employed solely as an interpreter and not an aide, was not as responsive to the needs of the teachers or students in areas other than interpretation. The authors also discussed the fact that there were no interpreter guidelines at the school and that both interpreters and teachers may have been acting with expediency in mind rather than understanding the issue of dependency on interpreters. This study emphasized the importance of clear expectations on the roles of interpreters by all team members. If roles were clearly delineated, then collaboration among team members would be facilitated and misperceptions of role responsibilities would be minimized. Special educators who are the liaison between general educators and interpreters might establish the roles by collaborating with the entire team. Collaboration on roles, responsibilities, and the necessity of encouraging full inclusion and limiting dependency on interpreters would contribute to a more effective practice for students who are deaf in inclusive settings.

CONCLUSION

This chapter was designed to give a brief overview of qualitative methodology and to provide examples of qualitative research in the field of special education. Hopefully, readers have gained a basic understanding of qualitative methods and more importantly of its potential and significance. I believe researchers should always select their methodology based on their research question. Qualitative methodology is applicable when one wants to obtain deep, rich, and complex perspectives of individuals who are involved in a particular phenomenon. These perspectives can guide policy, interactions, and interventions. Future research should focus on obtaining the voices of stakeholders in the field of special education. These stakeholders are numerous and include individuals with disabilities, general educators, special educators, special education directors, support personnel, paraprofessionals, family members of children with disabilities, administrators of special education programs, and employers in the community. The voices of individuals involved in the phenomenon of special education are not only numerous but are varied. For example, minority groups need to have their voices heard, individuals involved with Response to Intervention (RTI) need to be listened to concerning its effectiveness, and perhaps most importantly, those individuals who have disabilities need to have a voice. The value of qualitative research is that it allows these voices to be heard. However, the methodology and rigor must be strong to assure the audience, researcher, and participants that their views are expressed as they intended.

REFERENCES

Angell, M. E., Bailey, R. L., & Stoner, J. B. (2008). Family perceptions of facilitators and inhibitors of effective school-based dysphagia management. *Language, Speech, and Hearing Services in the Schools, 39*, 214–226.

Angell, M. E., Stoner, J. B., & Shelden, D. L. (2009). Trust in education professionals: Perspectives of mothers of children with disabilities. *Remedial and Special Education, 30*(3), 160–176.

Antia, S. D., & Kreimeyer, K. H. (2001). The role of interpreters in inclusive classrooms. *Annals of the Deaf, 146*(4), 355–365.

Bailey, R. L., Parette, H. P., Stoner, J. B., Angell, M. E., & Carroll, K. (2006a). Family members' perceptions of augmentative and alternative communication device use. *Language, Speech, and Hearing Services in the Schools, 37*, 50–60.

Bailey, R. L., Stoner, J. B., Parette, H. P., & Angell, M. E. (2006b). AAC team perceptions: Augmentative and alternative communication device use. *Education and Training in Developmental Disabilities, 41*(2), 139–154.

Barbour, R. S. (2001). Checklists for improving rigour in qualitative research: A case of the tail wagging the dog? *British Medical Journal, 322*, 1115–1117.

Bays, D. A., & Crockett, J. B. (2007). Investigating instructional leadership for special education. *Exceptionality, 15*(3), 143–161.

Blaska, J. (1998). *Cyclical grieving: Reoccurring emotions experienced by parents who have children with disabilities*. St. Cloud, MN: Department of Child & Family Studies, St. Cloud State University. (ERIC Document Reproduction Service No. ED419349).

Bogden, R., & Biklen, S. (1998). *Qualitative research in education: An introduction to theory and methods*. Boston, MA: Allyn and Bacon.

Brantlinger, E., Jimenez, R., Klingner, J., Pugach, M., & Richardson, V. (2005). Qualitative studies in special education. *Exceptional Children, 71*(2), 195–207.

Brown, K. S., Welsh, L. A., Haegle Hill, K., & Cipko, J. P. (2008). The efficacy of embedding special education instruction in teacher preparation programs in the United States. *Teaching and Teacher Education: An International Journal of Research and Studies, 24*(8), 2087–2094.

Butera, G. (2005). Collaboration in the context of Appalachia: The case of Cassie. *The Journal of Special Education, 39*(2), 106–116.

Charmaz, K. (2000). Grounded theory: Objectivist and constructivist methods. In: N. K. Denzin & Y. S. Lincoln (Eds), *Handbook of qualitative research* (pp. 509–536). Thousand Oaks, CA: Sage.

Creswell, J. (2008). *Educational research: Planning, conducting, and evaluating quantitative and qualitative research*. Upper Saddle River, NJ: Merrill Prentice Hall.

Fontana, F., & Frey, J. (2000). The interview: From structured questions to negotiated text. In: N. K. Denzin & Y. S. Lincoln (Eds), *Handbook of qualitative research* (pp. 645–672). Thousand Oaks, CA: Sage.

Harry, B., Klingner, J. K., & Hart, J. (2005). African American families under fire: Ethnographic views of family strengths. *Remedial and Special Education, 26*(2), 101–112.

Heyl, B. S. (1997). Talking across the differences in collaborative fieldwork: Unanticipated consequences. *The Sociological Quarterly, 38*, 1–18.

Janesick, V. (2000). The choreography of qualitative research design. In: N. K. Denzin & Y. S. Lincoln (Eds), *Handbook of qualitative research* (pp. 379–399). Thousand Oaks, CA: Sage.

Kinchin, I. M., & Hay, D. B. (2000). How a qualitative approach to concept map analysis can be used to aid learning by illustrating patterns of conceptual development. *Educational Research, 42*(1), 43–57.

Klassen, R. M. (2002). A question of calibration: A review of the self-efficacy beliefs of students with learning disabilities. *Learning Disability Quarterly, 25*, 88–103.

Klassen, R. M. (2007). Using predictions to learn about the self-efficacy of early adolescents with and without learning disabilities. *Contemporary Educational Psychology, 32*, 173–187.

Klassen, R. M., & Lynch, S. L. (2007). Self-efficacy from the perspective of adolescents with LD and their specialist teachers. *Journal of Learning Disabilities, 40*(6), 494–507.

Lake, J. F., & Billingsley, B. S. (2000). An analysis of factors that contribute to parent-school conflict in special education. *Remedial and Special Education, 21*(4), 240–251.

Leedy, P., & Ormrod, J. (2001). *Practical research: Planning and design* (4th ed.). Upper Saddle River, NJ: Merrill Prentice Hall.

Lincoln, Y., & Guba, E. (1985). *Naturalistic inquiry*. Newberry Park, CA: Sage.

Mastropieri, M. A., Scruggs, T. E., Graetz, J., Norland, J., Gardizi, W., & McDuffie, K. (2005). Case studies in co-teaching in the content areas: Successes, failures, and challenges. *Intervention in School and Clinic, 40*(5), 260–270.

McDuffie, K. A., & Scruggs, T. E. (2008). The contributions of qualitative research to discussions of evidence-based practice in special education. *Intervention in School and Clinic, 44*(2), 91–97.

Miles, M., & Huberman, A. (1994). *Qualitative data analysis*. Thousand Oaks, CA: Sage.

O'Brian, M. M., Stoner, J. B., Appel, K., & Gresens, J. J. (2007). The first field experience: Perspectives of preservice and cooperating teachers. *Teacher Education and Special Education, 30*(4), 264–275.

Purcell, M. L., Horn, E., & Palmer, S. (2007). A qualitative study of the initiation and continuation of preschool inclusion programs. *Exceptional Children, 74*(1), 85–99.

Scruggs, T. E., Mastropieri, M. A., & McDuffie, K. A. (2007). Co-teaching in inclusive classrooms: A metasynthesis of qualitative research. *Exceptional Children, 73*(4), 392–416.

Shank, G. D. (2006). *Qualitative research: A personal skills approach*. Upper Saddle River, NJ: Pearson Merrill Prentice Hall.

Stake, R. (1995). *The art of the case study research*. Thousand Oaks, CA: Sage.

Stake, R. (2000). Case studies. In: N. K. Denzin & Y. S. Lincoln (Eds), *Handbook of qualitative research* (pp. 435–454). Thousand Oaks, CA: Sage.

Stoner, J. B., & Angell, M. E. (2006). Parent perspectives on role engagement: An investigation of parents of children with ASD and their self-reported roles with education professionals. *Focus on Autism and Other Developmental Disabilities, 21*(3), 177–189.

Stoner, J. B., Angell, M. E., House, J. J., & Bock, S. J. (2007). Transitions: A parental perspective from parents of young children with autism spectrum disorder (ASD). *Journal of Developmental and Physical Disabilities, 19*, 23–39.

Stoner, J. B., Angell, M. E., House, J. J., & Goins, K. (2006a). Self-determination: Hearing the voices of adults with physical disabilities. *Physical Disabilities: Education and Related Services, 25*, 3–35.

Stoner, J. B., Bailey, R. L., Angell, M. E., Robbins, J., & Polewski, K. (2006b). Perspectives of parents/guardians of children with feeding/swallowing problems. *Journal of Developmental and Physical Disabilities, 18*(4), 333–353.

Stoner, J. B., Beck, A. R., Bock, S. J., Hickey, K., Kosuwan, K., & Thompson, J. R. (2006c). The effectiveness of the Picture Exchange Communication System (PECS) with nonspeaking adults. *Remedial and Special Education, 27*(3), 154–165.

Stoner, J. B., Bock, S. J., Thompson, J. R., Angell, M. E., Heyl, B., & Crowley, E. P. (2005). Welcome to our world: Parent perceptions of the interactions between parents of young children with autism spectrum disorder (ASD) and education professionals. *Focus on Autism and Other Developmental Disabilities, 20*, 39–51.

Strauss, A., & Corbin, J. (1998). *Basics of qualitative research: Grounded theory procedures and techniques*. Thousand Oaks, CA: Sage.

Woodward, J., & Brown, C. (2006). Meeting the curricula needs of academically low-achieving students in middle grade mathematics. *The Journal of Special Education, 40*(3), 151–159.

PART II
LANGUAGE, COMMUNICATION, AND EDUCATION

CHAPTER 3

BILINGUALISM AND EDUCATION: EDUCATING AT-RISK LEARNERS

Fabiola P. Ehlers-Zavala

THE SCHOOLING OF AT-RISK LEARNERS

The changing U.S. demographics, characterized by the rapid growth in immigration (Suarez-Orozco, 2003; U.S. Census Bureau, 2000), and the No Child Left Behind (NCLB) legislation are good reasons to prompt all educational stakeholders to seriously examine the practices of educating learners at risk of educational failure. Among at-risk learners, a significant portion is made up of English language learners (ELLs), especially those who are newcomers (i.e., ELLs who are fairly new to the school community in the United States with little or no English proficiency). The last census revealed that immigration accounts for more than "70% of the growth of the American population," and that "the foreign born-population reached 30 million" (Portes & Hao, 2004, p. 1). Of this group, Hispanic students comprise the fastest growing group, and among Hispanics born outside the United States, 44.2% drop out from the educational system between the ages of 16 and 24 years (National Center for Education Statistics, 2001). For this reason, discussions and debates on the best way to educate ELLs for effective English language acquisition leading to academic achievement in U.S. schools remain at the forefront of educational debates. At the core of this discussion, the question of whether or not to provide bilingual education services to learners for whom English is not their dominant or native language remains as one of the, if not *the*, greatest long-standing political, ideological, educational battles in the United States.

In addition to ideological and political differences of opinion among tax payers, scholars, and policy makers, the battle over the idea of promoting bilingualism in the United States, and offering bilingual programs to learners who do not speak English has been exacerbated due to various related issues. First, within bilingual education, there exist diverse programmatic alternatives to consider, so further disagreements continue to unfold regarding this single topic. Second, the nature of ELLs is vastly diverse, complicating matters even further because one approach is unlikely to meet the needs of diverse ELLs. Third, the oftentimes extremely linguistically and culturally diverse context of schools makes it challenging to offer bilingual programs because of the question of what to do with learners of less commonly taught languages present in the schools when no human/curricular resources exist to properly meet their needs. Fourth, in the United States, there is a shortage in the number of highly qualified bilingual teachers, which has prompted school districts to adopt measures that have not necessarily resulted in better educational practices (e.g., hiring foreign bilingual teachers who, despite their remarkable qualifications in their home countries, may lack the understanding of what it means to educate ELLs in the U.S. context). Fifth, even when political and ideological support exists for bilingual education, well-designed and implemented programs are sometimes still hard to come by for various additional problems that can be often summarized in one phrase: *lack of resources.*

Nevertheless, within this very challenging context, it remains necessary to have an adequate understanding of the possibilities that exist. The solution to the effective education of at-risk learners may not be reached overnight, but it is critical to understand that a brighter educational future for them is indeed possible. For this reason, in this chapter, the issues pertaining to at-risk ELLs first in the context of the learners themselves are discussed. The chapter begins with a discussion of the diversity among these learners, which shows why, in some cases, it is difficult, though not impossible, to embrace a single approach to a more effective education conducive to their academic success. Then, an overview of the phenomenon we have come to know as bilingualism is addressed. In doing so, core terminology related to the topic of bilingualism is introduced, and I discuss its connection to bilingual education, and bilingual special education. Finally, it is argued why the topics of bilingualism and bilingual education ultimately merit our attention and support.

DIVERSITY OF ENGLISH LANGUAGE LEARNERS IN THE UNITED STATES

ELLs are vastly diverse, so any attempts to describe ELLs must offer a fair acknowledgement of this critical aspect that characterizes them as such. The only common denominator to all ELLs is that English is neither their dominant nor their native language. For some of them, English may not even be their second language, rather their third or fourth language.

Some ELLs are recent arrivals. They may have come to the United States willingly (e.g., as part of an educational exchange program) or not (e.g., as refugees, as children of parents who made the decision willingly or not to migrate to the United States). Some of these ELLs may or may not have been exposed to English in their home countries. Some of these ELLs may be literate in their native language; others may not. This situation may relate to the length of time they may have spent elsewhere with or without the opportunity to attend school, which is often contingent upon family resources.

Other ELLs may have been born in the United States to families who do not speak English; therefore, they may not speak English because it is not the language of the household or of their immediate community. Others may have been born to families in the United States in which the parents speak one or more languages, so that several languages are used around them, and, consequently, these ELLs may be not bilingual, but multilingual. Some of them may be immersed in highly literate environments; again, others may not.

Furthermore, as readers of this chapter may anticipate, similar to what happens among monolingual learners, some ELLs are also exceptional learners. Some may exhibit one or more disabilities; others may be gifted. It is important to note that exceptional ELLs are difficult to account for in our communities due to the administration of inappropriate assessments that fail to take into account linguistic issues exhibited among ELLs. Because of inappropriate diagnostic assessment and varying definitional frameworks, historically, there have been both an overrepresentation of ELLs in special education (Cummins, 1991) and an underrepresentation of ELLs among the gifted, especially among those ELLs of Hispanic backgrounds (Kogan, 2001). Also, some ELLs with disabilities have not been properly diagnosed as such because of the language issue. Oftentimes, teachers who lack proper assessment training may have a difficult time distinguishing between a language acquisition problem and a learning disability or giftedness. In other words, the identification of either type of learner (with a learning disability or gifted) is continually challenged by the heterogeneity of the learners themselves as exceptional children. As with any other group of learners, those who have disabilities and those who are gifted are vastly diverse. Such diversity challenges any assessment practices, and calls for professionals with expertise on bilingual special education, of which there are only too few at any given educational location, if any.

Last, it should be mentioned that some other ELLs are also long-term language learners. They may have arrived as adults who may not be fully proficient in English and continue to struggle with their acquisition of English, as in the case of migrant workers (temporary or not) for whom it may not be easy to further their development of English, particularly when they are illiterate in their own dominant language. Other adult ELLs may come to the United States with advanced levels of proficiency in English, so that they are faced with a much smoother transition into their new life here.

Consequently, as it may be anticipated by now, there are many factors that will influence the depiction of ELLs. Their success or lack of success is influenced by many factors such as individual experiences, family language literacy experiences, community and socio-cultural factors, instructional factors, underlying cognitive abilities, print-related abilities, and oral language abilities (Genesee, 2005). In other words, their performance in English is mediated by their previous experiences, skills, and knowledge regarding both their native language or dominant language, and their second or foreign language, such as in English. That is to say, the nature of the learner together with the degree of bilingualism and biliteracy development achieved is closely connected to their social, academic and/or professional success in their new location. For this reason, it is highly inappropriate to either fully condemn or adopt a single approach to work with ELLs.

WHAT BILINGUALISM ENTAILS

The term bilingualism "has always been with us" (Dewaele, Housen, & Wei, 2003, p. 1). Yet, as a term, it remains as one of the most semantically open-ended linguistic items that exist. As such, it is capable of evoking a myriad of meanings, denotations, feelings, reactions (both negative and positive) on the part of human beings, leading to conflicting ideologies, and never ending political battles. Some scholars challenge the notion of being able to precisely define it. They argue that it is "essentially and ultimately impossible" (Baker, 2006, p. 16) to do, yet some sort of approximation may still be necessary to come to terms with it.

Bilingualism can be understood as an individual characteristic or as a characteristic of social group, whether it is a majority or minority group in society (Baker, 2006). Most commonly, when thought of as the characteristic of one individual, in the mind of the average person, bilingualism corresponds to the use of two languages by an individual with comparable levels of proficiency in both (Chin & Wigglesworth, 2007; Pavlenko, 2005). In turn, as a societal trait, bilingualism is observed when two languages exist in society, after all "there is no language without a language community" (Baker, 2006, p. 68). When two languages are used in society, existing geographically side by side, the term *diglossia* is used (Baker, 2006). It is important to clarify that the term diglossia is not equivalent to the term bilingualism, but together they can be used to illustrate distinct language situations that may be present in society. Consequently, in a given community, bilingualism and diglossia may, according to Baker (2006):

(a) coexist, as in the case where one sees that a language community comprises bilingual individuals who use languages for different purposes;
(b) exist without the other, as when there are bilinguals in a community, but no two languages are used to fulfill different purposes (bilingualism without diglossia); or in a community whew there are two languages used: one language is used by one group; the other language is used by the other group (diglossia without bilingualism);
(c) not practically exist (neither diglossia nor bilingualism), as in the case of communities that have "been forcibly changed to a relatively monolingual society" (p. 70).

The literature on bilingualism has undergone considerable growth over the past 20 years (Dewaele et al., 2003), and it offers ample evidence to account for the complexities of this phenomenon. For the past many years, scholars have problematized its definition and pointed at the oftentimes conflicting issues associated with this term. Pavlenko (2005, p. 6), for example, argues that some scholars view bilingualism and multilingualism as the language phenomena exhibited by those who "who use two or more languages or dialects in their everyday lives–be simultaneously (in language contact situations) or consecutively (in the context of immigration)." Pavlenko reiterates the claim that bilingual "speakers rarely exhibit equal fluency in all language skills, due to the complementarity principle – that is, the fact that their multiple languages are usually acquired and used in different contexts, with different people, and for different purposes" (p. 6). Indeed, the differing degrees of fluency in bilingualism are best understood when this phenomenon is carefully and adequately contextualized as it is being described. It is nevertheless fair to say that *bilingualism* is certainly a language competence–related matter that needs to be understood in light of the sociocultural and cognitive factors (linguistic and nonlinguistic) that shape this phenomenon on the part of language users. In other words, the use of either language on the part of the bilingual is largely done in accordance to the context to fulfill different purposes in light of different audiences and communicative demands. Diverse array of uses will lead to distinct types of bilingualism both as an individual characteristic and as a societal trait.

TYPES OF BILINGUALISM AND BILINGUAL ACQUISITION

Given that there is no single path to become bilingual, bilingualism is hardly a single-faceted phenomenon; therein the existence of diverse terms to describe different kinds of bilinguals and different types of processes to achieve bilingualism. On the basis of the path leading to bilingual acquisition, we may initially and broadly distinguish two basic terms: *sequential bilingualism* and *simultaneous bilingualism*. The former refers to the case in which bilinguals learn one language first, and later in life they add another language to their linguistic repertoire. For instance, this is often the case for many learners who learn a foreign language at school. Oftentimes, the literature of second-language acquisition (SLA) is most pertinent to understand and describe this situation. The latter, simultaneous bilingualism, is observed when an individual is exposed to two languages concurrently in the surrounding environment (i.e., the home), oftentimes from birth. This is typically the case in which children are born to bilingual or multilingual parents. In this case, children are exposed to two (or more) languages from the start in their households or immediate environments. This situation has come to be known as bilingual first-language acquisition (BFLA). De Houwer (2009, p. 2) defined BFLA, which, as she noted, appears to have been first introduced by Merrill Swain in her 1976 dissertation, as "the development of language in young children who hear two languages spoken to them from birth. BFLA children are learning two first languages. There is no chronological difference between the two languages in terms of when the children started to hear them." The research on BFLA is likely to help us more accurately understand the process of becoming bilingual when simultaneously exposed to two languages, as is the case of many ELLs in linguistically and culturally diverse countries such as the United States.

The fact that some individuals may be simultaneously exposed to two languages from birth does not mean that they will grow up to become bilingual. Changing circumstances in the personal lives of individuals certainly mediate the ultimate outcome. Likewise, not all children who hear two languages from birth may develop the ability to use the two eventually either. De Houwer (2009, p. 2) pointed out that "it is not uncommon for BFLA children to speak just one of the languages they have been addressed since birth. When BFLA children understand two languages but speak only one, they may be called 'passive' bilinguals, although there is nothing passive about understanding two languages and speaking one."

Moreover, not all bilingualism develops from birth. For many individuals, becoming bilingual is the result of changing circumstances over which they may or may not have had control. When individuals choose to become bilingual, we use the term *elective bilingualism*. This is the case when individuals choose to study another language for various reasons (i.e., personal fulfillment and professional advancement). Conversely, when individuals find themselves having to learn another language due to new circumstances in life, we use the term *circumstantial bilingualism*. An example of this type of bilingualism can be observed when becoming bilingual represents a matter of survival for an individual in a new environment, as is the case of refugees in a foreign land.

Additionally, the term bilingualism can also be described according to the levels of proficiency individuals exhibit in their performance or use of each of the two (or more) languages. At the most proficient end of the continuum, we can talk about *balanced bilingualism*, which is observed when an individual displays a strong command of the two languages. At the least proficient end, we can talk about *incipient bilingualism*, which is observed when individuals know enough about a language to manage in a communicative situation. As Baker (2006, p. 8) described, "the term *incipient bilingualism* allows people with minimal competence in a second language to squeeze into the bilingual category." This is the case of the typical traveler who knows a few phrases here and there and gets by in a foreign country. Additionally, there exists yet another term, *functional bilingualism*. It refers to how the bilinguals make use of their bilingualism in various contexts (i.e., work, hobbies, and religious meetings).

An exhaustive understanding of the term bilingualism as it relates to the nature of language use and abilities will call for a description that takes into account (a) degrees and abilities, (b) types of bilingualism, (c) types or contexts of use, (d) personal characteristics of individuals (i.e., age, culture, motivation, and development) as experienced or enacted by bilinguals or language users. For a more detailed description of these dimensions, see Baker (2006, pp. 3–4).

CONNECTING BILINGUALISM TO BOTH BILINGUAL EDUCATION AND BILINGUAL SPECIAL EDUCATION

Although the word bilingualism suggests the use of "two languages," for many, it often comes as a surprise to learn that, in the U.S. context, the term bilingualism connects to the term bilingual education in ways that may not be always indicative of the development of two languages on the part of the learner. Bilingual education in the U.S. context is an umbrella term that encompasses various programmatic alternatives that may or may not be available for ELLs. Whether they exist or not is contingent upon many factors, which are primarily mediated by whether or not a given state mandates one type of bilingual education over another, if any at all.

Bilingual education in the United States and abroad is not a new phenomenon. It has a long-standing history (Baca & Cervantes, 2004). What may be considered a fairly new phenomenon in the United States is federal support given to bilingual education, which was started on January 2, 1968, with the passage of the Bilingual Education Act, most commonly known as Title VII of the Elementary and Secondary Education Act. This piece of legislation set aside federal moneys to fund school programs, provide professional development to teachers, and conduct research. Since its original inception, this act underwent a number of amendments (1978, 1984, and 1988). In 2002, under the NCLB legislation, programs for ELLs were authorized under Title III. As Baca and Cervantes (2004, p. 91) noted:

> New provisions focus on promoting English acquisition and helping LEP [limited English proficient] students meet challenging content standards. Federal funds are allocated primarily to states, which issue subgrants to school districts and are held accountable for LEP and immigrant students' academic progress and English attainment. Professional development programs are also supported.

Following Baca and Cervantes (2004), it is important to clarify that, to date, there has been no federal mandate that has called for the provision of bilingual special education to bilingual exceptional learners. "Existing laws, however, in both bilingual education and special education do apply to bilingual exceptional children" (p. 96). This means that the fate that bilingual exceptional children face in the United States regarding programmatic alternatives offered to them is very similar to the one faced by children who are not identified as exceptional.

Within U.S. bilingual education, programmatic alternatives that exist vary in terms of their educational and societal aims. These programs with specific goals and aims could be visually plotted along a continuum. At one end of the bilingual educational continuum, we find programs that aim at ensuring that learners enrolled in those programs become fully bilingual and fully biliterate. Their societal aim is to contribute to a pluralistic society. These programs are additive in nature (Soltero, 2004). Also, these programs may be known under various labels, namely, two-way immersion, one-way immersion, and dual language – the most commonly known. Despite their exponential growth since the 1990s, they are not the most prevalent across the United States. It is important to note that even among these programs, and despite their common goals of biliteracy and bilingualism, there may be considerable variability in their design and implementation. Differences in design may be found in regard to the types of participants, and the ways in how the delivery of the curriculum and language use is set up. For instance, the main difference between two-way immersion and one-way immersion is that the former involves an equal number of both native and nonnative speakers of two languages in the classroom. One-way immersion programs do not. They aim at having a homogenous group of learners. That is, all learners in a one-way immersion class are native speakers of one same language, and they are all learning the same second/foreign language. Both, two-way immersion programs and one-way immersion programs are dual language programs because they aim at ensuring that their participants become fully bilingual and biliterate.

Despite their common goals of bilingualism and biliteracy, they may be designed and implemented differently, based on the resources available (both human and material), and the ideologies embraced by the various stakeholders (i.e., parents, tax payers, and school officials). In contexts, where stakeholders seem to exhibit a greater degree of tolerance and faith for how bilingualism and bilingual literacy development unfold, schools may be able to more successfully implement a 90/10 dual language education model that gradually shifts to a 50/50 model as learners make progress through the grade levels. This 90/10 or 50/50 proportion refers to how the percentage of language use during the instructional day is distributed across grade levels. In the 50/50 situation, both languages are distributed equally from the start of the program (Kindergarten or first grade) until the sixth grade. In the 90/10 design, broadly speaking, there is greater use of the non-English language in the earlier grades that shifts gradually to reach a 50/50 design around the fourth grade. For instance, in the 90/10 model, in the case of an English/Spanish dual language program:

> Ninety percent of the instructional day is devoted to content instruction in the target language (e.g., Spanish) and 10 percent in English in kindergarten and first grade. [...] In

second and third grades, students receive 80 percent instruction in Spanish and 20 percent in English. By fourth, fifth, and sixth grades, time of instruction in both languages becomes 50-50. (Calderón & Minaya-Rowe, 2003, p. 29)

Well-conceived dual language programs operate under the assumption that the learner will remain in the program for six years without major disruptions – which, in theory, is the minimum number of years that learners typically require to begin to exhibit and enjoy academic success, which is the natural consequence derived from having developed advanced levels of bilingualism, not only in the social but also in the academic context. For more details regarding other decisions related to design and implementation, see Calderón and Minaya-Rowe (2003).

At the other end of the bilingual education continuum, we identify programs that could be very well known as pseudo-bilingual programs because their goal is not to help learners become fully bilingual or biliterate. Because of their transitional nature, these programs are substractive (Soltero, 2004). Their societal aim is to promote assimilation, and even within this group, there is programmatic diversity. That is, they may be of different kinds: (a) submersion (sink or swim), (b) structured English immersion, or (c) transitional bilingual education (early exit or late exit). These transitional bilingual education programs are the most prevalent forms of bilingual education across the United States (Freeman, 2007). They have been more widely adopted and implemented in states that embrace bilingual education. Their goal is to transition learners into English (in the U.S. context), not to foster the development or maintenance of the learners' native or heritage language. The native language of the learners is used only during the transition to connect with the learners, and facilitate the process of ensuring that the learners are not academically falling behind. Clearly, learners in these programs may not become bilingual; thus, they have fewer chances of ever experiencing the benefits of reaching full bilingualism and biliteracy. What is worse, by not becoming fully bilingual and biliterate, they may be deprived from developing to their fullest potential. Any degrees of bilingual/biliteracy attainment of learners in these programs may be more closely related to non-school-related interventions. That is, it may be the result of the context outside the school that supports and fosters bilingualism (e.g., family and neighborhood). Oftentimes, these learners who have participated in transitional bilingual education programs realize later in life that they were deprived of a personal linguistic/cultural resource that could have given them an asset that oftentimes is recognized as such when entering college or pursuing a job in the United States or abroad.

When these bilingual education alternatives are not in place at a given school, meeting the needs of ELLs is typically attempted through English as a second language (ESL) classes. Sometimes, these ESL support programs unfold in different ways. For instance, in an ESL push-in model, the ESL specialist comes into a classroom to attend the needs of the ESL learner(s). In a pull-out model, learners leave the mainstream classroom to meet with the ESL specialist for additional support. In some contexts, learners receive their content instruction through sheltered classes so that they may have sheltered math, for instance, where the teacher utilizes specific techniques and engages in curricular modifications and adaptations to provide learners with meaningful access to the curriculum and foster English language development. However, it is important to note that ESL programs are not bilingual programs. In these programs, there is little or no use of the native language of the learners, and the goal is not to assist with the development or maintenance of the learners' native language. The sole goal is to help ELLs in the task of learning English to transition to the mainstream classroom. It should be pointed out that all well-designed bilingual programs should have an ESL component/offering delivered by properly trained and certified ESL professionals. Furthermore, some schools may even offer newcomer programs for the newly arrived learner in the school/country, among other family literacy programs.

Both transitional bilingual education programs and ESL programs in the United States are geared toward serving the needs of minority language learners. To meet the needs of majority language learners in the United States, outside the dual language or two-way immersion options, foreign language teaching and learning is the most prevailing form of bilingual education. This programmatic alternative may still not be enough for the true development and attainment of full bilingualism and biliteracy. The reason for this lack of success may obey to the fact that, in most cases, foreign language instruction starts in high school, and it lasts for a few years – in other words: "too little; too late." The short duration of these programs may not be enough to ensure the goal of helping learners become bilingual and biliterate.

WHY ATTENDING TO DEVELOPMENTS IN BILINGUALISM AND BILINGUAL EDUCATION MATTERS

There are many reasons why the topic of bilingualism and bilingual education merit our attention. Advocates of bilingual education, including myself, firmly believe that bilingualism and biliteracy are both individual and societal assets. First, bilingual education or the learning of a foreign/second language is a human right. All learners, including those with special needs, have the right to pursue bilingual education. This position is in direct alignment with the Salamanca guidelines drawn by UNESCO (1998), which constitute the first international document that addresses the specific needs and rights of learners with special needs. Basically this document states that, upon following proper design and implementation that considers and is responsive to learners' interests, abilities, and learning paths, all children have the right to learn languages other than their native language.

Second, bilingualism, or multilingualism, when made possible through the implementation of well-designed strong forms of bilingual education programs, contributes to the development of one's own fullest potential. Successful bilinguals can enjoy the benefits of bilingualism, such as reaching maximum cognitive development and self-growth, attaining greater educational and professional opportunities in adulthood, fostering and developing better intercultural or interethnic relations. The effectiveness of dual language education, for example, has been well documented in the United States (Lindholm-Leary, 2001; Thomas & Collier, 1997) and abroad (Dutcher, 1995). Research has shown that "English language learners who participated in dual language education programs outperformed comparable monolingually schooled students in academic achievement after four to seven years in the program" (Soltero, 2004, p. 15). For bilingual exceptional children, bilingualism, and bilingual education properly designed and implemented, may be the key to their ultimate success. Consequently, it is important to demystify the misconceptions surrounding exceptional children and the learning of foreign languages, which, according to Baca and Cervantes (2004, pp. 149–154), are the following: (a) students with exceptionalities cannot learn two (or more) languages; (b) parents of CLD students, with and without exceptionalities, should speak with their children at home in English; (c) acquiring more than one language is "difficult" and can lead to academic problems; and (d) some bilingual students do not speak any language to a real extent are "semilingual."

The truth is that students with exceptionalities can only benefit from developing their native language because it is the language they understand and can serve as the foundation for successfully acquiring English. However, it is important to understand that it is not enough to just send these students to bilingual education programs. Their inclusion in these programs needs to be done in appropriate ways, following the necessary modifications and interventions leading to a successful experience (Baca &

Cervantes, 2004). Bilingual educators with special education training must be employed in these programs. Parents should contribute to the maintenance of the native or heritage language to support the linguistic, cultural, social, and psychological development of their children. The learning of more than one language does happen in many contexts around the world in very natural ways, and when properly done or fostered, it can only lead to academic and personal successes in the long-run. Finally, as Baca and Cervantes (2004, p. 151) pointed out, "the idea of 'semilingualism' can be very compelling when we do not fully understand language development." But, as bilingual/multilingual education experts can attest, bilingual development takes time, and that there are many factors influencing the outcome. Not so positive outcomes, such as what may be perceived or described as semilingualism, are certainly possible. But they are typically observed when bilingual education programs are not properly designed or implemented. Negative outcomes are the direct result of the lack of knowledge on the part of stakeholders and those in decision-making positions regarding bilingualism and bilingual education. The opposite is true when experts are brought into the design and implementation of strong bilingual education programs that are supported and embraced from an informed position by all stakeholders (i.e., parents, teachers, staff, and community).

Third, bilingualism is a primary key to a nation's sustainable economic growth. In a global era, most individuals are increasingly confronted with the opportunity to become global citizens, and in turn, language learners (Kormos & Kontra, 2008). This situation is true regardless of whether or not an individual physically relocates to another part of the world. Thanks to the increasing access to technology, and business outsourcing, a greater number of people have an opportunity to interact with individuals around the globe. Oftentimes, this interaction is conducted through English, but effective intercultural understanding and communication is best understood and achieved when individuals have gone through the process of learning another language. Exceptional learners, those with special needs (e.g., deaf individuals, people with language and learning disorders, and/or with physical disabilities) and gifted, are not the exception to this fact. For exceptional learners, like for those who are not exceptional, learning another language helps them in "maintaining political and social relations, mobility in work and education, foreign trade, international companies, projects and cultural events, foreign travel and tourism all require that people have a shared language by means of which they can understand each other" (Kormos & Kontra, 2008, p. 1).

CONCLUSION

In the United States, the majority of ELLs are at-risk learners of educational failure. Exceptional ELLs, or bilingual/multilingual learners with exceptional needs, face the additional risk of being at-risk of learning a foreign language due to the misconceptions surrounding the topic. Historically, for the most part, their needs have not been properly met through the programmatic decisions that have been provided to them. Largely, the educational alternatives they have experienced have deprived them of reaching their fullest potential, as in the case when no bilingual education has been available or poor bilingual programs have been designed and implemented.

Because of the changing demographics of this nation, that is becoming increasingly linguistically and culturally diverse, and the country's commitment to leaving not a single child behind, it is particularly important that all citizens, and educators in particular, gain a better and informed understanding of topics such as bilingualism, multilingualism, bilingual education, and related matters. Because, in the United States the education of citizens is decided by each state, voters are the ones who, in the end, have the potential to advance or limit the educational opportunities of their children leading to their utmost success and personal development, and in turn, to the economic and sustainable growth of this nation. Consequently, it is up to educators to eventually help educate all stakeholders in their respective local communities as to the benefits of promoting full bilingualism and biliteracy. Individually, we may not be able to directly improve our nation, but collectively, we may be able have a greater positive impact if we focus on improving our children's schooling, and their schools.

REFERENCES

Baca, L. M., & Cervantes, H. T. (2004). *The bilingual special education interface* (4th ed.). Upper Saddle River, NJ: Pearson/Merrill Prentice Hall.
Baker, C. (2006). *Foundations of bilingual education and bilingualism* (4th ed.). Buffalo, NY: Multilingual Matters.
Calderón, M. E., & Minaya-Rowe, L. (2003). *Designing and implementing two-way bilingual programs.* Thousand Oaks, CA: Corwin Press, Inc.
Chin, N. B., & Wigglesworth, G. (2007). *Bilingualism: An advanced resource book.* New York: Routledge.
Cummins, J. (1991). *Bilingualism and special education: Issues in assessment and pedagogy.* Austin, TX: ProEd.
De Houwer, A. (2009). *Bilingual first language acquisition.* Buffalo, NY: Multilingual Matters.

Dewaele, J., Housen, A., & Wei, L. (Eds). (2003). *Bilingualism: Beyond basic principles*. Buffalo, NY: Multilingual Matters.

Dutcher, N. (1995). *Overview of foreign language students in the United States*. National Clearinghouse for Bilingual Education. Resource Collection Series, 6. Washington, DC: Center for Applied Linguistics.

Freeman, R. (2007). Reviewing the research on language education programs. In: O. García & C. Baker (Eds), *Bilingual education: An introductory reader* (pp. 3–18). Buffalo, NY: Multilingual Matters.

Genesee, F. (2005). Literacy development in ELLs: What does the research say? Paper presented at the Annual meeting of the National Association for Bilingual Education, San Antonio, TX.

Kogan, E. (2001). *Bilingual students: A paradox?* New York: Peter Lang Publishing.

Kormos, J., & Kontra, E. H. (Eds). (2008). *Language learners with special needs: An international perspective*. Buffalo, NY: Multilingual Matters.

Lindholm-Leary, K. J. (2001). *Dual language education*. Buffalo, NY: Multilingual Matters.

National Center for Education Statistics (Producer). (2001). *Dropout rates in the United States:1999*. Available at http://nces.ed.gov/pubs2001/dropout/StatusRates3.asp

Pavlenko, A. (2005). *Emotions and multilingualism*. New York: Cambridge University Press.

Portes, A., & Hao, L. (2004). The schooling of children of immigrants: Contextual effects on the educational attainment of the second generation. *Proceedings of the National Academy of Sciences of the United States of America, 101*(3). Advance online publication. Retrieved on April 20, 2009. doi: 10.1073/pnas.0403418101.

Soltero, S. W. (2004). *Dual language: Teaching and learning in two languages*. New York: Pearson/Allyn and Bacon.

Suarez-Orozco, C. (2003). Identities under siege: Immigration stress and social mirroring among the children of immigrants. In: A. C. M. Robben & M. M. Suarez-Orozco (Eds), *Cultures under siege, collective violence and trauma* (pp. 194–226). Cambridge, UK: Cambridge University Press.

Thomas, W., & Collier, V. (1997). Two languages are better than one. *Educational Leadership, 55*(4), 23–24.

UNESCO (Producer). (1998). *Declaração de Salamanca sobre pincípios, política e prácticas na area das necessidades educativas especiais* [The Salamanca statement and framework for action on special needs education]. Available at http://unesdoc.unesco.org/images/0013/001393/139394por.pdf

U.S. Census Bureau (producer). (2000). *Projections of the resident population by race, Hispanic origin, and nativity: Middle series, 2050 to 2070* (Available at http://www.census.gov/population/projections/nation/summary/np-t5-g.pdf). Washington, DC: U.S. Census Bureau.

CHAPTER 4

MASTERING ENGLISH TO ENHANCE EDUCATION

Dike Okoro

Mastering English, no doubt, has innumerable advantages to students, educators, civil servants, and professionals worldwide, irrespective of ethnic background or nationality. For example, immigrants who become proficient in English are likely to earn about 20 percent more than those who do not (Fish, 2002). History has shown that English is the language of business and the language preferred by most educators and business owners in the United States and worldwide (see Fish, 2002). As the editor of three anthologies of modern Anglophone African poetry, I value and respect my views regarding the many benefits mastering English provides for both speakers and writers. I have used English to present, project, and interpret African poetry to students, scholars, and educators. At the end of my presentation, my audience felt enlightened and appreciated. To me, my goal was not to share a message; I wanted to bridge the gap that exists when works translated from non-English languages into English language are misinterpreted. I never felt disturbed by the fact that the work translated might lose some of its original meaning; however, I felt satisfied with the positive feedback I received from my audience. My satisfaction, as I believed then and still do now, is predicated on the realization that English language is used for educational purpose. And this is why I wholeheartedly agree with the Jamaican writer Robotham's (2007, p. 1) assertion that

> Emancipation and Independence celebrations may strike some as an inappropriate time to insist that mastering English is the key to improving our educational performance. But, as pointed out last week in the article on youth education, substantially raising the educational and skills levels of our young people is critical to improving their economic circumstance. This cannot happen without mastering English.

Robotham's statement is crucial if we consider the fact that economics and the politics of language are intertwined. Governments in Third World nations such as Jamaica and elsewhere often make laws that affect their education system. And what better way to bring awareness to lawmakers than the reminder presented by Robotham's statement. It is no longer enough to dwell on impractical methods of teaching English to young people; they have to be educated on why mastering the language will help them to become productive citizens of their nation and the world. This, I believe, is at the base of Robotham's argument. But if arguments such as Robotham's are to be considered meaningful, we have to examine the problems associated with making mastering English to young people and adults a success.

EXTENT OF THE PROBLEM

This brings us to the question of the extent of the problem and how it might be alleviated. Well, because it is widely accepted that those who live in glasshouses should not throw stones, I shall be careful with my analysis of the problems associated with mastering English. In addition to English, I speak five languages. The adjustments I make on a daily basis to retain fluency in these non-English languages are quite tedious. Nevertheless, I have learnt to use these languages for situational purposes. I suppose students desiring to master English ought to do the opposite when it comes to embracing English and mastering its component. Should they choose to do so, they stand a good chance of reaping the benefits of mastering English in the United States or globally. Statistics and documented evidence shows that US immigrants who devote time and space to mastering English stand a good chance of enhancing their education and securing employment (see Miller & Ward, 2005). This is true because the United States is not yet a bilingual nation. Furthermore, documented evidence shows teachers in most American schools are working hard at implementing new approaches and methods that will help immigrant children and students in schools to succeed (see Ramakrishan, 2002). This is a positive sign for education in the United States. English is the language of commerce and the language that is used to educate the world when literature is disseminated at major international circuits and business transactions. As such, it is important that we make its usage and mastery a pivotal part of the education immigrant students receive irrespective of ethnic background. To provide key factors for my reasons, I will reference critical points made by teachers, politicians, writers, lawmakers, and educators concerning the mastery of English and the immigrant population in the United States. Much as I am interested in explaining why and how the mastery of English will help to enhance education for non-English-speaking immigrants, I am also interested in explaining why they need to master English.

BENEFITS OF MASTERING ENGLISH

In many ways Robotham's (2007) previous statement that "mastering English is key to improving our educational performance" confirms what we already know about the mastery of English in a society where English is the dominant language. In the case of the United States, the mastery of English is important for the young people from immigrant families. For example, there have been documented reports that reveal how students from non-English-speaking communities in Latin America, Africa, and Asia struggle in American schools as they try to adapt to the education system and American culture. In truth, majority of the problems these students face emanate from their inability to communicate effectively in English. While the difficulty to communicate effectively in English may not be linked to the education level of these students, because most of them arrive in the United States armed with undergraduate or graduate degrees, their ability to master English often determines their success in school and the workforce.

As noted earlier, Robotham's (2007) statement is shaped by the premise that "mastering English is the key to improving our educational performance." We deceive ourselves if we negate this fact. This is a clear statement directed at every sector imaginable in the social and educational fabric of American society. English proficiency is needed today for those who seek success or progress in the workforce. Moreover, majority of those in today's workforce were once students or have, by virtue of their job duty, encountered literature or text with instructions in English. They have graduated from the school systems that prepared them for the challenges of the real world. They have painstakingly exhausted time and energy in mastering reading and writing. Much of their experiences have normalized their mastery of grammar and other relevant aspects of the English language as they prepared for graduation. But not all those involved in the workforce today have a smooth transition in the learning of English. Some, as a result of language barrier, had to go to war with their own personal struggles to adopt and master a new language. This is where the challenge lies for most of those non-English-speaking immigrants to the United States attempting to master English or attain English proficiency. Because most of them already have a language of their own, the mastery of a new language becomes a burden and a challenge they must tackle. But most business transactions in the United States and other countries across the globe are conducted with English, a fact that further strengthens the relevance of mastering English. According to Ramakrishan (2002, p. 30),

> Whether we like it or not, English is the primary language of knowledge and technology. The primacy of English is obvious when one visits a library or enters a bookshop, or one accesses the internet or watches TV. Even in Europe, French is fast losing to English in popular use.

It is evident from Ramakrishan's statement that English is "the primary language of knowledge and technology." Unless we are discussing the possibility of mastering English in a non-English-speaking country, say France, which in this case will be irrelevant, it is essential for any non-native speaker of English in the United States to master English. For good reasons, mastering English provides many benefits for non-native speakers of English. Mastering English obviously will help a non-native speaker of English to overcome obstacles experienced during communication. For the non-native speaker, the ability to function in a literate society will open doors to effective communication, friendships, jobs, and the ability to read and write in English. These points are all advantages that will be enjoyed by those who work hard to master English.

How will we know the benefits non-native speakers of English in the United States stand to gain should they master English and enhance their education? Obvious answers to this question can be found in Robotham (2007) contention:

> Moving skills from the semi-to the fully skilled level in today's world, not to mention further technical and professional education, is inconceivable without a mastery of the written forms of the relevant language, whatever that language may be. In our case, this language is English. All the talk about business process outsourcing and 'job creation' will come to naught unless this issue is tackled frontally. So it is of the utmost urgency that we make mastering written English the real priority in our educational policy.

In examining Robotham's statement, we have to consider the logic involved in his claim. Education and the workforce go hand in hand. Communication in the workforce, as far as we know, is conducted in a language that is relevant. In the case of the United States, the language of communication or business is English. Although educators whose support for bilingual education remains uncontested may think otherwise, their views regarding this issue, even at the administrative level, remain divided.

GOVERNMENT SUPPORT/POLITICAL RESISTANCE TO MASTERING ENGLISH

According to Fish (2002, p. 1),

> The recent vote in favor of Question 2 by Massachusetts voters underscores the importance an overwhelming number of voters place on making our school children proficient in English but what of their parents? While English proficiency is seen as one of the leading determinants in students' success in school, proficiency in English is often the first rung on the ladder for the thousands of non-English speakers who come here searching for Economic opportunity. These first-generation Americans have become a critically important part of the economy of our Commonwealth.

The ideal situation for advocates of English proficiency for both parents and children of immigrant families would be to master English or acquire proficiency. Such accomplishments, by national standard, will make living in a society such as America useful to them and the society they live. For instance, they will make an easy transition into the society's social network, and assimilation will be attained sooner. Unless fortune smiles on them, in which case they choose or elect to lead an affluent lifestyle such as hiring interpreters so that they do not have to deal with the constant need for interpretation, non-English-speaking immigrants to the United States will assimilate quicker and find success sooner if they master English language. However, the level of mastery of English language will depend on the goals or plans adopted for the future. If they are simply interested in jobs, then they must learn at least the basic form of the English language. Also, should they elect to pursue education in high school or college, they will have to prepare their diction and command of English by taking preparatory classes. These steps are essential and cannot be avoided.

The United States is a nation blessed with the legacies of people from ethnic backgrounds across the globe, with most of its immigrant population from non-English-speaking countries without the ability to speak or communicate in the English language. This is one of the reasons why it is important for a vast majority, if not all of the immigrant population from non-English-speaking countries, to embrace the idea of mastering English to enhance education. If they succeed in doing so, in no time, employers and educators will be faced with fewer communication problems in the classroom. And accessing the difficulty of dealing with non-English-speaking employees or finding effective English Second Language (ESL) Programs will help new comers to the country with limited exposure to English language. But, for the record, let me stress the obvious here: the goal of encouraging the mastery of English is a favor done to actually help those non-native speakers. They stand the chance of increasing their productivity at work, assimilating quicker in a new society, and finding common ground with their children at home.

Unlike the much-maligned wave of criticism that has been directed at government officials who champion the cause for English mastery or proficiency, the truth remains that immigrant families from non-English-speaking countries will benefit immensely from mastering English. Former House Speaker Newt Gingrich, cited in an article titled "Gingrich says English should get official status" (Moscoso, 2007), contends, "Immigrant parents want their children to compete in the core American economic system and to have the highest possible income. That inherently requires mastering English" (p. 2). Today, criticisms by educators and critics whose views differ from that espoused by Gingrich and his likes have yielded little or no results whatsoever to suggest that immigrant families from non-English-speaking ethnic backgrounds do not need mastering English.

We live in a society that is constantly adapting to change, and the advancement of technology in the workforce is not making the ability to function in public easy for those who lack the mastery of English. Take, for example, the case of Gennadiy Stryzhak, 50, an immigrant from Ukraine who remembers visiting a doctor and laments: "With no English, it's really difficult to communicate" (Steinbacher, 2006, p. 25). Although Stryzhak's dilemma is a major problem experienced by new Americans from non-English-speaking countries, it provides for us ample reason to support the need for mastering English. Furthermore, Stryzhak's dilemma echoes the point made by Steinbacher (2006), who contends that "Learning the ABCs of English might be a rite of passage for those born in America, but mastering it takes some work for many foreigners arriving later." And indeed we do have a classic case in Gennadiy Stryzhak. But more and more, there are cases that warrant attention and support the need for advocates to reexamine the view expressed by Gingrich. And, as difficult as it might be to embrace wholeheartedly Gingrich's take on this matter, I find it hard to accept his reasons. It should be noted that in continuation of his statement, based on the same article, Gingrich asserted, "We should have a principle that government documents are in English" (Moscoso, 2007, p. 6). I find this notion unacceptable for two reasons. First, it puts immigrants and American citizens from non-English-speaking countries in a difficult situation. I have already cited the case of Stryzhak as an example. What, then, should non-English-speaking Americans and immigrant residents in America do if they are unable to communicate in English language, according to Gingrich? Second, Gingrich's stance on this matter infringes on freedom of speech. In fact, some states and counties in the United States have already adopted programs that encourage the translations of government documents. This move suggests a change from the view expressed by Gingrich. Furthermore, Miller and Ward (2005, pp. 22–23) reported,

> In response to the growth in the number of those who do not speak English in Washington, D.C., Mayor Anthony A. Williams in April signed into law the Language Access Act of 2004 that requires written translations of all "vital documents" and interpreters at most agencies for any foreign language spoken by at least five hundred residents. The Language Access Act provides translations and interpretation services for about 38,000 city residents who do not speak or read English well at a cost of about $440,000 a year. The new law will make city government documents available in Spanish, Korean, Mandarin, Chinese, Vietnamese, and Ethiopian Amharic.

Moscoso (2007, p. 7) reacted to Gingrich's suggestion that government documents ought to be in English as follows:

> Immigrant advocates and civil rights groups say that making English the nation's language would infringe on people's right to free speech, would encourage discrimination against immigrants and could make it difficult for people with limited or no English to receive basic public services such as health care.

What we need is a structured program that addresses the needs of immigrants in need of English proficiency. If implemented, such programs might advocate for basic level English classes for adults, because documented evidence shows that children from foreign countries can adapt easily through the school system. Embracing an idea such as that suggested by Gingrich hints at autonomous control of laws and imperialism. Ndebele (1987, p. 230) addressed the problem of control in a society dominated by the English language in his essay by commenting that

> It has been shown that the corporate world in the United States, controlling vast sums of money, also effectively controls thought in that country, a fact which renders problematic the much vaunted concept of freedom of speech in that country.

Furthermore, John Trasvina, president and general counsel of the Mexican American Legal Defense and Educational Fund, in reacting to Gingrich's view stated, "Latinos and Immigrants do not need a law to tell them that

English is the language to get ahead in the United States ... A conservative like Newt Gingrich ought to know that you don't pass a law, you provide classes" (Moscoso, 2007, p. 9).

EDUCATIONAL INTERVENTION LEADS TO MASTERY OF ENGLISH

By far, and without question, the government and numerous organizations running the school systems and educational outlets in the United States have helped non-native speakers of English to master English. For many years, immigrants new to the United States and those who do not speak English but were born here have been receiving help in the form of educational classes designed to help people with limited English proficiency to master the language. These community and public school English proficiency classes for adults and children are available in small towns and major cities through the United States. Students enrolled in these classes are finding ample time to enrich their knowledge with American education while also bridging the gaps that exists in their level of English proficiency. These students come from countries distant and near. Jason (2003) commented that for these students there is a hope, that learning a language early on in education allows them the opportunity to learn other things.

Accordingly, classes aimed at teaching English proficiency will help immigrant students to embrace the many opportunities that abound in their new country (Stoeltje, 2004). Communication is key to almost every facet of life in a thriving society. Not being able to communicate in the language used for in either commerce or education places children or students in a handicapped position. Unfortunately, that language, in our own case, is English. To help most children in this position to master English, schools within the United States have begun to structure educational programs and English mastery classes that will benefit newcomers. These steps, though sometimes problematic for students and children from non-English-speaking backgrounds, have proved to be useful for the most part. Griffith (1992), in her article titled "The Struggle to Adapt in Arlington: Immigrant Sisters Make Some Strides on Road to Mastering English," shares anecdotes that illustrate the efforts teachers have been making in helping students in the Washington area (see below). The highlights of Griffith's points rest in the value found in communication. Communication opens doors, helps those learning

English to practice the language, and gives them a sense of hope as they assimilate and embrace certain aspects of their new culture.

> Like thousands of other immigrant students in the Washington area who began the school year not knowing how to speak English, the Sereke Sisters have rapidly absorbed U.S. language and culture and are able to carry on simple conversations. Now, their teachers say, the Serekes need to continue learning during summer, and avoid getting frustrated as their schoolwork becomes more complex and the pace of their progress inevitably slows. (Griffith, 1992, p. 5)

The kind of commitment shown by the Serekes teachers helps students to succeed. Their teachers are encouraging and inspiring. By giving the girls ample time to develop, in spite of the frustrations they experience in learning a new language, their teachers are slowly helping them to realize the benefits that are abound in courage, patience, and perseverance. Furthermore, mastering English, like the process that takes place when students try to master a new language, takes time. Typically, it takes 2–4 years for non-English-speaking students to become proficient in a language (Griffith, 1992). But the good news about the experience is that the various techniques applied by teachers in the United States is working.

MEASURING ENGLISH MASTERY WITH STANDARDIZED TESTS

Aside from educational programs designed to help students master English, there are documented cases of standardized tests designed to measure the progress made in helping immigrant students or children to enhance their English proficiency (see Sheridan, 2003). Records and statistics show that tests of this nature have been highly criticized by parents and teachers. Sheridan (2003) provides support for the logic behind such a test in his statement that "The goal is to improve student achievement and eliminate the performance gap between white, Asian and middle-class students and lower-scoring minority and poor students" (p. 7). While tests such as this succeed in identifying the statistic required to measure the progress in its continuation, its failure rests in the simple fact that teachers and administrators whose students continue to fail stand the risk of being replaced or transferred elsewhere. The idea of having standardized tests that examine students whose native language is not English and those who are native English speakers creates inequality in the assessment of records. There is no basis for such an assessment. However, if its sole purpose is to see whether schools are helping students to progress, then it is a good idea. After all, one good way to monitor students' progress is through evaluation or review of statistics and records. And standardized testing falls under this process. The sad part is that students who are still mastering English will struggle.

CONCLUSION

Whether we like it or not, mastering English helps to facilitate education. The ability to speak or write in English, as we note today, is essential for anyone wishing to succeed in the workforce. While this chapter covered a wide range of topics and viewpoints, they are intended to show how English proficiency, whether at a young age or in adulthood, can be of immense benefit to non-English-speaking immigrants in the United States. And for those immigrants from non-English-speaking countries who end up studying for college degrees in English after taking ESL classes to master English, they represent the symbol of hope for those struggling with the language. Anything is possible. And if they can do it successfully, so can those who have just arrived in the United States. But studying a new language takes time, and there is no easy way out of this process. Commitment, patience, attention, and perseverance are all key factors involved in the study process. Much as students or adults who do not speak English struggle in their English classes at schools or adult learning centers across the nation, they will reap the benefits of their sacrifices if they put their hearts to learning. After all, at the end of the day, they stand to gain massively when they are employed or promoted at work as a result of their mastery of English.

REFERENCES

Fish, L. K. (2002). Mastering English for economic reasons. *Boston Globe*, November 23. Retrieved on May 22, 2009, from ProQuest database.

Griffith, S. (1992). The struggle to adapt in Arlington: Immigrant sisters make strides on road to mastering English. *The Washington Post*, January 14. Retrieved on May 22, 2009, from ProQuest database.

Jason, K. (2003). Language and identity are two separate issues. *Malaysiakini: News and views that matter*, July 27. Available at http://www.malaysiakini.com/news/100194. Retrieved on May 22, 2009.

Miller, S. A., & Ward, J. (2005). English: A vital element in immigrants' success. Available at http://www.worldandi.com/subscribers/feature_detail.asp?num = 245321. Retrieved on May 22, 2009.

Moscoso, E. (2007). Gingrich says English should get official status. *The Atlanta Journal-Constitution*, January 25. Retrieved on May 22, 2009, from ProQuest Database.

Ndebele, N. S. (1987). The English language and social change in South Africa. In: D. Bunn, D. Taylor, R. Gibbos & S. Plumpp (Eds), *From South Africa: New writing, photographs & art* (p. 230). Evanston, IL: Northwestern University Press.

Ramakrishan, P. (2002). A national will to mastering English: Reflections on the "English language" question. Available at http://www.aliran.com/oldsite/monthly/2002/4b.html. Retrieved on May 22, 2009.

Robotham, D. (2007). Mastering English. *Jamaican Gleaner*. Available at http://www.jamaicagleaner.com/gleaner/20070805/cleisure/cleisure2.html. Retrieved on May 22, 2009.

Sheridan, M. B. (2003). Immigrants to take standardized tests: Exams called a key to better evaluation. *The Washington Post*, January 23. Retrieved on May 22, 2009, from ProQuest database.

Steinbacher, M. (2006). Mastering English: Classes for learning language on the rise. *The Pantagraph*, August. Retrieved on May 22, 2009, from ProQuest database.

Stoeltje, M. F. (2004). Deciphering illiteracy: Mastering English is still a struggle for many. *San Antonio Express News*, September 5. Retrieved on May 22, 2009, from ProQuest database.

PART III
TECHNOLOGY AND STUDENTS WITH DISABILITIES

# CHAPTER 5

USING ASSISTIVE TECHNOLOGY TO SUPPORT THE INSTRUCTIONAL PROCESS OF STUDENTS WITH DISABILITIES

Howard P. Parette, Jr. and
George R. Peterson-Karlan

Students with disabilities who participate in 21st century classrooms benefit from both the legal mandates of and the achievement expectations embedded in the No Child Left Behind Act of 2001 (NCLB) and the Individuals with Disabilities Education Improvement Act of 2004 (IDEIA, 2004). NCLB clearly articulates the responsibility of public schools to ensure that all children participate in the general education curriculum *and* demonstrate academic progress (Bakken & Parette, 2008). IDEIA 2004 requires that students with disabilities have individual program plans (IEPs) developed for them that (a) emphasize special education services provided within the general education program [20 U.S.C. 1401 § 601(C)(5)(A)] and (b) require "consideration" of assistive technology [AT; 20 U.S.C. 1401 § 614(B)(v)] to support their participation in special education programs (Center for Technology in Education, Johns Hopkins University, and Technology & Media Division [TAM] of the Council for Exceptional Children, 2005). The IDEIA 2004 definition of AT refers to "any item, piece of equipment or product system, whether acquired commercially or off the shelf, modified, or customized, that is used to increase, maintain, or improve functional capabilities of individuals with disabilities" [20 U.S.C. 1401 § 602(1)(A)]. As noted by Parette and Peterson-Karlan (2007, p. 387), the federal definition "places emphasis on the 'compensatory' nature of AT, i.e., it compensates for something a student *cannot* functionally do or perform" at an "expected level of performance" (Parette, Peterson-Karlan, Wojcik, & Bardi, 2007).

This expanded concept of AT is supported by the Supreme Court case, *Hedrick Hudson School District v. Rowley* (1982), in which the issue of a "floor of opportunity" being required for all students participating in special education was addressed (Parette & Peterson-Karlan, 2007). In essence, this case clarified that schools must provide services ensuring that children with disabilities have the *opportunity* to participate in the curriculum. As noted in Fig. 1, the demonstrated performance of students with disabilities on academic tasks is often below that expected of peers (i.e., the expected performance level to participate in the curriculum). The nature of their disabilities is such that without some type of AT compensatory support they would not have a floor of opportunity to participate and succeed in the curriculum, that is, perform targeted academic or life skills tasks having clear performance expectations that they could not otherwise achieve without use of these tools. Having a floor of opportunity, in turn, "creates the potential for achievement (educational progress) in the curriculum" (Parette & Peterson-Karlan, in press) by providing needed supports for the instructional process.

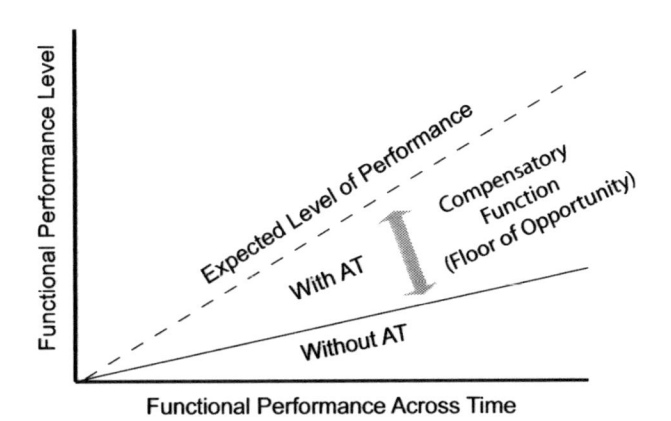

Fig. 1. AT Provides Compensatory Support for Functional Performance of Tasks to Students with Disabilities, Thereby Affording a "Floor of Opportunity." *Source:* Reproduced with permission from © 2009, SEAT Center.

AT CONSIDERATION IN THE INSTRUCTIONAL PROCESS

Although AT consideration has been mandated since 1997 (Individuals with Disabilities Education Act Amendments of 1997) and subsequently echoed in IDEIA 2004, there is no consensus in the field regarding how education professionals approach the task of making decisions about AT devices that can support the instructional process. Numerous models and frameworks have been proposed to provide guidance in the consideration of AT (e.g., Blackhurst, 2005; Bowser & Reed, 1995; Center for Technology in Education, Johns Hopkins University; and Technology & Media Division [TAM] of the Council for Exceptional Children, 2005; Chambers, 1997; Edyburn, 2000, 2005; Melichar & Blackhurst, 1993; Parette & VanBiervliet, 1990, 1991; Zabala, 1993). More recent clarifications of this process have been presented (Parette et al., 2007). However, at Illinois State University, we have developed an approach used in our undergraduate preparation program that has been effective in helping future teachers understand this process and more effectively make decisions about appropriate AT solutions for students with disabilities. The following sections present an overview of this process, preceded by an introduction to the role of tools in our society.

Clarification of the Role of Tools

Generally, for students to participate in the academic or life skills curriculum, they must complete tasks that require them to (a) remember, (b) interpret symbols, (c) do something, or (d) say something. Examples of tasks include eating, storing materials in a desk or locker, performing computations, reading a book, taking notes, and writing a paper. Each task with which the student is confronted has varying demands that include (a) *physical* (i.e., the student must *do* something), (b) *cognitive* (i.e., the student must *remember* or *make sense of* something), (c) *linguistic* (i.e., the student must *interpret* printed and visual symbols), and (d) *social-communicative* (i.e., the student must speak and interact with others).

There are two ways in which humans respond to task demands, either by human ability alone or by human ability mediated by tool use; the history of humans is one of developing tools to meet every increasing task demands. To complete tasks within school curricula, students also use or have access to tools created to meet educational task demands. For example, a spoon is designed to help a student eat; a lock and handle are components of a locker; and a calculator is designed for computation. All tools increase the student's effectiveness (the ability to complete the task at all) or efficiency (i.e., within the expected performance level) of completing such tasks (King, 1999).

Although any task presents varying demands on students, mere use of tools also presents demands. Physical demands may require the student to initiate, pursue, and complete a task using the tool by (a) sustaining his or her body position, maintaining balance, or using muscle strength and endurance; and (b) making and repeating movements (i.e., range, resolution, repetition/combination of movements; speed/duration of movement).

Cognitive demands in tool use require "thinking" to use the tool. Thinking includes processing of perceptual/sensory input (i.e., visual, auditory, tactile-kinesthetic perception) to (a) discriminate (differentiate among stimuli), (b) recognize patterns, and (c) associate the technology use with experiences (either real or virtual). Cognitive demands also include remembering such as factual memory (i.e., recall of bits of information, such as a name), and (b) sequential memory (e.g., recall of order, such as digits, steps/procedures, and actions). Additionally, cognitive demands may require the student to use "executive function," or putting perception and memory to work in a specific situation, as well as using problem-solving or adaptive thinking (e.g., What is wrong? How can I get help?). Often there are linguistic demands in using the tool, and the student is confronted with the challenge of interpreting symbols, including printed text, icons, and graphics associated with or affixed to the tool. In using the tool, the student may also have to remember symbol sequences, for example, a combination of keystrokes on a computer, such as <Shift+a> to produce a capital "A."

Many tools are used in the context of socializing and/or communicating with others. When such social-communicative demands are present, an array of communication rules must be adhered to which may be challenging to the student (e.g., initiating, sustaining, and terminating conversations; organizing thoughts for expressing oneself; not engaging in behaviors that distract others).

Thus, AT tools are developed by either adapting an existing tool (e.g., adapting a spoon or pencil grip) or creating a new tool (e.g., a wheelchair). This can be accomplished in one of two ways: (a) tool *adaptation*, that is, changing the tool demands or features of the tool, or (b) creating a *new* tool with features that alter task demands (Fig. 2).

We feel that the AT decision-making approach requires consideration of four interrelated areas that impact the student in the context of the educational setting, resulting in compensatory supports that create a

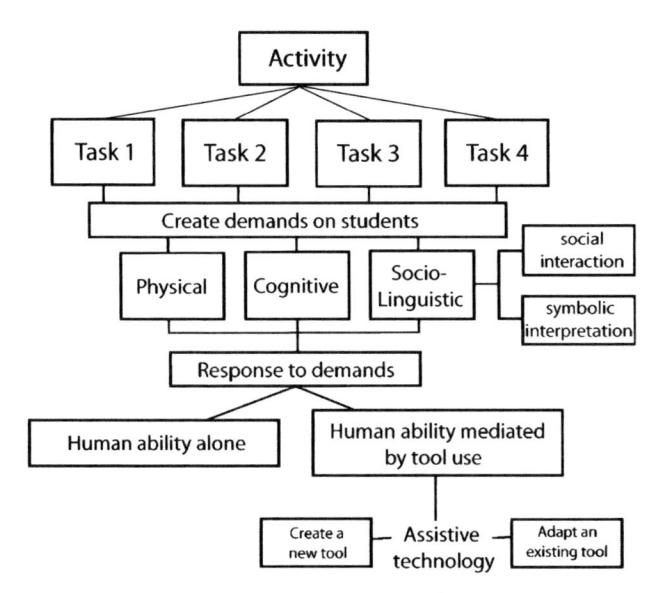

Fig. 2. Activity-Task-Tool Demand Framework for AT Consideration. *Source:* Reproduced with permission from © 2009 George Peterson-Karlan.

"floor of opportunity" for participation in the curriculum. These include (a) understanding the student; (b) examining aspects of the student's environment, activities, and tasks; (c) identifying the discrepancies that exist between student abilities and challenges and demands placed on the student for participation in the curriculum; and (d) identifying the tools needed to provide the necessary compensatory supports. Each of these processes is described in the following section.

UNDERSTANDING THE STUDENT

The first phase of AT decision making in the instructional process focuses on understanding the student and requires the education professional to address two principal questions: "What are the student's *current abilities*?" and "What are the student's *special needs*?" Answers to these questions are revealed as the education professional considers the student's basic human abilities, including "physical abilities" (i.e., manipulation, positioning, and mobility skills); "cognitive abilities" (i.e., sensory perception and memory skills); "linguistic skills" (i.e., symbolic interpretation abilities); and "social-communicative" skills (i.e., socially appropriate and language-based interpersonal skills). Student skills in each of the executive function areas must also be considered (i.e., abilities in personal management, reading, writing, and math).

The education professional must also ask the question, "What is it that the student *needs* to do?" This question has numerous embedded considerations, as thought must be given to the curriculum – whether it is life skills or academic – in which the student participates. This includes a broad examination of activities and tasks presented to the student, what the participation performance expectations are, and resources that are available. Fig. 3 presents a sample planning format that can assist the education professional in examining both (a) abilities/strengths and (b) needs/weaknesses of the student. To most effectively understand a student, the education professional should examine these two areas in terms of physical,

Reading	
Abilities/Strengths	Justin can scan, perceive, and decode text.
Needs/Weaknesses	It takes Justin a long time to read.
	Justin must read text over and over to understand it.
	Reading is one of his two most difficult subjects.
	He has difficulty keeping up with class reading.
	He has IEP goals focusing on reading.
Writing	
Abilities/Strengths	He can grip a pencil and transcribe some text.
	He has good ideas.
	Justin completes multiple drafts while writing.
Needs/Weaknesses	Justin tries to take good notes, but cannot figure out what he has written when he later reviews them.
	He fatigues after writing for more than 10 minutes.
	Writing is one of Justin's two hardest subjects.
	Justin has a hard time writing down what he is thinking.
	Justin has poor spelling skills and must use spell check often.
	Justin has hard time keeping up on writing assignments.
	Justin has lots of issues with placing the letters on the line and reversing the orientation of the letters.

Fig. 3. Sample Excerpts from a Planning Format for Reading and Writing Student Characteristics. *Source:* Reproduced with permission from © 2009, SEAT Center.

cognitive, social-communicative-linguistic, attitude/motivation, personal management, reading, writing, and math aspects. It must be kept in mind that this format and other planning documents discussed herein are to help organize the education professional's thinking in the AT decision-making process *before* decisions are made about AT tools for any particular student.

UNDERSTANDING THE ENVIRONMENT, ACTIVITIES, AND TASKS

The second component of the AT decision-making process is understanding demands placed on students while performing academic and life skills tasks (Parette & Peterson-Karlan, in press). The school environment for each student with a disability can vary markedly and have an impact on AT decisions made for a particular student. Questions that must be asked include (a) What are the settings (i.e., school, home, community, and work) or locations (e.g., classroom, gym, kitchen, bathroom, reading center, art table, and science lab) in which the student participates? (b) What are the physical and instructional features of these environments (i.e., available equipment and materials, physical structure of the environment, and existing barriers to access; instructional groupings; instructional formats; barriers to student participation, including attitudes; anticipated changes in curriculum, grade level, or school)? (c) What are the resources available in these environments? (i.e., family and personal supports, peer supports, related services, and other school-based supports); and (d) Who are the typical participants (i.e., adults, peers, and family members) in these activities?

Education professionals must carefully examine the environmental arrangement and instructional settings in which the student participates. This may include such factors as organization of the school (e.g., classrooms and multi-floor placements), arrangement of desks, window configurations, and type of instructional environment (e.g., lecture, group work, and laboratory; see Fig. 4). Such issues could potentially impact the size or transportability of an AT tool selected, as well as the features reflected in a tool considered (e.g., surfaces that reflect light and create glare if intense light sources are present, a lightweight vs. heavy communication tool that would have to be transported up and down stairs).

An additional component of understanding the student's environment is examination of available instructional materials and resources used in the curriculum. Once these resources are identified (Fig. 5), it is much easier

Features of the Environment Describe the school; the classroom environment, including typical classroom layout, (e.g., orientation and location of desks, tables activity centers, etc.); and any other locations in which the student participates (e.g., lockers, restrooms, lunchroom, office, etc.)	Justin attends high school in an urban, Midwestern city. The school is set up across two-levels and is generally shaped like a 'plus' sign. The cafeteria and gymnasium are located on the first floor, along with English, Foreign language, Math, Art, and Special Education classes. The second floor houses science classes and a computer lab. Justin spends his educational time in five different classrooms for an hour each, as well as the gymnasium and cafeteria. Justin also spends time in the library and the PE locker room daily. He visits the restroom, and sometimes the office, guidance office, and nurse. Justin has his own locker on the second floor and stops at his locker multiple times during the day. His Art, Algebra II, and Physics classrooms have multiple desks in rows, with the teacher lecturing at the front of the class near the board. He works in discussion groups in his English class and small groups, or one-on-one, during his Resource period. The Resource Room is filled with desks or tables without much floor space in which to move around. Since his H.S. uses a tracking system, he is in a lower track due to his placement in special education and his uncertainty about his future. This may be a barrier because he may not have access to opportunities to further his education. There are no physical barriers to Justin's education.

Fig. 4. Sample Planning Sheet for Features of a Student's Environment. *Source:* Reproduced with permission from © 2009, SEAT Center.

to understand other elements of the AT decision-making process and make informed decisions about potential tool solutions to support the student in the curriculum.

Fig. 6 presents an excerpt of a planning document for resources and supports and participant attitudes and expectations within the educational environment. A clear understanding of the performance expectations is an underpinning of the AT decision-making process. Attitudes of all participants – the student, education professionals, and family members – are also important considerations, as both positive and negative attitudes toward the student may potentially affect varying AT solutions that are considered later in the decision-making process.

Materials and Instructional Technology Describe the educational materials, resources, and instructional technology typically found in a classroom environment at the student's grade level.	Justin has a textbook for every class. Other educational materials for Justin's Physics class include lab equipment, safety equipment, and manuals. For English there are books and journals. Algebra class requires a calculator, protractors, rulers, and compasses. He has many art supplies for his Art class, including paint, brushes, crayons, markers, colored pencils, paper, canvas, and other materials. PE requires an array of athletic equipment. Instructional technologies include computers, laptops, overhead projectors, document cameras, white boards/chalkboards, Smart Boards, TVs, and VCR/DVD players. Teachers use the Internet, colleagues, and teacher's manuals as resources.

Fig. 5. Sample Planning Sheet for Compiling Information Related to Instructional Materials and Resources. *Source:* Reproduced with permission from © 2009, SEAT Center.

UNDERSTANDING ACTIVITIES

Consideration of the environment must include examination of *all* the student's "activities." In the life skills curriculum, activities might include personal hygiene and care, domestic living, recreation and leisure activities, community transportation, shopping or work, each having embedded tasks. In the academic curriculum, activity areas are the broad curriculum areas under which daily academic activities are organized. At the preschool level such activities might include circle time, snack time, show and tell, and reading activity area. At the elementary level, typical activity areas might include math, language arts (including reading, writing, and spelling), science, and social studies (Parette & Peterson-Karlan, in press). At the junior and high school levels, activities would be the specific subject area classes such as English, history, geometry, civics, and consumer economics.

UNDERSTANDING TASKS

Although identifying the student's typical activities is important, it is critical that natural routines and tasks that are embedded in these activities be clearly identified to facilitate effective AT decision making. Each task has a *distinct purpose*, or outcome, and is often composed of numerous steps (or critical events). A task analysis is typically used to determine the steps. We feel that there are four specific components to understanding tasks.

Resources and Supports Describe the resources and supports available to the student and significant others, including family and personal, peer supports, related services, and other supports.	General education teacher provides additional assistance; general education teacher frequently spends time sitting with Justin helping him process through what he is reading and going through multiple drafts of his writing. Special education teacher sees Justin daily for about 50 min a day for resource; teacher focuses on whatever assignments he has at the time. Accommodations made for Justin at school include: - Extended time on tests - Extended time on assignments - Peer Reader

Participant Attitudes and Performance Expectations
 	
Describe any performance expectations or attitudes of participants evident that might affect the student's performance in activities and tasks positively or negatively.
	General education teacher feels that Justin works hard or harder than most of her students.
	
	General education teacher wants a way to let Justin express his knowledge and feelings.
	
	Special education teacher believes he is an average student.
	
	Special education teacher believes Justin has an exceptional work ethic.
	
	Justin is the pride of the family and that they are impressed and amazed with the work he does.
	
	Mother recognizes that Justin has difficulty reading and writing, but feels he is a bright student.
	
	Mother feels he will definitely do well at whatever he chooses.
	
	Justin's father is not available for support.
	
	√ Performance expectations:
	- Produce legible written work
	- Produce organized and accurately spelled written compositions
	- Analyze classical literature and develop analytical writing skills by writing about discussions of theme and other literary elements
	- Educational goals reflected in Justin's IEP include that he will:
	  o read grade level text.
	  o accurately complete writing assignments given in classes.
	  o accurately complete math assignments given in classes.

Fig. 6. Sample Planning Sheet for Resources and Supports within a Student's Environment. *Source:* Reproduced with permission from © 2009, SEAT Center.

All activities have a beginning (i.e., some type of preparation), middle, and ending (completion) routines. Key questions that should be considered by the education professional when examining tasks embedded within activities include (a) What is the transition from the previous activity? (b) What are the preparation tasks? (c) What are the tasks (routines) needed to carry out the activity? (d) What are the ending tasks? and (e) What is the transition to the next activity? Regardless of the activity area – whether it is life skills or academic – each of these questions provides insights that can assist the education professional in supporting the student in the instructional process.

For example, in the life skills curriculum, the activity area of "community transportation" might include tasks such as getting to a bus stop on time, calculating time needed to arrive at a destination, and having/providing correct change for a fare. Each of these tasks also has varying physical (What needs to be *done*?), cognitive (What needs to be *perceived* or *remembered*?), linguistic (What symbolic information must be *interpreted*?), and/or social-communicative (What needs to be *said* and to whom?) demands that may require different AT solutions for the student.

In the preschool activity of "show and tell," students might be expected to complete the tasks of sitting with peers, attending to the teacher, retelling a story about a previous event, and answering questions. Each of these tasks also has varying physical, cognitive, linguistic, and/or social-communicative demands placed on the students. In the elementary curricula, "learning to write" is typically an important activity. Writing is *not* a single task but includes several different embedded tasks including (a) planning and organization of the composition, (b) transcription of ideas into text form, (c) revising and editing the composition, and (d) "publishing" a document. Each of these embedded writing tasks has its own cognitive, physical, and linguistic demands requiring different types of compensatory tools (e.g., content-specific outlines, pencil grips or keyboarding devices, editing guides with embedded prompts). Beyond the early elementary level, learning to read, write, and spell are no longer specific instructional focus areas, but are skill processes employed across multiple curricular areas (e.g., reading and writing for content are learning in history, English, and geometry classes).

Extending Task Examination

To further understand tasks and their varying demands, we have found it helpful to give particular attention to the complex cognitive processes that are inherent in the tasks. These include (a) degree of problem-solving required; (b) extent of reading, writing, and math computation needed; and (c) management of things (objects), time, events, and/or procedures required of the student to complete activities. Furthermore, the education professional must examine the typical tools used in and performance expectations for completion of tasks. With many tasks presented to students with disabilities in activity areas, there are tools that typical students may use to complete the tasks. In writing, typical tools might include a pencil and lined paper and/or a word processor on a desktop computer. In reading, a typical tool might include textbook, handout, or a web site.

With each task, there are performance expectations for the typical student to succeed in completing the task. And each task may also have expectations related to *rate* (e.g., turning in homework daily), duration (e.g., maintaining attention for 30 minutes during a group activity), quantity (e.g., completing a 10-item math worksheet), and quality (e.g., no more than three spelling errors per submitted paper). A sample examination of the tasks, demands, and typical tools used within an activity area is presented in Fig. 7.

Activity:	English	
Tasks	**Task Demands** What must a typical student do, say, or remember to complete the task? Include the reading, writing, math, or personal management requirements of the task.	**Typical Tools Used (if any)**
Transition & Preparation Tasks	Retrieves and organizes materials from backpack—textbook, notebook, and paper.	
Task 1	Attends to teacher and transcribes notes during 20-minute lecture	Pencil, lined paper
Task 2	Scans, perceives, decodes, and comprehends text in English textbook	Dictionary
Task 3	Writes papers, to include identifying a topic (prewriting), organizing his thoughts, creating a draft, revising the draft, and publishing his final submission	Pencil, lined paper, Computer, Word processor
Task 4	Completes and submits homework assignments	Textbook
Ending & Transition Tasks	Stores materials in personal bin and replaces personal items in backpack	Assignment bin

Fig. 7. Sample Planning Excerpt for Tasks within the Activity Area of English. *Source:* Reproduced with permission from © 2009, SEAT Center.

DISCREPANCY ANALYSIS

The third phase of the AT decision-making process – one which is a *key difference* from other approaches reported in the literature – is the "discrepancy analysis." This enables the education professional to identify *discrepancies* that exist between the student's abilities and the activity/task demands. In developing any individualized education program, a discrepancy analysis is conducted to identify a student's strengths and challenges requiring special education accommodations and interventions. The discrepancy analysis that evolves during AT decision-making, and which may or may not be a routine part of the IEP development process, requires identification of *target activities and associated tasks* that need to be met effectively or efficiently and the *specific task demands* that the student *cannot* effectively or efficiently meet. Having previously identified tasks within various activity areas of the curriculum (and their embedded tasks and demands), this phase simply requires the education professional to examine unmet demands which then become potential foci of tool consideration in the final phase of the process. Fig. 8 presents an organizational format that can assist the education professional in determining discrepancies within various tasks across activity areas for a student with a disability. Organizing one's thoughts within this framework should be done across all activity areas in which tasks are presented that present problems to students.

SELECTING AT TOOLS TO PROVIDE COMPENSATION

Parette and Peterson-Karlan (in press) have offered specific recommendations regarding the AT tool selection process to guide AT decision making. The final phase of decision making – selecting specific AT tools – meshes identification of unmet demands of tasks with "features" needed in tools that might provide compensatory supports. Cook and Hussey (2002) defined an AT "feature" as the particular "implementation of a characteristic" (p. 168). Pufpaff (n.d.) noted that "'input device' is a characteristic whereas 'standard keyboard' and 'alternative keyboard' are features." All AT devices have features, including such descriptors as voice output, text-to-speech, word prediction, customizable interface, cursor control options, input options (e.g., one-hand keying, on-screen keying, and scanning), text display, and text-embedded prompts. To assist education professionals,

Activity – English

Description of Activity – Student writes essays, takes notes, uses oral language, reads books, participates in class discussions, completes homework.

List the Tasks and what the student is expected to complete

Task 1: Write Essay

Task Demands	Student: Abilities & Needs
Justin must grip a pencil/pen, transcribe text legibly, identify a topic during prewriting, organize his thoughts regarding a topic, create a draft, edit his draft, revise his draft based on teacher feedback, publish a final paper for submission	**Describe how student <u>meets</u> the task demands effectively or efficiently**
	Justin holds a pencil and legibly transcribes text for about 10 minutes.
	He has good ideas for topics.
	Justin uses spell check for spelling and grammar using a word processor.
	Describe how student *does not meet* the task demands effectively or efficiently
	Justin does not finish assignments on time in class.
	He cannot organize his thoughts on paper prior to writing.
	He cannot write legibly after 10 minutes of transcription.

Fig. 8. A Discrepancy Analysis Reflecting Task Demands for Writing an Essay and Identification of Met and Unmet Demands. *Source:* Reproduced with permission from © 2009, SEAT Center.

technology matrices for AT, reading, writing, and math are available at the National Center for Technology Innovation web site (see http://www.techmatrix.org/; Fig. 9). These matrices are organized based on features of AT devices that are available to provide compensatory supports.

To support the education professional's thinking about this final phase of AT decision making, we have found it helpful to use the following format for considering potential tools (Fig. 10). First, list the unmet demands for target tasks that are deemed important and for which AT solutions might be considered. For example, in Justin's case (Fig. 8), unmet demands for the task of "writing an essay" included (a) does not finish assignments on time in class, (b) cannot organize his thoughts on paper prior to writing, and (c) cannot

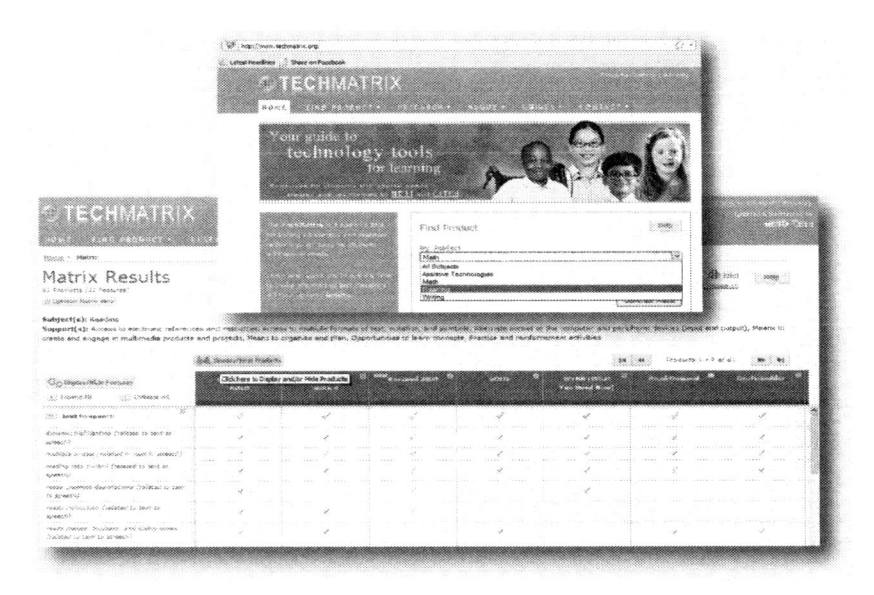

Fig. 9. Screen Shot of Tech Matrix for Reading Presenting Features of Devices and Products Available Having These Features.

write legibly after 10 minutes of transcription. Each of these unmet demands requires device features that are different and that may call for differing AT tools. In the first instance, to provide compensatory support for Justin to complete assignments on time, it was determined that several AT features might be important: a device that presents visual and/or auditory prompts related to the passage of time, and auditory/visual reminder of steps involved in the writing task. Proposed tools, then, that have most or all of these features could be identified, allowing the education professional to choose one (or a combination) of the tools that provides the needed compensatory support.

CONCLUSION

The process of AT decision making for any student involves consideration of numerous factors described in this chapter. Using the steps noted herein, education professionals may become more aware and better prepared to participate in effective decision making for their students with disabilities in classroom settings.

Target Task:	Writing an essay	
Unmet Demands	**AT Features Needed**	**Proposed Set of AT Tools**
Justin does not finish assignments on time in class.	Visual and/or auditory prompts re: passage of time Auditory or visual reminder of steps in assignments	Graphics-based checklist of writing task steps Electronic timer √ StepPad device Large-faced wrist watch
He cannot organize his thoughts on paper prior to writing.	Customizable interface outlining capability Text-to-speech Embedded resources (dictionary)	Inspiration˚ software SOLO software √
He cannot write legibly after 10 minutes of transcription.	Text-to-speech Word prediction	Hand-held recorder Voice recognition (in Microsoft Word) SOLO software √

Fig. 10. Sample AT Tool Decision-Making Chart for the Target Task of "Writing an Essay." *Source:* Reproduced with permission from © 2009, SEAT Center.

REFERENCES

Bakken, J. P., & Parette, H. P. (2008). Self-determination and persons with developmental disabilities. In: A. F. Rotatori, F. E. Obiakor & S. Burkhardt (Eds), *Autism and developmental disabilities: Current perspectives and issues* (Vol. 18, pp. 221–234). Bingley, UK: Emerald Group Publishing Ltd.

Blackhurst, A. E. (2005). Historical perspective about technology applications for people with disabilities. In: D. Edyburn, K. Higgins & R. Boone (Eds), *Handbook of special education technology research and practice* (pp. 3–29). Whitefish Bay, WI: Knowledge by Design.

Bowser, G., & Reed, P. (1995). Education TECH points for assistive technology planning. *Journal of Special Education Technology, 12*, 325–338.

Center for Technology in Education, Johns Hopkins University; and Technology & Media Division [TAM] of the Council for Exceptional Children. (2005). *Considering the need for assistive technology within the individualized education program.* Columbia, MD: Author.

Chambers, A. C. (1997). *Has technology been considered: A guide for IEP teams.* Reston, VA: Council for Exceptional Children.

Cook, A. M., & Hussey, S. M. (2002). *Assistive technologies. Principles and practices* (2nd ed.). St. Louis, MO: Mosby.
Edyburn, D. L. (2000). Assistive technology and students with mild disabilities. *Focus on Exceptional Children, 32*(9), 1–24.
Edyburn, D. L. (2005). Assistive technology and students with mild disabilities: From consideration to outcome measurement. In: D. Edyburn, K. Higgins & R. Boone (Eds), *Handbook of special education technology research and practice* (pp. 239–270). Whitefish Bay, WI: Knowledge by Design, Inc.
Hedrick Hudson School District v. Rowley, 458 U.S. 206, 102 S. Ct. 3051. (1982).
Individuals with Disabilities Education Act, Amendments, 20 U.S.C. § 1400 *et seq.* (1997).
Individuals with Disabilities Education Improvement Act, 118 Stat. 2647. (2004).
King, T. W. (1999). *Assistive technology: Essential human factors*. Boston: Allyn and Bacon.
Melichar, J. F., & Blackhurst, A. E. (1993). *Introduction to a functional approach to assistive technology [training module]*. Lexington, KY: Department of Special Education and Rehabilitation Counseling.
No Child Left Behind Act 20 U.S.C. §§ 6301 *et seq.* (2001).
Parette, H. P., & Peterson-Karlan, G. R. (2007). Facilitating student achievement with assistive technology. *Education and Training in Developmental Disabilities, 42,* 387–397.
Parette, H. P., & Peterson-Karlan, G. R. (in press). Integrating assistive technology into the curriculum. In: P. Peterson, B. McGaw & E. Baker (Eds), *International encyclopedia of education* (3rd ed.). Oxford, England: Elsevier.
Parette, H. P., Peterson-Karlan, G. R., Wojcik, B. W., & Bardi, N. (2007). Monitor that progress! Interpreting data trends for AT decision-making. *Teaching Exceptional Children, 39*(7), 22–29.
Parette, H. P., & VanBiervliet, A. (1990). *Assistive technology and disabilities. A guide for parents and students*. Little Rock, AR: University of Arkansas at Little Rock (ERIC Document Reproduction Services No. Ed364026).
Parette, H. P., & VanBiervliet, A. (1991). *Assistive technology curriculum: A module of in-service for professionals [and] instructor's supplement*. Little Rock, AR: University of Arkansas at Little Rock (ERIC Document Reproduction Service No. ED324887).
Pufpaff, L. (n.d.). *Feature match: Assistive technology*. Available at http://www.idealindiana.com/ideal/modules/48/narrative.php. Retrieved on May 17, 2009.
Zabala, J. (1993). *The SETT framework: Critical issues to consider when choosing and using assistive technology*. Paper presented to the Closing the Gap, Minneapolis, MN.

CHAPTER 6

TECHNOLOGY AND STUDENTS WITH DISABILITIES: DOES IT SOLVE ALL THE PROBLEMS

Emily C. Bouck

"Remarkable new technology is introduced into the school system and experts predict education will be revolutionized" (Lewis, 1988). This quote from a 1988 *New York Times* column on personal computers by Peter H. Lewis referenced the perception of many regarding personal computers. However, it could be considered applicable to almost any innovative technology as it could describe the feelings in the years after 1988 toward liquid crystal display (LCD) projectors, document cameras, and the Internet. But this quote was referencing the introduction of the blackboard in the 1840s. However, neither the blackboard nor personal computers have revolutionized education. As Lewis wrote, "the magic fail[ed] to materialize."

One should not be surprised that the invention and implementation of any one piece of technology does not revolutionize education. Any technology, whether it be personal computers or specific technology designed for particular populations (i.e., augmentative and alternative communication (AAC) devices, and text-to-speech), will not radically transform education. After all, technology is not a panacea; technology is a tool (Edyburn, 2001). Technology use in education is just one tool in an educator's toolbox; a tool to assist in educating students in academic, social, or functional skills.

It has great potential, but the expectations of technology typically far-succeed what it is capable of doing and hence leave feelings of frustration and dissatisfaction.

While many cannot think of living without our current modern technology (e.g., the Internet, cell phones, mp3 players, and notebook computers), we recognize while these tools can make our lives easier, they do not fix all aspects of our lives. Technology does not solve all the problems we face in modern society; in fact, the innovative technologies that have become commonplace in society have actually created some challenges (e.g., some contend modern technology has enslaved us [Lahm, 2008], and others indicate that it has made cheating easier [Dick et al., 2003]). Yet, we continue to use these technologies and hold them in high esteem.

This chapter will address technology for students with disabilities and specifically will question whether technology for students with disabilities solves all the problems. While the quick answer is no, the question is actually more complicated. Technology – including assistive technology – makes things possible for some students with disabilities that would otherwise not, yet it does not solve all the problems these students encounter in and out of school. Despite the potential of technology to improve the lives of students with disabilities, it is still a tool facing obstacles to address all problems.

TECHNOLOGY: THE GREAT EQUALIZER

Technology, particularly for students with disabilities, is often viewed as "the great equalizer" (Wyer, 2001, p. 1). It is perceived as a means of providing access and opportunity, promoting independence, and encouraging empowerment (Edyburn, Higgins, & Boone, 2005b). Technology can greatly benefit students with disabilities and solve many of the challenges these students face. Perhaps, this was put most profusely by former Assistant Secretary of the United States Department of Education, Office of Special Education Programs Judy Heumann, "For most of us, technology makes things easier. For a person with a disability, it makes things possible" (Edyburn et al., 2005b, p. xiii). The potential of technology is enormous for students with disabilities. For example, technology can provide a voice to those students who may not otherwise have one per their disability (i.e., AAC devices), read a text to a student who struggles with reading as a result of his/her disability (i.e., text-to-speech devices, screen readers, and Reading Pens), grant access to a computer and other electronic tools (i.e., switches and speech recognition), and offer low-tech devices such as pencil grips or lined paper to aid students in writing.

Yet, technology is sometimes more hype than reality; its potential highlighted more by intuition and belief than research and actual in-practice evidence. Hannaford (1993, p. 12) captured this sentiment years ago for one particular piece of technology, stating,

> Much of what is presented as being known about the use of computers with exceptional persons is actually what is believed, felt, or hoped. While there is an increasing amount of research and evaluation support associated with various uses of the technology, there is still relatively little empirical support for many statements found in the popular literature.

While almost two decades have passed since the sentiment was expressed, the field still lacks a substantial research base for an array of technology for students with disabilities, but especially for students with mild disabilities (Edyburn, 2007). While an increase in attention has been made (i.e., the relatively recent *Handbook of Special Education Technology Research and Practice*), additional research is needed, especially research involving robust designs (Edyburn, Higgins, & Boone, 2005a).

Although technology for students with disabilities has it supporters and research to validate its effectiveness, it also has its critics. Specifically, technology can be criticized for failing to deliver on its perceived promise to solve the problems faced by this population (Edyburn et al., 2005a). Technology for students with disabilities does not live up to its proclaimed potential for many reasons, including (1) it is not well understood and (2) there is a general failure to address contextual issues related to technology use.

UNFULFILLED PROMISES ... UNREALISTIC EXPECTATIONS

A Definition of Confusion

Technology for students with disabilities will not solve all the problems faced by these students because, for one, technology for this population is not well understood. Technology for students with disabilities is typically referred to as assistive technology, which is defined as "any item, piece of equipment, or product system, whether acquired commercially off the shelf, modified, or customized, that is used to increase, maintain, or improve functional capabilities of a child with a disability" (Individuals with

Disabilities Education Improvement Act [IDEIA], 2004, 602.1A). This definition is broad, convoluted, and open to interpretation. For example, debate exists over what is, or more aptly what is not, assistive technology given the word *any* that appears in the commonly accepted definition (Edyburn, 2005). Some believe anything can be assistive technology given the vagueness of the federal definition, whereas others apply a more conservative interpretation, excluding tools not commonly associated with technology (i.e., concrete manipulatives) (Edyburn, 2005). Thus, leaving the following questions unanswered (a) is a stepladder assistive technology?, (b) is a hearing aid assistive technology?, and (c) is an instructional strategy assistive technology?

The confusion over what is or is not assistive technology is further fueled by the division of assistive technology into categories of low-tech and high-tech; no-tech, low-tech, and high-tech; or low-tech, moderate tech, and high-tech; and the different interpretations applied to these terms (Blackhurst, 1997; Edyburn, 2005; Johnson, Beard, & Carpenter, 2007; Vanderheiden, 1984) (Table 1). Depending on one's perspective, no tech can mean (1) no assistive technology is deemed appropriate for the student; (2) a tool is selected for a student that requires no technology per se, such as a strategy; or (3) a nonelectronic device (Behrmann & Jerome, 2002). Low-tech, or light tech, is typically considered as (1) a tool that requires

Table 1. Categories of Assistive Technology.

Category	Definition	Examples
No-tech[a]	No assistive technology deemed appropriate	
	Tools requiring no technology (e.g., strategy)	POSSE (Englert & Mariage, 1991)
	Nonelectronic devices	PECS (Bondy & Frost, 1994)
Low-/light tech[b]	Tools requiring little technology and lower in cost	Pencil grip, concrete manipulatives
	Nonsophisticated electronic devices	Tape recorder, four-function calculator
Moderate tech	Tools with electronic components but not computerized	Graphing calculator
High-tech[c]	Tools using computers and higher in cost	Microsoft Reader (Microsoft, n.d.a)

[a]Behrmann and Jerome (2002).
[b]Behrmann and Schaff (2001).
[c]Edyburn (2005), Johnson et al. (2007) and Vanderheiden (1984).

little technology and is lower in cost, or (2) a nonsophisticated electronic device (Behrmann & Schaff, 2001). Moderate technology, when referenced as a category, is commonly referred to as technology that has electronic components but is not computerized and is generally more reasonable in cost. High-tech is then technology that uses the computer and has a higher cost factor (Edyburn, 2005; Johnson et al., 2007; Vanderheiden, 1984).

Given the above distinctions, or more aptly overlap in distinction, many are often left to wonder what is *not* assistive technology, or what specifically makes something technology for students with disabilities. A debate truly does exist regarding what is assistive, and issues are more often taken with the *low-tech* or *no-tech* options. For example, are concrete manipulatives assistive technology, albeit a low-tech or no-tech tool? Concrete manipulatives are common tools used with all students in mathematics classrooms, yet also a standard evidence-based accommodation for students with disabilities in mathematics (Maccini & Gagnon, 2000). Students with disabilities are probably given concrete manipulatives by teachers on a daily basis, without regard for the challenges this tool addresses or how using a particular concrete manipulative can help students with disabilities access the general education curriculum. Given the aforementioned duties of concrete manipulatives, one can stipulate that this tool helps to increase, maintain, or improve students' functional capabilities relative to mathematics.

Furthermore, some technology for students with disabilities has become so commonplace in everyday teaching and learning that it is not recognized as being assistive technology, and hence, its benefits are understated or unnoticed (Hitchcock et al., 2005). Technology use in general has increased in schools, with computers becoming necessities not luxuries in the education of all students, and teaching tools standard in many classrooms (Prensky, 2001a, 2001b). Because many of the technologies considered assistive technology for students with disabilities potentially benefit all students (e.g., computer-based concept mapping, virtual manipulatives, and software programs), the distinction between technology for students with disabilities and technology for teaching is blurry. In this case, the technology is not solving a problem; it is merely doing its job.

Standing in the Way

Another reason technology does not, or cannot, solve all problems is the current failure to fully address contextual issues related to technology use for students with disabilities. It may be technology does not solve all the problems because as a field and a society we do not allow it. Although technology holds great promise, its potential can only be achieved if it is used, and many factors influence students with disabilities getting access to assistive technology, using assistive technology, and not abandoning it.

Technology for students with disabilities can only be used if students actually have access to it. Access to technology is not equivocal across contextual factors for students with disabilities; issues such as socioeconomic status and culture interact with access to technology (Hitchcock et al., 2005). Students with disabilities from lower socioeconomic status typically have less access to technology (Bray, Brown, & Green, 2004; Warschauer, 2007), and research suggests individuals from some cultures have different reactions toward using assistive technology (Heur, Parette, & Scherer, 2004). To address problems faced by students with disabilities – and particularly diverse students with disabilities – greater attention needs to be paid to the equality of access, the equality of options for assistive technology, and the knowledge of assistive technology service providers toward issues of culture and diversity and its intersection with assistive technology selection and use.

Aside from access, appropriate selection of assistive technology is critical, as inappropriate selection sets up students with disabilities to fail (Alper & Raharinirina, 2006). Assistive technology selection should involve consideration of the person–technology match (Bryant & Bryant, 2003; Raskind & Bryant, 2002), ensuring a fit (i.e., compatibility) between the student and the device (Lahm & Sizemore, 2002). Compatibility includes examining not only the student's strengths and limitations to see if they align with a device, its features, and the tasks it is to be used for, but also the student's attitude and interest toward the device. If a student is disinterested in the particular assistive technology device or assistive technology in general, it will not work. Furthermore, if a student is embarrassed about using the tool, abandonment will occur, as some assistive technology can create a stigmatizing effect given the student will stand out in the classroom from its use. Educators involved in making assistive technology decisions need to carefully consider a range of factors when making decisions, such as the tasks for which the students will be using the assistive technology, the context in which the assistive technology is to be used, the individual, and the actual device (Bryant & Bryant, 2003; Raskind & Bryant, 2002).

Aside from a mismatch between student and technology, another major reason why assistive technology is abandoned or not used is insufficient training. Training is a key factor to assistive technology use and implementation (McGregor & Pachuski, 1996; Riemer-Reiss & Wacker, 2000).

Without training, students with disabilities may have technology and not know how to use it or use it to its full potential. Training is essential not only for the students but also for teachers and family members. Teachers have indicated a lack of training impacts their use and acceptance of assistive technology in their classrooms (Alper & Raharinirina, 2006; Lee & Vega, 2005). Challenges encountered by students with disabilities and their teachers cannot be solved, let alone addressed even, if the assistive technology is not used, and its use is compromised without proper training.

A final reason why technology for students with disabilities does not solve all the problems is the negative connotations surrounding technology for students with disabilities and the lack of effort to counteract these perceptions. The true value of the assistive technology will not be realized if negative connotations continue to prevent its use. This is particularly so for students with high-incidence disabilities in which assistive technology more often addresses academic content and access to the general education curriculum. Educators need to understand as well as help parents and others comprehend when and why one uses assistive technology to bypass or compensate for a student's disability and how use of the assistive technology supports and helps to teach the student academic content (i.e., reading, mathematics) (Edyburn, 2007). Edyburn (2005) illuminated this idea through a story of parents of a child with a disability who expressed frustrated that their child's school had given up on her because they recommend she be given a calculator for her struggle in learning (aka memorizing) math facts.

Similar concerns arise with other technology that supports basic skills students with disabilities struggle with, such as decoding (i.e., text-to-speech software, screen readers, and Reading Pens). According to Edyburn (2005), there is concern or prejudice about technology being a "cognitive prostheses" and a belief that what students with disabilities are able to do with a technology is less valued than what they can do without one (p. 246). This is related to the apprehension that assistive technology can become a crutch for students with disabilities; the technology is not assisting the students in gaining a skill (e.g., reading, computation) but rather substituting for that skill (Rapp, 2005). In other words, technology for students with disabilities is not viewed as a tool offering the same support as a "more knowledgeable other" which students with disabilities can utilize to help them make sense of and demonstrate what they are capable of within a content area, but rather as a replacement for actual instruction in the area that students struggle (Ferdig, 2007; Scardamlia & Bereiter, 1991).

Another negative pervasive attitude toward technology limiting its use is concern over fairness (Parette, Peterson-Karlan, Smith, Gray,

& Silver-Pacuilla, 2006). Some educators indicate providing students with disabilities technology, which may not be offered to other students, is unfair as it gives students with disabilities an undue advantage. This is particularly so for students with more high-incidence disabilities whose recommended assistive technology may be more commonplace in the classroom and perceived to be beneficial to all students (e.g., calculators and pencil grips) (Ashton, 2005). Yet, this notion applies a child's definition of fairness – giving everyone the same thing, rather than the true definition of fairness which involves giving each child what she/he needs (Edyburn, 2006; Welch, 2000). These negative attitudes toward technology limit its use and its potential to truly assist students with disabilities.

TECHNOLOGY'S POTENTIAL

Despite the criticism and concern, technology for students with disabilities solves a lot of problems, or at the very least, helps to alleviate them. The beauty of assistive technology is its capability to address the challenges faced by students with high-incidence disabilities (i.e., mild), those encountered by students with low-incidence disabilities (i.e., severe), and its role in creating a Universal Design for Learning (UDL) experience for students with and without disabilities (Bryant & Bryant, 2003; Council for Exceptional Children [CEC], 2005; Edyburn et al., 2005a, 2005b). There are the notable *heroes* of assistive technology (e.g., AAC devices and text-to-speech programs) and, as Langone (2005) stated, "unsung heroes," such as the low-tech devices of switches, adaptive utensils, and pencil grips (p. xi). There are also the frequently, and unfortunately, unknown heroes, such as Microsoft Reader (Microsoft, n.d.a) – a free, downloadable ebook reader from Microsoft that also allows users to convert Microsoft Office documents into ebooks, CLiCk Speak – a free screen reader for the browser Firefox (Chen, 2008), and a magnifier that comes as part of the accessibility options with the Windows Operating System to enlarge a screen (Microsoft, n.d.b).

Technology for students with disabilities can assist students in the content areas, providing a means to engage in the domain of study (e.g., literacy, mathematics, science, and social studies) which might not otherwise be possible. This is particularly so for Web-based technology and the Internet. For example, advanced technology now allows virtual science labs for students who may struggle with fine motor skills or visual impairments (Schaff, Jerome, Behrmann, & Sprague, 2005). Web-based technology allows students to use virtual manipulatives, such as those in the National

Library of Virtual Manipulatives, to explore and understand mathematical concepts in a manner that enables interactivity and immediate feedback (Bouck & Flanagan, in press; Cannon, Dorward, Duffin, & Heal, 2004). For social studies, a Web-based learning environment – the Virtual History Museum – provides access and interest in learning about history and geography by utilizing images, sound, teacher-controlled text, and video as well as relying on free assistive technology (e.g., text-to-speech and spell-check) (Okolo, Englert, Bouck, & Heutsche, 2007).

Specific technology for students with disabilities can also solve generic access problems. For example, technology can help students with print disabilities (i.e., reading disabilities and visual impairment) and students with physical disabilities get access to printed text, and in a manner that promotes greater independence. With technology, these students can read text independently through a text-to-speech or screen reader program (i.e., JAWS and Universal Reader), or through separate hand-held devices (e.g., Reading Pen), rather than being reliant on a teacher or a peer (Anderson & Anderson, 2005; Banks & Coombs, 2005). While these technologies have their limitations, they grant access and, more importantly, independence in controlling one's own learning and knowledge acquisition. Similarly, speech recognition technology can provide greater access and independence in general education curriculum (e.g., writing a paper or email, using a calculator on the computer, and controlling a computer) (Higgins & Raskind, 2000; Raskind & Higgins, 1999).

Technology for students with disabilities is not only for school but involves lifelong tools (e.g., employment), helping students to access, increase, maintain, or improve their performance in a particular area (i.e., reading, communicating) at a particular time. Assistive technology are tools promoting success in school by helping students to access material, environments, and learning as well as promoting independence at home, work, and the community. Technology can make things possible for students with disabilities that at once seemed improbable, and work to solve various problems – common and more obscure – students with disabilities encounter (see Edyburn et al., 2005a).

THE FUTURE ...

Given the noted benefits of technology for students with disabilities, another answer to the question if technology solves all problems is not yet. New, innovative technology is continually being developed. The technology of tomorrow can solve the problems of today. Think back to when reading printed text was a challenge for students with reading disabilities or visual impairments, and no options existed (aside from perhaps books on tape). Then text-to-speech software, screen readers, and Reading Pen technologies were developed and marketed for educational purposes. We can only guess what future technologies might entail considering today's technology allows students with disabilities to write papers using only their voice (i.e., speech recognition) (Jeffs, Behrmann, & Bannan-Ritland, 2006), receive prompting from a pentop computer (i.e., FLY Pen) (LeapFrog, 2008; Pogue, 2005), and use an AAC tool from cell phones or personal digital assistants (PDAs) (Bryen & Pecunas, 2004).

Although technological innovations have provided increasingly sophisticated, effective, and efficient technologies for addressing the challenges faced by a range of students with disabilities, problems still exist. These existing problems are a result of both technology not overcoming the depth or breadth of the challenges and technology not currently existing to address the problem. For example, a problem the field still faces is providing accessible graphing calculators for students with disabilities (i.e., talking or speech-output graphing calculators), and at an affordable cost. Students with visual impairments often face challenges getting access to higher level mathematics and science education, and one reason is the limiting nature of technology (Banks & Coombs, 2005). While talking scientific calculators exist, these calculators do not support graphing, and the options for students with visual impairments in terms of sophisticated calculators for advanced mathematics are limited.

CONCLUSION

Given the allure of the potential of technology and society's apparent obsession toward it (e.g., smart phones and mp3 players), a return to the original question is needed – does technology for students with disabilities solve all the problems? While the quick answer may be no, to truly answer the question one needs to ask if technology for students with disabilities has done what it has intended to do. And perhaps that should be the question; does technology for students with disabilities do what it needs to do? Possibly technology for students with disabilities has been set up to fail, to be under-appreciated and devalued by being viewed as the solution to all the problems faced by students with disabilities. Perhaps, technology for students with disabilities needs to be viewed for what it does do, what it has contributed, and the potential it still offers.

One could argue that technology for students with disabilities was never intended to solve all problems. By its very definition, assistive technology does not have to solve problems; it can simply help students maintain the status quo. Furthermore, according to the Technology-Related Assistance for Individual with Disabilities Act (1988, p. 1044), known as the Tech Act, the goal of assistive technology is to

> enable individuals with disabilities to (a) have greater control over their own lives, (b) participate in and contribute more fully to activities in their home, school, and work environments, and in their communities, (c) interact to a greater extent with nondisabled individuals, and (d) otherwise benefit from opportunities that are taken for granted by individuals who do not have disabilities.

When one stops to reflect on these ideas, technology for students with disabilities is addressing what it has been asked, and can reasonably be expected, to do.

Technology for students with disabilities does allow individuals with disabilities to have greater control over their lives. From the simple example of wheelchairs allowing students with physical disabilities to control their mobility to the more complex example of computer-based voice input speech output tools that give students with visual impairments greater control over their participation in school and employment, technology enables independence. Technology also allows students to participate in their environments, such as talking microwave ovens and vibrating alarm clocks (Freitas & Kouroupetroglou, 2008; Kordas, 2008). Furthermore, AAC devices, from the low-tech Picture Exchange Communication Symbols to the high-tech Tango, encourage interaction between students with and without disabilities (Bondy & Frost, 1994; Ellenson, 2006). Finally, technology, such as text-to-speech, helps make opportunities (i.e., reading) possible for students with disabilities that many individuals without disabilities take for granted.

REFERENCES

Alper, S., & Raharinirina, S. (2006). Assistive technology for individuals with disabilities: A review and synthesis of the literature. *Journal of Special Education Technology, 21*(2), 47–64.

Anderson, K. M., & Anderson, C. L. (2005). Integrating technology in standards-based instruction. In: D. Edyburn, K. Higgins & R. Boone (Eds), *Handbook of special education technology research and practice* (pp. 521–544). Whitefish Bay, WI: Knowledge by Design.

Ashton, T. M. (2005). Students with learning disabilities using assistive technology in the inclusive classroom. In: D. Edyburn, K. Higgins & R. Boone (Eds), *Handbook of special education technology research and practice* (pp. 229–238). Whitefish Bay, WI: Knowledge by Design.

Banks, R., & Coombs, N. (2005). Accessible information technology and persons with visual impairments. In: D. Edyburn, K. Higgins & R. Boone (Eds), *Handbook of special education technology research and practice* (pp. 379–391). Whitefish Bay, WI: Knowledge by Design.

Behrmann, M., & Jerome, M. K. (2002). Assistive technology for students with mild disabilities: Update 2002. *ERIC Digest*. Available at http://www.ericdigests.org/2003-1/assistive.htm. Retrieved on March 10, 2009.

Behrmann, M., & Schaff, J. (2001). Assisting educators with assistive technology: Enabling children to achieve independence in living and learning. *Children and Families*, 42(3), 24–28.

Blackhurst, A. E. (1997). Perspectives on technology in special education. *Teaching Exceptional Children*, 29(5), 41–48.

Bondy, A. S., & Frost, L. A. (1994). The picture exchange communication system. *Focus on Autism and Other Developmental Disabilities*, 9(3), 1–19.

Bouck, E. C., & Flanagan, S. M. (in press). Virtual manipulatives: What are they and how can teachers use them? *Intervention in School and Clinic*.

Bray, M., Brown, A., & Green, T. D. (2004). *Technology and the diverse learner*. Thousand Oaks, CA: Corwin Press.

Bryant, D. P., & Bryant, B. R. (2003). *Assistive technology for people with disabilities*. Boston: Allyn & Bacon.

Bryen, D. N., & Pecunas, P. (2004). Augmentative and alternative communication and cell phone use: One off-the-shelf solution and some policy considerations. *Assistive Technology*, 16(1), 11–17.

Cannon, L., Dorward, J., Duffin, J., & Heal, B. (2004). National library of virtual manipulatives. *The Mathematics Teacher*, 97, 158–159.

Chen, C. (2008). CLiCk, Speak. Available at http://clickspeak.clcworld.net/. Retrieved on March 10, 2009.

Council for Exceptional Children (2005). *Universal design for learning: A guide for teachers and education professionals*. Boston: Pearson.

Dick, M., Sheard, J., Bareiss, C., Carter, J., Joyce, D., Harding, T., & Laxer, C. (2003). Addressing student cheating: Definitions and solutions. *ACM SIGCSE Bulletin*, 35(2), 172–184. Available at http://doi.acm.org/10.1145/782941.783000. Retrieved on March 2, 2009.

Edyburn, D. (2007). Technology-enhanced reading performance: Defining a research agenda. *Reading Research Quarterly*, 42, 148–152.

Edyburn, D. L. (2001). Models, theories, and frameworks: Contributions to understanding special education technology. *Special Education Technology Practice*, 4(2), 16–24. Available at http://cte.jhu.edu/accessibility/primer/resources/data/assistivetech/brochure_edy_burn.pdf. Retrieved on April 29, 2009.

Edyburn, D. L. (2005). Assistive technology and students with mild disabilities: From consideration to outcomes measurement. In: D. Edyburn, K. Higgins & R. Boone (Eds), *Handbook of special education technology research and practice* (pp. 239–270). Whitefish Bay, WI: Knowledge by Design.

Edyburn, D. L. (2006). Assistive technology and mild disabilities. *Special Education Technology Practice*, 8(4), 18–28.

Edyburn, D. L., Higgins, K., & Boone, R. (Eds). (2005a). *Handbook of special education technology research and practice*. Whitefish Bay, WI: Knowledge by Design.

Edyburn, D. L., Higgins, K., & Boone, R. (2005b). Preface. In: D. Edyburn, K. Higgins & R. Boone (Eds), *Handbook of special education technology research and practice* (pp. xiii–xvi). Whitefish Bay, WI: Knowledge by Design.

Ellenson, R. (2006). Two who tango!: A father, a son, and a new generation of speech generating devices. *Exceptional Parent* (June), 29–31. Available at http://www.blink-twice.com/tango/news.html. Retrieved on March 6, 2009.

Englert, C. S., & Mariage, T. V. (1991). Making students partners in the comprehension process: Organizing the reading "POSSE". *Learning Disability Quarterly, 14*, 123–138.

Ferdig, R. E. (2007). Editorial: Examining social software in teacher education. *Journal of Technology and Teacher Education, 15*(1), 5–10.

Freitas, D., & Kouroupetroglou, G. (2008). Speech technologies for blind and low vision persons. *Technology and Disability, 20*, 135–156.

Hannaford, A. E. (1993). Computers and exceptional individuals. In: J. D. Lindsey (Ed.), *Computers and exceptional individuals* (pp. 3–26). Austin, TX: Pro-Ed.

Heur, M. B., Parette, H. P., & Scherer, M. (2004). Effects of acculturation on assistive technology service delivery. *Journal of Special Education Technology, 19*(2), 31–41.

Higgins, E. L., & Raskind, M. H. (2000). Speaking to read: The effects of continuous vs. discrete speech recognition systems on the reading and spelling of children with learning disabilities. *Journal of Special Education Technology, 15*(1), 19–29.

Hitchcock, C., Khalsa, A., Malouf, D. B., Parette, P., Zabala, J. S., & Edyburn, D. L. (2005). Forum: The future of assistive technology. *Thresholds*, 10–14. Available at www.ciconline.org/c/document_library/get_file?folderId = 30&name = T-Win05-ATForum.pdf. Retrieved on March 5, 2008.

Individuals with Disabilities Education Improvement Act. (2004). P.L. 108-446, 108.

Jeffs, T., Behrmann, M., & Bannan-Ritland, B. (2006). Assistive technology and literacy learning: Reflections of parents and children. *Journal of Special Education Technology, 21*, 37–44.

Johnson, L., Beard, L. A., & Carpenter, L. B. (2007). *Assistive technology: Access for all students*. Upper Saddle River, NJ: Pearson.

Kordas, T. (2008). Meeting the listening needs of adolescents: FM and other technologies. *Perspectives on Hearing and Hearing Disorders in Childhood, 18*, 30–34.

Lahm, A. (2008). Is your daily life enslaved by the electronic world? *AlterNet*, (April). Available at http://www.alternet.org/mediaculture/83228. Retrieved on March 18, 2009.

Lahm, E. A., & Sizemore, L. (2002). Factors that influence assistive technology decision making. *Journal of Special Education Technology, 17*, 15–26.

Langone, J. (2005). Foreword. In: D. Edyburn, K. Higgins & R. Boone (Eds), *Handbook of special education technology research and practice* (pp. xi–xii). Whitefish Bay, WI: Knowledge by Design.

LeapFrog. (2008). Personal learning tools. Available at http://www.leapfrogschoolhouse.com/do/findpage?pageKey = plt. Retrieved on October 21, 2008.

Lee, Y., & Vega, L. A. (2005). Perceived knowledge, attitudes, and challenges of AT use in special education. *Journal of Special Education Technology, 20*(2), 60–63.

Lewis, P. H. (1988). Ex machina; the computer revolution revised. *The New York Times*, August 7. Available at http://query.nytimes.com/gst/fullpage.html?res = 940DE4DF1F38F934A3575BC0A96E948260&sec = &spon = &pagewanted = 1. Retrieved on March 2, 2009.

Maccini, P., & Gagnon, J. C. (2000). Best practices for teaching mathematics to secondary students with special needs. *Focus on Exceptional Children*, *32*(5), 1–22.

McGregor, G., & Pachuski, P. (1996). Assistive technology in schools: Are teachers ready, able, and supported. *Journal of Special Education Technology*, *13*, 4–15.

Microsoft. (n.d.a). Microsoft reader. Available at http://www.microsoft.com/Reader/default.aspx. Retrieved on March 10, 2009.

Microsoft. (n.d.b). Turn on and use magnifier. Available at http://www.microsoft.com/windowsxp/using/accessibility/magnifierturnon.mspx. Retrieved on March 10, 2009.

Okolo, C. M., Englert, C. S., Bouck, E. C., & Heutsche, A. M. (2007). Web-based history learning environments: Helping all students learn and like history. *Intervention in School and Clinic*, *43*(1), 3–11.

Parette, H. P., Peterson-Karlan, G. R., Smith, S., Gray, T., & Silver-Pacuilla, H. (2006). The state of assistive technology: Themes from an outcome summit. *Assistive Technology Outcomes and Benefits*, *3*(1), 15–33Available at http://www.atia.org/i4a/pages/index.cfm?pageid = 3314. Retrieved on March 2, 2009.

Pogue, D. (2005). Review: The fine points of a high-performing pen. *International Herald Tribune*, November 18. Available at http://www.iht.com/articles/2005/11/18/news/ptpogue19.php. Retrieved on October 21, 2008.

Prensky, M. (2001a). Digital natives, digital immigrants. *On the Horizon*, *9*(5), 1–6.

Prensky, M. (2001b). Digital natives, digital immigrants, Part 2: Do they really think differently? *On the Horizon*, *9*(6), 1–9.

Rapp, W. H. (2005). Using assistive technology with students with exceptional learning needs: When does an aid become a crutch? *Reading and Writing Quarterly*, *21*, 193–196.

Raskind, M., & Bryant, B. R. (2002). *Functional evaluation for assistive technology*. Austin, TX: Psych-Educational Services.

Raskind, M. H., & Higgins, E. L. (1999). Speaking-to-read: The effects of speech recognition technology on the reading and spelling performance of students with learning disabilities. *Annals of Dyslexia*, *49*, 251–281.

Riemer-Reiss, M. L., & Wacker, R. R. (2000). Factors associated with assistive technology discontinuance among individuals with disabilities. *Journal of Rehabilitation*, *66*, 44–50.

Scardamlia, M., & Bereiter, C. (1991). Higher levels of agency for children in knowledge building: A challenge for the design of new knowledge media. *The Journal of Learning Sciences*, *1*(1), 37–68.

Schaff, J. I., Jerome, M. K., Behrmann, M. M., & Sprague, D. (2005). Science in special education: Emerging technologies. In: D. Edyburn, K. Higgins & R. Boone (Eds), *Handbook of special education technology research and practice* (pp. 643–661). Whitefish Bay, WI: Knowledge by Design.

Technology-Related Assistance for Individuals with Disabilities Act. (1988). PL 100-407. (August 19, 1988). Title 29, U.S.C. 2201 et seq: *U.S. Statutes at Large*, *102*, 1044–1065.

Vanderheiden, G. (1984). High and light technology approaches in the development of communication systems for the severely physically handicapped person. *Exceptional Education Quarterly*, *4*(4), 40–56.

Warschauer, M. (2007). A teacher's place in the digital divide. *Yearbook of the National Society for the Study of Education*, *106*(2), 147–166.

Welch, A. B. (2000). Responding to student concerns about fairness. *Teaching Exceptional Children*, *33*(2), 36–40.

Wyer, K. (2001). The great equalizer: Assistive technology launches a new era in inclusion. *Teaching Tolerance*, *19*, 1–5.

PART IV
MULTICULTURAL EDUCATION

CHAPTER 7

MULTICULTURAL EDUCATION: A NECESSARY TOOL FOR GENERAL AND SPECIAL EDUCATION

Satasha L. Green

This chapter examines the use of multicultural education as a necessary tool for general and special education. Multicultural education is essential in a pluralistic classroom, and it allows for students' diverse ways of learning and knowing. Increasingly, special educators are working with culturally, racially, ethnically, and linguistically diverse student populations with a wide range of abilities in their classrooms, whereas the vast majority of teachers continue to be monolingual, white, middle-class, and female. Of nearly 48.2 million students receiving a public school education in the United States (Lips, 2006), African Americans represent more than 30% of the students in special education, yet they make up only 17% of the total school age population (Green & Qualls, in press; Obiakor, 2007). Native Americans represent less than 1% of the school population and 1% of the special education population. Asian Americans represent less than 2% of all students in special education, while they make up 4% of the school-aged population. European-American students are the most proportionate of all of the groups relative to the overall school age population (67%), with placement in special education at 43.2% (National Center for Educational Statistics, 2005; Obiakor, 2007).

Traditionally, Latino American students have been overrepresented in all categories of special education, particularly speech and language disorders and learning disabilities; they are 16% of the national school population and 14% of the children in special education (National Center for Educational Statistics, 2005).

Educators must become aware of differences in cultural experiences, language, and learning styles when instructing students. Teachers must instruct from a culturally responsive perspective even though they may be culturally different from their students (Lane, 2006). Since there is an apparent cultural mismatch between many teachers and students, teachers need to be more sensitive to diversity in the classroom and promote the use of multicultural education because student's culture and language may contribute to the development of their identity, self-worth and academic achievement (Lovelace & Wheeler, 2006; Weinstein, Tomlinson-Clark, & Curran, 2004; Zeichner, 1993). Effective teachers should understand that both institutional and individual biases have negative effects on culturally and linguistically diverse (CLD) students, themselves, and teacher–student relationships. These biased perceptions may impact teacher–student interactions and make it less likely to meet the needs of CLD students whose attitudes, values, beliefs, and behavioral patterns may vary from their non-CLD peers. Multicultural education as a tool in general and special education can help to provide a more positive view by educators of their CLD students. It may provide an avenue to prevent the incongruity between the home culture and the school culture of a CLD student (Gay, 2000).

Often times in school CLD students struggle for acceptance and acknowledgement of their strengths that do not fit the conventional definition. Frequently educators may interpret cultural and linguistic differences of these students as academic deficits (Webb-Johnson, 1999). CLD students can easily become outsiders in the existing educational system that is fundamentally developed and implemented, to a large degree around European-American middle-class values and perspectives (LeCompte & McCray, 2002). CLD students who have special needs may face compounded obstacles of cultural, linguistic, and ability differences. The challenge for teachers to successfully provide curriculum and instruction that meet these students' needs is difficult and quit complex. Therefore, this chapter makes the argument for the use of multicultural education as a necessary tool for general and special education because of the growing CLD student population in U.S. public schools. Theories have been offered relative to the disproportionate representation of CLD students in special education and to the educational disparity of these students in both general and special education. The fundamental question "Is multicultural education a necessary tool for general and special education?" will guide the argument for the use of multicultural education in schools in the following sections.

MULTICULTURALISM: ORIGIN AND NATURE OF THE SCHOOL PROBLEM

Schools maintain a monocultural approach to teaching even with a growing CLD school population. Multiculturalism supports the idea that school curriculum should represent and reflect the cultural make-up of the school population. Multicultural education is democratic, and it promotes cultural differences as assets rather than liabilities.

Multicultural education grew out of the civil rights movement of the 1960s (Banks, 2001; Banks & Banks, 1997, 2001), and it has gone through many transformations in both theory and practice. It utilizes a combination of concepts, paradigms, and theories from various fields of study such as ethnic and women studies, history, social and behavioral sciences, humanistic education, behavioral education, and cognitive education methodologies. Multicultural education incorporates content from these fields and disciplines into pedagogy and curriculum development in educational settings (Banks, 2001; Banks & Banks, 1997, 2001; Smith, Richards, MacGranley, & Obiakor, 2004).

Researchers in the field have coined several definitions for the term multicultural education (Gollnick & Chinn, 2002; Gorski, 2000). Different conceptualizations for it exist, and one conception is that multicultural education is an education movement that proposes to increase equity for particular victimized groups without limiting the opportunities of another (Banks, 2001; Banks & Banks, 1997; Diaz, 2001). Banks and Banks (1995) define multicultural education as a field of study that aims to create equal educational opportunities for students from CLD backgrounds (Obiakor, 2007; Smith et al., 2004). A major goal of multicultural education is to assist all students in acquiring the knowledge and skills needed to navigate effectively in a pluralistic society (Banks, 2001; Banks & Banks, 2001; Gorski, 2000). Multicultural education, as an approach, focuses on reversing current shortcomings, failures, and discriminatory practices in our educational school system in several ways (Banks, 2001; Banks & Banks, 2001; Gorski & Covert, 2000). First, it helps students to appreciate diversity and develop a greater potential for learning. Second, multicultural education focuses on long denied social and education equity for CLD students (Davidman & Davidman, 2001; Gorski & Covert, 2000). Third, it teaches both students and teachers to view students with different ethnic and racial identities as assets (Banks, 2001; Gay, 2002; Rhee, 2002; Tantum, 1997). Chisholm and Wetzel (1997) indicate that multicultural education is as essential to teaching as nurturing is to human development, and it is based on the premise that teachers must understand and appreciate their students' cultural diversity. Multicultural education, as a strategy, may assist in alleviating the mislabeling and misdiagnoses of CLD students who are referred and placed into special education at a disproportionate rate (Webb-Johnson, 1999). Special education has generated much attention because CLD students are greatly affected by the current referral and placement processes. For example, these students' cultural differences are many times perceived as deficits and treated like disabilities, which often leads to the over-identification of these students in special education (McCray & Garcia, 2002; Patton, 1998; Webb-Johnson, 1999). There is a lack of research in the field of special education concerning culturally responsive research-based pre-referral interventions designed for CLD students who have special needs (LeCompte & McCray, 2002; McCollum & McBride, 1997). To successfully and effectively identify the physical, developmental, and socio-cultural needs of CLD students, teachers must begin to align instruction with multicultural education (Ladson-Billings, 2001). Multiculturalism represents a holistic approach in the education process (e.g., assessments, evaluations, special education referrals, and special education placements), and this practice can help to alleviate disparities and social injustices in our current educational system. Multicultural education is a nontraditional technique that provides a blueprint for teachers to convey knowledge and skills reflective of students' culture and language, which may contribute to a more positive and productive reciprocal relationship.

MULTICULTURAL EDUCATION: TEACHERS' PERCEPTIONS

Teachers should understand how forms of racism and cultural biases affect students. Research on multicultural education and its effectiveness in the teaching and learning process indicate that educators' low expectations for students have negative effects on their academic performance (National

Research Council, 2002). Teachers who apply multicultural education have more positive perceptions and expectations of underachieving CLD students than those who do not utilize multicultural education. Many educators are reluctant and uncomfortable with acknowledging that racial and cultural differences exist among teachers and students. Educators often teach as if they live in a color-blind society and that all students are afforded the same opportunities. Teachers use phrases such as "I don't see color I see the student" and "I treat all my students the same regardless of their race or ethnicity." These are unrealistic clichés and unsound expressions that go against the very foundation for appreciation of multiculturalism and cultural diversity in the classroom. Although it may be easier for teachers to claim that all students are the same and to ignore students' differences in the classroom, this may also aid in the creation of a conscious or unconscious racist and ethnocentric school environment (Green, 2007, 2009). Bos and Reyes (1996) suggest teachers should focus on the students' cultural resources not necessarily their ethnic differences to alleviate conditions where some teachers feel uncomfortable with acknowledging these differences.

Teachers who are aware that behavior is culturally defined will provide a more flexible classroom where multicultural education is utilized to serve the diverse needs of CLD students. For example, research shows that some African-American boys' social lifestyles are developed more in classrooms that allow them greater movement and interaction (Dandy, 1990; Sheets & Gay, 1996). Educators who utilize multicultural education in their curriculum and instruction recognize, accept, and focus on strengths CLD students bring into the classroom. Gay (2000) indicates classrooms should be more consistent with students' cultural orientations. The use of cultural knowledge, prior experiences, frames of reference, and performance styles of ethnically diverse students makes learning more relevant and effective. Another example, of effective use of multicultural education is the inclusion of bilingual education and English as a second language (ESL) programs for English language learners (ELLs). Both teachers and students benefit from knowing when teaching linguistically diverse students, it is important to incorporate their native language into curriculum and instruction (e.g., utilize dictionaries in English and their native language/native dialect). When students are provided multicultural education in their classrooms, learners may view their culture and language as important and valued within the classroom, school, and in society. This may have a positive impact on the achievement gap between CLD learners and non-CLD peers.

MULTICULTURALISM: IN REHABILITATION COUNSELING, NEXT STEP IN SPECIAL EDUCATION

Educators are ill-equipped to provide culturally responsive curriculum and instruction for CLD students who have special needs. Therefore, multicultural education has expanded in scope to the field of special education, and it is called *Multicultural Special Education*. Obiakor (2007) indicates multicultural special education encompasses education programs that help all learners who are at risk for misidentification, misassessment, miscategorization, misplacement, and misinstruction because of their racial, cultural, and linguistic differences. Academic disparities between CLD students and their non-CLD peers in school exist and explanations for this may be provided through the use of scientific theory, a blueprint for research. The "double whammy" and "triple threat" theories are used to give accounts for the educational achievement gap between CLD students who have special needs and non-CLD students.

DOUBLE WHAMMY THEORY

Marshall (1987) developed a theory based on clients of color who encountered a double dose of discriminations based on racial prejudice and ability bias called the *Double Whammy Theory*. This research was done with African Americans with disabilities in the rehabilitation counseling system. The principles of this theory may be applied to CLD students in special education. There is a potential double bias associated with being CLD and having a disability. CLD students in the current educational system often deal with cultural and linguistic discrimination, and at the same time, they must face discrimination based on their cognitive or physical disabilities. Alston, Russo, and Miles (1994) indicate there are similarities in stigmas and inequities experienced by CLD students and persons with disabilities. Both groups have been excluded from mainstream American life, and they share underprivileged status. Walker (1988) suggests persons with disabilities are "tolerated but not allowed to participate fully in society" and they are "consistently relegated...to economic deprivation and dependency" (Alston et al., 1994). Persons of color in the United States have endured the negative effects of such stigmas, which ultimately pose serious and unique challenges for educators and learners (Alston & Mngadi, 1992).

Students with disabilities, similar to CLD students, are less likely to receive encouragement and recognition for their efforts and their academic achievements, and they are less likely to be recommended for participation in enrichment programs (Walker, 1988). The combination of having a disability and being a person of color may engender a double whammy stigma that poses a barrier to full participation in education, employment, and social opportunity (Herbert & Cheatham, 1988). CLD students who have disabilities may encounter prejudice from individuals and groups who lack awareness and sensitivity of the potential combined effects of being CLD and having a disability (Alston & Mngadi, 1992).

CLD students who have disabilities as all groups are not monolithic and may not solely view themselves with respect to culture and race (Reynolds & Pope, 1991). Their disability may be an equally salient aspect of their identity, and these students may consequently identify more with individuals who share their disability than their culture and race. Cultural and racial identity development for some CLD students who have disabilities may be disability specific, which means that it may not apply as strongly to persons with certain disabilities. For example, an African-American student who is blind may have a greater connection with the "blind culture," and it may be more difficult for him/her to understand the concept of racial identity than for an African-American student with a learning disability who interacts with persons of other cultures and races (Alston, Bell, & Feist-Price, 1996). Multicultural education may help to foster an understanding of similar situations in the classroom.

TRIPLE THREAT THEORY

Over the past 25 years, students from linguistically diverse backgrounds have increased rapidly comparative to mono-English speakers in California and in the rest of the United States (California Linguistic Minority Research Institute, 2006). A large number of students with disabilities have limited English proficiency (LEP) as well as a low socio-economic status (SES). In the early 1990s, the number of pre-K students with LEP enrolled in U.S. schools grew at nearly 10 times the rate of native-English-speaking students (Echevarria, Vogt, & Short, 2000). In the year 2000, there were an estimated 3.4 million students with LEP between the ages of 5 and 14 years in U.S. public schools (California Linguistic Minority Research Institute, 2006). In 2005 more than 10 million children, in the United States between the ages of 5 and 17 years, spoke a language other than English (California Linguistic Minority Research Institute, 2006). This population of students represented 20% of school-age children (United States Census Bureau, 2005). For example, in California, 44% or 3.9 million school-age children spoke a language other than English. This population increased by 187%, whereas mono-English speakers increased by only 8% (California Linguistic Minority Research Institute, 2006). Similarly, national statistics for linguistically diverse students increased by 130%, whereas mono-English speakers decreased by 1.3% (University of California Linguistic Minority Research Institute, 2006). As a result, the majority of the 5 million additional school-age children in the United States over the past 25 years were from linguistically diverse backgrounds (California Linguistic Minority Research Institute, 2006).

This population of students who have a disability, who are LEP, and who have low SES have been referred to as "triple threat" students in the literature (Baca, 1990). Baca used the term "triple threat" students to focus on the obstacles faced by many children and youth with disabilities from CLD backgrounds even before they enter the school system. Baca and Cervantes (1991) indicated these students have three strikes against them before they get an opportunity to even go to school. The first strike triple threat students may face is having a disability that places them into special education. The second strike they encounter is their limited classroom English proficiency as defined by bilingual education. The third strike that many of these students may confront is low SES (Baca & Cervantes, 1991). However, some scholars have suggested that there may even be a fourth strike, which may consist of the students' cultural backgrounds (Baca & Cervantes, 1989, 1991). The research, literature, and legislation support the position that a negative relationship exists between educators who have a lack of respect for students who have cultural differences, disabilities, LEP, and low SES. Teachers who support cultural diversity in the classroom can contribute to the academic success of CLD students by providing multicultural education. Educators who utilize multicultural education for CLD students who have special needs focus on cultural diversity in the classroom and find ways for students to connect with the content and materials (Montgomery, 2001). Students who are provided multicultural education are more motivated to learn, engage in school activities, and perform better academically (McIntyre, 1996).

Multicultural education allows CLD students and their teachers to engage in teaching–learning environments that cause students to become motivated and to succeed in academic settings. Since schools are not culturally neutral terrains, multicultural education may be used as an alternative to rectify this situation by considering students' varied backgrounds (Boykin, 2000). Emerging research supports the efficacy of engaging in multicultural education because schools have typically practiced traditional instruction, which is often characterized by tracking (Banks & Banks, 2001; Oakes & Wells, 1998).

Tracking is undemocratic in nature, and teachers who use this tactic limit or exclude the contributions of people of diverse cultures and languages (Banks & Banks, 2001; Gollnick & Chinn, 2002; Green, 2009). Denbo (2002) indicates that the effectiveness of a school is influenced by a school's culture, which may be expressed through its policies, practices, and beliefs. School culture may affect the quality of the social and emotional climates of the education system, student achievement expectations, student and teacher relationships, and community associations.

Multicultural education allows teachers and learners to accept and focus on the strengths CLD students bring into the classroom; therefore, classroom teachers must be consistently conscious of students' cultural and particularly linguistic orientations (Gay, 2000). Educators who incorporate multicultural education acknowledge that there is cultural and linguistic diversity within the classroom, and they find ways for students to connect with various content and materials (Gay, 2002; McIntyre, 1996; Montgomery, 2001).

IMPLICATIONS FOR USING MULTICULTURAL EDUCATION IN DIVERSE GENERAL AND SPECIAL EDUCATION CLASSROOMS

This chapter implies that without utilizing multicultural education as a tool in general and special education, teachers will not become effective brokers of culturally responsive teaching and may not successfully provide interesting and relevant materials that will motivate and engage CLD students academically. It is also implied that without multicultural education the responsibility for the academic success of CLD students is determined by monocultural approaches to teaching that may contribute to low self-esteem and academic failure (Green, 2009). The educational system must ensure that all students are provided a fair and equal opportunity to learn. A monocultural approach to teaching is counter-productive to the academic health, well-being, and future aspirations of society, and this approach is detrimental for all students and CLD students in particular. A monocultural approach to teaching perpetuates the idea that there is a "one size fits all" model and that this model is the standard for academic success (Green, 2007; Pierre-Pipkin, 2004). Academic success is the product of a team effort consisting of the school and the student's community. The message that is conveyed in schools to CLD students who do not conform to mainstream cultural views is that they are resistant and uncooperative

(Green, 2007). It is important for teachers to recognize that in educating the whole students their culture, language, attitudes, and belief systems must be taken into account when developing curriculum and providing instruction (Wayman & Lynch, 1991). A "critical cultural consciousness" that entails an awareness and encouragement of students is essential to become effective educators (Gay, 2002). Educators should address cultural consciousness so that they can begin to reflect and assess their own values, biases, and stereotypes that they bring into their teaching (LeCompte & McCray, 2002). Teachers who acquire these attitudes and behaviors will allow themselves to move toward a multicultural education approach to teaching in their classrooms that meets the academic needs of their CLD students. Hopefully, educators may come to view multiculturalism and human diversity as assets to their knowledge and skill sets.

MULTICULTURAL EDUCATION: A NECESSARY TOOL FOR ALL STUDENTS

"Is multicultural education a necessary tool for general and special education?" The achievement gap between CLD students and their non-CLD peers and the disproportionate referral and placement of CLD students in special education helps to address this fundamental question. Some efforts have been made to address these devastating disparities in the field of education; however, many of these attempts have fallen far short and are ineffective. Nontraditional education techniques such as multicultural education are offered as a solution (Gay, 2002; Harry, 1992, 2002; LeCompte & McCray, 2002). Multicultural education may effectively meet the diverse academic and emotional needs of CLD students in general and special education by providing culturally appropriate and relevant materials (Green, 2007). Scholars (Fogel & Ehri, 2006; Irvine, 2003; Lane, 2006; Villegas & Lucas, 2002) have offered several suggestions that may be applied to help begin the application of multicultural education in U.S. classrooms. First, provide professional development for preservice and inservice teachers in multicultural education to help prepare them to teach the growing CLD population of students found in today's classrooms (Fogel & Ehri, 2006; Villegas & Lucas, 2002). Second, emphasize that the critical role of a teacher entails the ability to incorporate the daily experiences and prior knowledge of students when teaching new concepts (Irvine, 2003). Third, teachers should connect students' personal knowledge to objectives that learners must master by utilizing culturally familiar ways of instruction that gives teachers the opportunity to encourage and include the cultural knowledge of students (Irvine, 2003). Teachers should ensure that learners are culturally grounded and become potential agents of positive change in their communities (Lane, 2006).

WEAVING THE FABRIC TOGETHER

Teachers must develop specific knowledge and skills to assist them in promoting respect for diversity in the classroom when working with diverse student populations. It is beneficial for educators to recognize that cultural and linguistic differences include patterns of communication as well as behavior. Teachers may incorporate multicultural education to embrace students' cultural patterns of socialization, and they must recognize that behavior should not be interpreted homogeneously and that expectations are different across cultures. Multicultural education is needed to build bridges between the students' backgrounds and experiences and the teacher's frame of reference when teaching CLD students with and without disabilities. Instruction must be responsive to students' learning needs, adapted to their learning styles and enhance their existing skills. A multicultural approach accommodates students who are culturally and linguistically different by using teaching strategies that promote successful academic outcomes (Bennett, 2003; Gollnick & Chinn, 2002).

Multicultural education is a progressive holistic approach for transforming current shortcomings, failings, and discriminatory practices into positive, fair, and just practices in education. It is grounded in the ideals of social justice, education equity, and facilitating diversified educational experiences. Multicultural education focuses on students reaching their full potentials as learners and their becoming socially aware and active beings in their community and society. The approach emphasizes the necessity of the school to lay the foundation for teachers and students to transform society and help to eliminate oppression and injustice (Gorski, 2000).

Serious attention must be given to *multicultural education as a necessary tool in general and special education* concerning CLD students who have disabilities, disproportionate academic failure rates, erroneous labeling and diagnosis, and reckless referral and placements into special education programs. Educators must become aware of the specific difficulties facing CLD students, and they must acknowledge the role teachers play in the educational disparities of this population. Educators must begin, upon recognition of its importance, the process of facilitating multicultural education to suit the needs of CLD students in schools. For example, teachers should begin the process by eliminating the label "culturally disadvantaged" that is often used to describe CLD students. If teachers simply examined the terms they use to describe students, this would be a step in the right direction. A learner who has a difference should not be perceived as a student with a deficit, as having deviant behavior or who is culturally disadvantaged, which inherently relegate many CLD students to inferior status in schools. Furthermore, educators are in positions to mediate curriculum and instruction that are provided to their students. Consequently, teachers are obligated to critically evaluate the roles in promoting multicultural education and culturally responsive teaching. Whether through ignorance, indifference, or blatant disregard for CLD students they encounter, many educators have not considered the needs of these students particularly if the student has a disability. No longer can educators ignore the changing demographics of the education system in the United States. Movement toward a curriculum that is culturally responsive is necessary because all our students deserve an equitable education.

Teachers who are uncertain about the importance of implementing multicultural education in the classroom may devalue their CLD students, and it may cause these students to doubt themselves and their abilities. However, teachers who use multicultural education (1) build on students' cultural knowledge to teach students academic knowledge, (2) use students' prior experiences to make connection with new academic experiences, (3) incorporate students' frames of reference into materials and content being discussed in the classroom, (4) encourage and evaluate students strengths to help develop new academic strengths, and (5) recognize students multi-intelligence as assets to help motivate and engage students in classroom activities (Gay, 2002; Green, 2009; Lane, 2006). Therefore, multicultural education assists in the production of students who achieve academically, demonstrate cultural competence, and are able to understand and critique the existing social order (Ladson-Billings, 2001). Educators who support multicultural education as a necessary tool in general and special education have the responsibility to transform the educational system and they must make decisions about instruction and evaluation that consider the whole student their culture, language, attitudes, belief systems, and abilities (Green, 2009; Wayman & Lynch, 1991).

REFERENCES

Alston, R. J., Bell, T. J., & Feist-Price, S. (1996). Racial identity and African American with disabilities: Theoretical and practice. *The Journal of Rehabilitation, 62*(2), 11–16.

Alston, R. J., & Mngadi, S. (1992). The interaction between disability status and the African American experience: Implications for rehabilitation counseling. *Journal of Applied Rehabilitation Counseling*, 23(2), 12–16.

Alston, R. J., Russo, C. J., & Miles, A. S. (1994). Brown v. board of education and the Americans with disabilities act: Vistas of equal educational opportunities for African Americans. *Journal of Negro Education*, 63(3), 349–357.

Baca, L. M. (1990). *Theory and practice in bilingual/cross cultural special education: Major issues and implications for research, practice and policy. Proceedings of the First Research Symposium on Limited English Proficient Student Issues.* ERIC Document Reproduction Service No. ED341267. Washington, DC.

Baca, L. M., & Cervantes, H. T. (Eds). (1989). *The bilingual special education interface* (2nd ed.). Columbus, OH: Merrill.

Baca, L. M., & Cervantes, H. T. (1991). Bilingual special education. Learning disabilities online. Document reproduced from ERIC Digest No. E496. Available at http://www.ldonline.org/ld_indepth/bilingual_ld/esl_ld_eric.html. Retrieved on August 19, 2003.

Banks, J. A. (2001). Multicultural education: Its effects on students' racial and gender role attitudes. In: J. A. Banks & C. A. McGee Banks (Eds), *Handbook of research on multicultural education* (pp. 123–150). San Francisco: Jossey-Bass.

Banks, J. A., & Banks, C. A. M. (Eds). (1995). *Handbook of research on multicultural education*. New York: Macmillan.

Banks, J. A., & Banks, C. A. M. (1997). *Multicultural education: Issues and perspectives* (3rd ed.). Needham Heights, MA: Allyn and Bacon.

Banks, J. A., & Banks, C. A. M. (2001). *Multicultural education: Issues and perspectives* (4th ed.). New York: Wiley.

Bennett, C. I. (2003). *Comprehensive multicultural education: Theory and practice* (5th ed.). Boston, MA: Allyn and Bacon.

Bos, C. S., & Reyes, E. I. (1996). Conversations with a Latina teacher about education for language-minority students with special needs. *The Elementary School Journal*, 96, 343–351.

Boykin, A. W. (2000). The talent development model of schooling: Planning students at promise for academic success. *Journal of Education for Students Placed At Risk*, 5(1&2), 3–25.

California Linguistic Minority Research Institute. (2006). The growth of the linguistic minority population in the U.S. and California, 1980–2005. Available at http://lmri.ucsb.edu

Chisholm, I. N., & Wetzel, K. (1997). Lesson learned from a technology-integrated curriculum for multicultural classrooms. *Journal of Technology and Teacher Education*, 5(4), 293–317.

Dandy, E. B. (1990, March). Sensitizing teachers to cultural differences: An African-American perspective. Paper presented at the National Dropout Prevention Conference, Nashville (ED323479).

Davidman, L., & Davidman, P. T. (2001). *Teaching with a multicultural perspective: A practical guide* (3rd ed.). New York: Longman.

Denbo, S. J. (2002). Why can't we close the achievement gap? In: S. J. Denbo & L. Moore Beaulieu (Eds), *Improving schools for African American students: A reader for educational leaders* (pp. 13–18). Springfield, IL: Charles C. Thomas.

Diaz, C. F. (2001). *Multicultural education in the 21st century*. New York: Longman.

Echevarria, J., Vogt, E., & Short, D. J. (2000). *Making content comprehensible for English language learners: The SIOP Model.* Needham Heights: Allyn and Bacon.

Fogel, H., & Ehri, L. C. (2006). Teaching elementary students who speak black English vernacular to write in standard English: Effects of dialect transformation practice. *Contemporary Educational Psychology, 25*, 212–235.

Gay, G. (2000). *Culturally responsive teaching: Theory, research and practice.* New York: Teachers College Press.

Gay, G. (2002). Culturally responsive teaching in special education for ethnically diverse students: Setting the stage. *Qualitative Studies in Education, 15*(6), 613–629.

Gollnick, D. M., & Chinn, P. C. (2002). *Multicultural education in a pluralistic society.* Washington, DC: Merrill-Prentice Hall.

Gorski, P. (2000). Narrative of whiteness and multicultural education. *Electronic Magazine of Multicultural Education [online], 2*(1), 43. Paragraphs received from http://www.eastern.edu/publications/emme/2000spring/gorski.html

Gorski, P., & Covert, B. (2000). Working definitions. *Teaching Children Mathematics, 9*(3), 179–183.

Green, S. L. (2007). Preparing special educators to work with culturally and linguistically diverse students. *The Black History Bulletin, 70*(1), 12–19.

Green, S. L. (2009). *Motivating African American learners in reading: Using culturally and linguistically responsive scientifically-based reading instruction.* Germany: VDM Publishing House.

Green, S. L., & Qualls C. D. (in press). Educating children with speech and language problems. In: P. Peterson, B. McGraw & E. Baker (Eds), *International encyclopedia of education.* Oxford, England: Elsevier.

Harry, B. (1992). Developing cultural self-awareness: The first step in values clarification for early interventionist. *Topics in Early Childhood Special Education, 12*, 333–351.

Harry, B. (2002). Trends and issues in serving culturally diverse families of children with disabilities. *Journal of Special Education, 36*(3), 13–16.

Herbert, J. T., & Cheatham, H. E. (1988). Africentricity and the Black disability experience: A theoretical orientation for rehabilitation counselors. *Journal of Applied Rehabilitation Counseling, 19*(4), 50–54.

Irvine, J. J. (2003). *Educating teachers for a diverse society: Seeing with the cultural eye.* New York: Teachers College Press.

Ladson-Billings, G. (2001). *Crossing over to Canaan.* San Francisco, CA: Jossey-Bass.

Lane, L. S. B. (2006). Black in the red zone: A study of disproportionate suspension of African American males. *Dissertation Abstracts International, 68*(1A), 55.

LeCompte, K. N., & McCray, A. D. (2002). Complex conversations with teacher candidates: Perspectives of whiteness and culturally responsive teaching. *Curriculum & Teaching Dialogue, 4*(1), 25.

Lips, D. (2006). America's opportunity scholarships for kids: School choice for students in underperforming public schools. Research Education. Available at http://new.heritage.org/Research/Education/bg1939.cfm

Lovelace, S., & Wheeler, T. R. (2006). Cultural discontinuity between home and school language socialization patterns: Implications for teachers. *ERIC, 127*(2), 303–309.

Marshall, M. (1987). Fighting for their rights. *Ebony* (October), 68–70.

McCollum, J. A., & McBride, S. L. (1997). Ratings of parent-infant interaction: Raising questions of cultural validity. *Topics in Early Childhood Special Education, 17*(4), 16.

McCray, A. D., & Garcia, S. B. (2002). The stories we must tell: Developing a research agenda for multicultural and bilingual special education. *Qualitative Students in Education*, *15*(6), 599–612.

McIntyre, T. (1996). Earning the respect of streetwise youngsters. *Reclaiming At-Risk Youth*, *4*(4), 38–41.

Montgomery, W. (2001). Creating culturally responsive, inclusive classrooms. *Teaching Exceptional Children*, *33*(4), 4–9.

National Center for Educational Statistics. (2005). National assessment of educational progress: The nations' report card. Available at http://nces.ed.gov/nationsreportcard/. Retrieved on April 10, 2006.

National Research Council. (2002). *Minority students in special education and gifted education*. Washington, DC: National Academy Press.

Oakes, J., & Wells, A. (1998). Detracking for high student achievement. *Educational Leadership*, *55*(6), 38–41.

Obiakor, F. E. (2007). *Multicultural special education: Culturally responsive teaching*. Upper Saddle River, NJ: Pearson Merrill/Prentice Hall.

Patton, J. (1998). The disproportionate representation of African American in special education: Looking behind the curtain for understanding and solutions. *The Journal of Special Education*, *32*(1), 25–31.

Pierre-Pipkin, J. (2004). Placing NCLB in perspective for children of African descent: The facts, myths and realities of No Child Left Behind legislation. Presented at the 32nd Annual National Alliance of Black School Educators Conference, Dallas, TX.

Reynolds, A. L., & Pope, R. L. (1991). The complexities of diversity: Exploring multiple oppressions. *Journal of Counseling and Development*, *70*, 174–780.

Rhee, E. (2002). Professor researches the effects of racial identity on children. Available at http://www.udel.edu/PR/UDaily/01-02/rhee112202.html. Retrieved on March 30, 2004.

Sheets, R. H., & Gay, G. (1996). Student perceptions of disciplinary conflict in ethnically diverse classrooms. *NASSP Bulletin*, *80*(580), 84–94.

Smith, T. B., Richards, P. S., MacGranley, H., & Obiakor, F. E. (2004). Practicing multiculturalism: An introduction. In: T. B. Smith (Ed.), *Practicing multiculturalism: Affirming diversity in counseling and psychology* (pp. 3–16). Boston: Pearson/Allyn & Bacon.

Tantum, B. D. (1997). *Why are all the black kids sitting together in the cafeteria? And other conversations about race*. New York: Basic Books.

United States Census Bureau. (2005). American community survey. Available at http://www.census.gov/acs/www/index.html. Retrieved on October 5, 2006.

Villegas, A., & Lucas, T. (2002). Preparing culturally responsive teachers: Reshaping the curriculum. *Journal of Teacher Education*, *53*(1), 20–32.

Walker, S. (1988). Toward economic opportunity and independence: A goal for minority persons with disabilities. In: S. Walker, J. W. Fowler, R. W. Nicholls & K. A. Turner (Eds), *Building bridges to independence. Proceedings of national conference on employment successes, problems, and needs of black Americans with disabilities*. Washington, DC: The Center for the Study of Handicapped Children and Youth.

Wayman, K. I., & Lynch, E. W. (1991). Home-based early childhood services: Cultural sensitivity in a family systems approach. *Topics in Early Childhood Special Education*, *10*(4), 56–76.

Webb-Johnson, G. C. (1999). Cultural contexts: Confronting the overrepresentation of African American learners in special education. In: L. Meyer & J. Scotti (Eds), *Behavioral intervention: Principle, models, and practices* (pp. 449–464). Baltimore, MD: Brookline Publishers.

Weinstein, C., Tomlinson-Clarke, S., & Curran, M. (2004). Toward a conception of culturally responsive classroom management. *Journal of Teacher Education, 55*(1), 25–38.

Zeichner, K. (1993). Rethinking the practicum in the professional development school partnership. *Journal of Teacher Education, 43*, 296–307.

CHAPTER 8

MULTICULTURAL EDUCATION: NOT A GENERAL AND SPECIAL EDUCATION PANACEA

Festus E. Obiakor

> Education must have the tendency, if it is education, to form attitudes. The tendency to form attitudes which will express themselves in intelligent social action is something very different from indoctrination ... There is an intermediary between aimless education and the education of inculcation and indoctrination. The alternative is the kind of education that connects the materials and methods by which knowledge is acquired with a sense of how things are done; not by impregnating the individual with some final philosophy, whether it comes from Karl Max or Mussolini or Hitler or anybody else, but by enabling him [her] to so understand existing conditions that an attitude of intelligent action will follow from social understanding. (Dewey, 1958, p. 56)

Dewey's quote is very revealing, especially as it relates to multicultural education, general education, and special education. The literal thinking is that any form of education must have the power to change attitudes and uplift humanity. In reality, this thinking appears to be an assumption that is not frequently matched by measurable actions. Should our knowledge of multicultural education not influence our positive attitudes toward others or how good we treat or value each other?

We all have endured some form of discrimination at some point in our lives. This experience can be damaging, educational, and transformational.

As a teacher, scholar, and professional, I have endured discrimination from different individuals. Even though I am a US citizen, in some quarters, I am not Black enough, and in other quarters, I am too Black in my quest for an end to unfairness and racism. Discrimination does not only exist in the United States. Even in my country of origin, Nigeria, in some quarters, I have endured some discrimination in the form of tribalism because I belong to the Igbo tribe, and among my tribesmen and women, I suffer from some discrimination because I am married to a woman outside my tribe and country. In my life, people have attempted to define me based on their personal values and idiosyncrasies, and sometimes, I have attempted to define others to protect or defend my own personal values and integrity. Apparently, our perceptions of others, whether right or wrong, affect how we relate to them, how we learn from them, how we teach them, and how we work with them (Brooks, 2004; Cortes, 2000; Duvall, 1994; James, 1958; Minton & Schneider, 1980; Obiakor, 1999, 2001a; Watkins, Lewis, & Chou, 2001). In other words, our perceptions of others influence our expectations of them and the limits we set for them (Comer, 1997; Gould, 1981).

Dember (1961), many years ago, acknowledged that perception is an imprecise scientific concept that cannot be rigorously and thoroughly defined. Logically, perception is loaded with unwarranted assumptions and illusory conclusions that affect how people teach, learn, and interact with others (Obiakor, 1999, 2001a, 2007, 2008, 2009; Obiakor & Algozzine, 2009). Because of the influence of perceptions on how we frame or construct knowledge, it is difficult to use them to improve teaching, learning, human valuing, and human interactions, the very essence of multicultural education or multiculturalism (Banks, 1998, 1999, 2002; Banks & Banks, 2007; Clark, 1963). Going back to Dewey's quote, some important questions come to mind. Has our emphasis on multicultural education today improved our attitudes toward our teaching, learning, and interactions with people different from us? If it has, how far have these attitudes expressed themselves in intelligent social actions? Also, how have general and special education programs measurably changed because of the impact of multicultural education? This chapter responds to these critical questions.

THE HEART OF THE MATTER

Multiculturalism, in theory and practice, has become an important educational phenomenon in today's schools, colleges, and universities.

It seeks inclusive avenues that equalize opportunities for all individuals (Sue, 2004). To a large measure, it incorporates multiple voices, including those of culturally and linguistically diverse (CLD) persons and communities in solving local, national, and global problems. As it appears, CLD learners are the majority in some of the largest school districts in the United States (Grossman, 1995, 1998; Ladson-Billings, 1994; Obiakor, 2004; Obiakor & Beachum, 2005). For instance, Ladson-Billings (1994) noted that these learners "represent 30 percent of the public school population. In the twenty largest school districts, they makeup over 70 percent of total school enrollment" (p. x). This revelation is particularly important today, especially because the composition of educational professionals and service providers still does not reflect the changing cultural and linguistic compositions of children in schools (Obiakor, 2007, 2008). At some levels, rather than progressive measures of desegregation, we are seeing retrogressive measures of resegregation. While this might not be a necessarily bad idea for some urban schools, the progressive goals of the 1954 Brown versus the School Board of Education in Topeka, Kansas case have somehow failed (Obiakor & Utley, 2004).

In today's school programs, we are either using the right medication for the wrong problem or the wrong medication for the right problem. Somehow, we are failing to ask the right questions in general and special education. As a result, we seem to be using wrong simplistic answers to tackle serious educational problems confronting today's CLD children and youth. With legislative, technological, and multicultural advances, it would appear that traditional general and special education problems would have been resolved. We have seen some demographic and multicultural changes in our schools, communities, and our nation. For example, at a national level, the election of President of Barack Obama (the son of a Kenyan father and a mother from the state of Kansas) as the first African American President of the United States is an historic reality. This is not a fad that will soon disappear. The world is getting smaller and smaller, and multicultural education has played a key role in this. While these changes appear to be progressive movements, there is a plethora of evidence to suggest that savage inequalities have continued to exist in schools and communities, across the nation (Kozol, 1991; Obiakor, Grant, & Dooley, 2002). Clearly, some knowledge of multicultural education is a good thing; however, it has become increasingly evident that "having the knowledge is not enough anymore – knowledge must be followed by measurable commitment and action" (Obiakor & Algozzine, 2009, p. ii).

Following are a few samples of how our knowledge of multicultural education has not led to measurable actions and results (see Obiakor, 2004):

- The Brown case was supposed to terminate discrimination or prejudicial exclusion in public schools. Rather, it has led to White flight to the suburbs which then has led to one-way bussing of CLD learners to the suburbs. Today, we have what seems to be resegregation of public schools in most urban areas.
- The Civil Rights Act (1964, PL 88–352) was supposed to protect all persons, including those initially disenfranchised by discriminatory laws. Today, the civil rights of many CLD learners are consistently violated (e.g., the frequent use of culturally, racially, and socioeconomically biased tools to measure how intelligent they are or how appropriate they behave).
- Affirmative action regulations were instituted to increase the visibility of CLD persons in public institutions. Today, they are consistently challenged and viewed as "quota." Ironically, the same institutions that intentionally recruit, hire, and promote incompetent minorities refuse to recruit, hire, and promote confident and competent minorities because they might be intellectually superior and socially progressive to the liking of these institutions. As a result, terms such as "not fitting in," "loose cannon," "trouble-maker," and "arrogant" are used to describe these confident and competent minorities.
- The Education of All Handicapped Children's Act 1975 (PL 94-142) and its amendments and reauthorizations have been instituted to provide students with (a) free appropriate public education, (b) proper identification, (c) nondiscriminatory assessment, (d) procedural safeguards, (e) placement in the least restrictive environment, (f) confidentiality of information, and (g) the development of an Individualized Education Plan (IEP). Today, the burning issue is the disproportionate representation of CLD learners in special education and gifted programs. While many of these students are placed in programs for students with behavior disorders, few of them are placed in programs for students with gifts and talents.
- The No Child Left Behind Act (2001, PL 107–110) and Individuals with Disabilities Education Improvement Act (2004, PL 108–446) are supposed to increase accountability, educate *all* learners, and "leave no child behind." Today, they are viewed as poorly funded mandates that have failed to answer critical accountability questions in general and special education programs. In the end, they have created more educational problems than they are supposed to solve.

MISMEASURING MULTICULTURAL EDUCATION

I strongly believe multicultural education is here to stay, but I also believe multicultural knowledge must be expressed through measurable commitments and actions. We have played many devastating games with multicultural education in our schools, institutions, communities, and governments. In today's general and special education programs, multiculturalism has been mismeasured, misrepresented, abused, and bastardized. The response to current demographic changes have been half-baked, half-hearted, disingenuous, and somewhat strange (Cortes, 2000; Obiakor, 2004). For example, many general and special educators have falsely responded to multiculturalism by (a) *practicing tokenism* (i.e., when a CLD faculty or staff is hired as a figure head to appease requests for inclusion and equanimity); (b) *engaging in suicide mission* (i.e., when a culturally sensitive faculty or staff, especially White, is intentionally made irrelevant, destroyed, or victimized because he/she dared to support equity); (c) *playing the divide-and-conquer game* (i.e., when CLD faculty or staff are set up to fight against each other based on the White supremacist idea of "goodness"); (d) *encouraging the crab-bucket syndrome* (i.e., when proactive efforts are made to pull down or devalue a high-performing CLD faculty or staff); (e) *favoring quota* (i.e., when an incompetent and mediocre CLD faculty or staff, or administrator is hired in place of qualified ones); (f) *engaging in fraudulent multiculturalism* (i.e., when multiculturalism is discussed in a half-hearted fashion to appease the masses or accreditation bodies and create a phony sense of community); (g) *silencing of voices* (i.e., when the White supremacist strategy of one-person-one vote is adopted to impose majority views on a situation); (h) *playing the revolving door game* (i.e., when a CLD faculty or staff is hired to serve a major purpose and let go after that purpose is achieved); and (i) *making visible talents invisible* (i.e., when talented CLD faculty and/or staff are made invisible by underutilizing them or pretending that they do not exist).

Clearly, the above practices appear archaic, racist, and not prudent, at least from the perspective of some CLD people. While many general and special educators know that these practices have been counterproductive to the advancement of their profession and reputation, they continue to be reintroduced and repackaged in different forms to produce the same retrogressive results (Algozzine & Obiakor, 1995; Obiakor & Algozzine, 2009). To fully understand how multicultural education has been mismeasured, it is important to discuss below the devastating political games that both the so-called liberals and the anti-multiculturalists play to masquerade their bigotry.

How Multicultural Are the So-Called Liberals?

We have heard time and time again that general and special educators are very liberal. That sounds good! However, this statement is far from the truth even though we have a seen a handful of efforts (e.g., teachers and leaders who come from CLD backgrounds, in mainstream programs and institutions). If general and special educators are that liberal, why do they continue to rely on standardized tests that have reliability and validity problems for many CLD students in their programs? Why do they continue to struggle with recruitment, retention, and promotion of CLD faculty, staff, and administrators? Why do they continue to struggle with collaborating, consulting, and cooperating with CLD communities in which the schools are located? Finally, why do they continue to mismeasure human talents and attributes in their programs and institutions? These critical questions will continue to haunt general and special education programs as long as school leaders and practitioners continue to resist visionary voices and contemporary imperatives.

In many instances, when it comes to multicultural education, we have not been true to ourselves. We continue to masquerade our prejudices under one cloak or the other, and as a result, we mismeasure multicultural education or multiculturalism. Consider the case of the "Danshiki Man" below (see Obiakor, 2001a, pp. 140–141):

> The "Danshiki Man" was an African American who directed a Black program at a major university. He was known for his pride about Africa. In fact, he was the faculty sponsor for the Black Students' Union and the Organization of African Students. For instance, he invited Africans to support his programs and wore African attire to school. As a result, the university administration never wanted to mess with him – they were scared that this man who knew so much about Africa would take them to task. Nobody tried to bother him! He was virtually free to do whatever he wanted to do. The Danshiki Man had two daughters who were also students at the same university. These daughters were "beautiful, black and brilliant" and commanded great respect on campus. Before long, one handsome Nigerian who was pursuing a graduate degree in chemical engineering became captivated by one of the Danshiki Man's daughters. He came from a rich royal family. He made a pass at the daughter, and she accepted. The two of them began to date, and she started strategizing on how to introduce him to her family. The Danshiki Man heard through the grapevine that his daughter was dating a Nigerian. He confronted the daughter with the news, and she honestly acknowledged that she was falling in love this Nigerian. The Danshiki Man was angry and asked the daughter, "Why are you dating an African? Could you not see other African American men?

> Do you really know what you're doing? How will your kids look? Do you plan to live with him in the jungle? What will people say when they hear that my daughter is married to an African?" The daughter responded, "I thought you loved Africans, Daddy. I can't believe you are bigoted and closed-minded toward them." The Danshiki Man repeated, "I don't care what you say. Do not marry an African! Africans are backward." Out of respect for the Danshiki Man, the daughter stopped dating the Nigerian, and their wonderful relationship ended. They were both emotionally devastated.

The aforementioned case might be far-fetched; however, it depicts the kind of games that we play with multiculturalism and how we masquerade our ignorance and closed-mindedness. Even though the Danshiki Man always wore African attires to show his pride for Africa, he was phony. As other fraudulent multiculturalists, he preached what he never practiced. Some teachers, programs, and institutions play this kind of self-destructive game today. They think that being multicultural means wearing cultural attires, eating at Taco Bell, or using chopsticks instead of a fork at Chinese restaurants. Multicultural education is not a feel good simplistic liberal gimmick. It has enormous psychological, philosophical, and educational implications (Obiakor, 2001a, 2001b; Obiakor & Algozzine, 2009).

How Unity-Oriented Are Anti-Multiculturalists?

My criticisms of multicultural education do not necessarily mean that I am an anti-multiculturalist. In fact, I disagree with anti-multiculturalists who see multicultural competencies in general and special education as anti-quality or a move away from the basic traditional goals of the US schools, which are to (a) teach traditional value-oriented skills to students, (b) increase quality through higher test scores, (c) participate in the shared national culture, (d) promote allegiance to the values of the nation, (e) become competent in English, and (f) insure national unity (Ceaser, 1998; Chavez, 1998; D'Souza, 1991; Ravitch, 1991–1992, 2000; Schlesinger, 1992; Sowell, 1993). For example, D'Souza argued that acknowledging cultural difference is divisive and will destroy European-based heritages in the United States. In his opinion, multicultural programs tend to create a "monolithic ideological focus that places minority sentiments on a pedestal while putting majority ones on trial" (pp. 214–215). Ravitch (1991–1992) emphasized the threatening nature of multicultural education to American's unity. She indicated that inclusion of other histories and cultures in education curricula causes "ethnic chauvinism" (p. 11). Similarly, Schlesinger (1992) noted that when multicultural education is carried to the extreme, the emphases on cultural differences usually have serious negative ramifications, which include (a) the rejection of the vision of unifying individuals from all national origins into a single nation and culture, (b) decreased interests in integration and assimilation, and (c) increased levels of segregation and separatism among ethnic and racial groups.

In his opposition to multicultural education, Sowell (1993) reiterated that American education is undermined by dogmas that have little to do with quality education. He noted that "while it is undoubtedly true that there are many negative factors at work in many low-income neighborhood schools, especially those in inner-city shelters and barrios, that does not automatically explain away the declining academic performances of American schools in general" (p. 9). This point was supported by scholars who advocated (a) understanding the different minority groups (Ogbu & Simon, 1998) and (b) reframing educational and psychological programs for multicultural students (Obiakor & Barker, 1993). For instance, Ogbu and Simon (1998, p. 161) wrote,

> Structural barriers or discriminations in society and school are important determinants of low school achievement among minorities. However, they are not the sole cause of low school performance; otherwise all minorities would not do well in school since all are faced with such discriminations ... It is true that cultural and language differences do cause learning problems. But cultural and language difference explanations do not account for school success of some minority groups that face similar discontinuities as do others that are less successful.

Many opponents of multicultural education have wondered if it enhances liberal democracy in the United States (Ceaser, 1998; Melzer, Weinberger, & Zinman, 1998; Ravitch, 2000). With regard to this issue, for example, Ceaser (1998) concluded that multicultural education is major threat that perpetuates a perverse psychology. He explained that "people of different groups thus vie in unseemly process to claim that they have been oppressed – even in cases when they manifestly have not been. The real differences among various groups are thus over-looked" (p. 155). In the same dimension, Chavez (1998, p. 167) added,

> The more diverse we become racially and ethnically, the more important it is that we learn to tolerate difference – and also to celebrate what we all have in common. Whether we come to the United States voluntarily or involuntarily, we all choose to live here now. And more people want to live here than anywhere else in the world. No other country accepts as many immigrants as we do. Surely, even those who criticize our so-called Eurocentric society must admit that it has something to offer or there would not be such long lines of those waiting to get in – very few of them European, by the way.

Reconciling the Bigotry of the So-Called Liberals and Anti-Multiculturalists

Based on the above discussions, it is clear that multicultural education has been used politically by some so-called liberals in the "left" to masquerade their bigotry and by anti-multicultural laggards in the "right" who are close-minded about change. Both camps are wrong! Multicultural education involves not just change in thinking but also change in practice. It is not a "feel-good" liberal or conservative appeasement, and it is not an anti-unity endeavor. It is ethnocentric to think that one culture can assimilate or dominate other cultures. We must value our differences, but not at the expense of peace and unity. For example, if general educators have continued to reach all their learners, maybe special education would be unimportant today. Then, if special educators have continued to do a good job, many CLD learners would not have been misidentified, misassessed, miscategorized, misplaced, and misinstructed (Obiakor, 1999, 2001a, 2001b, 2007, 2008; Utley & Obiakor, 2001). Some traditionalists in special education (e.g., Kauffman, 2002, 2003a, 2003b; Lieberman, 2001; Sasso, 2003) seem to be infuriated about criticisms levied against special education, especially with regard to the disproportionate placement of CLD learners in programs for students with emotional and behavioral disorders (E/BD). The fundamental question is, Why should it not bother us that predominantly CLD learners are placed in programs for students with E/BD and only a few of them are placed in programs for students with gifts and talents? The other related questions are, How do we prove that a student, staff, or faculty has experienced racial discrimination in general and special education because it is very difficult to legally prove racial discrimination? and Why is it not racist to get rid of CLD students, staff, or faculty in programs and organizations because they look, learn, or act differently? The fact remains that it is psychologically debasing to be expelled from a program or fired from a job because of learning styles and behavioral patterns.

While there is a great need for evidence-based practice in general and special education today, I strongly disagree with scholars and educators who downplay human feelings because they are not measurable. For instance, I disagree with Kauffman's (2003a) assertion that "if you discount science as a way of finding things out and believe that special education is fundamentally flawed, second rate, ineffective, unfair, and oppressive, then you are not going to use it for prevention" (p. 206). I believe that science is necessary; however, the indiscriminate use of scientifically proven medication to cure every illness or everyone is dangerous, unethical, and immoral

(Obiakor, 2004). The "heart" or respect for humanity must be incorporated into whatever we do as professionals even though one's "heart" or spirituality cannot be measured. Science may not always be the only answer; feelings matter too! Even in the medical field, the touch of a doctor and the feeling of the patient can facilitate and advance the healing process. Why should general and special education be any different? In their study titled, "Do race of student and race of teacher influence ratings of emotional and behavioral problem characteristics of students with emotional disturbance?", Cullinan and Kauffman (2005) concluded that "results did not support the position that, among students with ED [emotional disturbance], overrepresentation of African Americans arises from racial bias in teacher perceptions of emotional and behavioral problems" (p. 393). Coupled with the study's limitations and weaknesses as identified by Cullinan and Kauffman, there is the presumption of innocence of teachers just because of their race or culture. In many urban schools, there are CLD professionals who through their actions have devastated the lives of CLD students and their parents (Obiakor, 2001b, 2008). In the same dimension, there are many Black policemen or women who shoot and kill fellow Blacks and continue to engage in serious police brutality against Blacks. Their race or culture must never be an alibi that exonerates them from being criticized or sued for violating the civil rights of others (Prater, 2006). Clearly, on issues of misidentification, misassessment, miscategorization, misplacement, and misinstruction of students, a poorly prepared culturally incompetent general and special educator will not advance the education of CLD learners (Obiakor, 1999, 2001b, 2004, 2007, 2008; Obiakor & Beachum, 2005).

We need accountability at all multicultural and educational levels. Instituting a multicultural education program is not enough, and it is not even enough to apply it based on our comprehension of it. We need to begin to analyze, synthesize, and evaluate what has resulted from its implementation or infusion whether we are from the "left" or "right." In general and special education programs, our goal must be to maximize the fullest potential of all learners, whether they are White, African American, Latino/a, Asian American, or Native American. In the long run, if done right, the race of the student, teacher, or professional may not matter – what may matter is whether the student's potential is fully maximized by a well-prepared culturally sensitive teacher or professional. As a society, we cannot allow any group or institution to mismeasure multiculturalism. We do not need to patronize CLD students and faculty or simplify the seriousness of racism, discrimination, and unfairness. Of late, it appears that we have mixed apples and oranges in the guise of "quality" and "equity." We must be skeptical about those who want to assimilate and silence any voice, no matter how heretical (Ellison, 1972). We cannot afford to exclude and destroy other voices and talents. As a matter of urgency, we must practice the kind of multicultural education that allows students, families, schools, communities, and governments to work together (Obiakor, 2001a, 2001b).

BEYOND THE MULTICULTURAL RHETORIC: THE NEED FOR RISK-TAKERS

For multicultural education to be truly "multicultural," it must involve commitment, action, and risk-taking. We must take advantage of the current demographic "season" of change by taking risks. We all have the potential to change, but we must challenge ourselves and others for such a change to occur. Chittister (1999, p. 53), in her book, *There is A Season*, argued that

> The thought of constant change colors our sense of the future. We wear it like a logo as we race from place to place, and now, in our time, from idea to idea, from concept to concept, from social revolution to social revolution ... change, after all, is not a given. Change follows in the wake of something that preceded it, quiet as a shift in the wind. It does not just happen; it is not a timed process. "If we're just patient; if we just wait long enough it has to come," we say when we do not want to be responsible ourselves for the change. But change does not just come; change is brought somehow.

It is apparent that multicultural education has attracted many skeptical and opposing viewpoints. We have gone to court to fight for our rights; we have passed laws to give us more rights; we have designed programs to see that everyone's rights are protected, but, we seem to flounder in mediocrity when it comes to producing positive results. In my frustrations, I have been tempted to believe racism and discrimination in education will never end (see Bell, 1985, 1992; Grier & Cobbs, 1968). While I continue to believe race matters (West, 1993) and that there are usually some underlining motives behind societal initiatives, I strongly believe change is an inevitability in life. This is not in consonance with the "what will be, will be" natural law. We need risk-takers who can think outside the box and challenge the status quo (Chomsky, 2000). From my perspective, positive change results from risk-taking and some risky actions. For example, where would the Socratic question-and-answer method be today without the risk taken by Socrates to challenge the wealthy Greek Sophists who were more interested in maintaining the status quo than in challenging the Athenian youth to maximize their fullest potential? Though his ideas seemed innovative and far-reaching, he was accused of impiety to the gods and of corrupting the Athenian youth.

In the end, he became a great equalizer who wanted the masses to be involved in the socioeducational discourse of his time (Sagal, 1983). Proponents of multicultural education seem to have a similar equalizing effect – they challenge the status quo to educate all persons from different cultural, linguistic, and racial backgrounds. Like the Sophists, opponents of multicultural education, whether they are from the "left" or "right," appear to be more interested in assimilating all persons in spite of cultural differences and personal idiosyncrasies. In the face of these conflicting views, many of today's children with atypical manifestations are improperly identified, unfairly assessed, disproportionately placed, and misinstructed (Artiles & Trent, 1994; Obiakor, 2001a, 2001b, 2007, 2008). Is it any surprise that many CLD learners continue to be involved in educational programs that frequently fail to assist them in maximizing their fullest potential?

Clearly, multicultural education involves novel thinking that goes beyond modern day liberal or conservative rhetoric. To a large measure, it involves risk-taking that leads to change. A robber who knows that there is a camera in the bank and still goes there to rob is a risk-taker, but his/her risk-taking behavior will not lead to positive change. On the contrary, a young woman who protects an elderly woman from being robbed by some armed marauders has taken some risk, and her risk is a positive one. Consider my experience with Mr. C. W. Sisemore below (see Obiakor, 2001a, pp. 138–139):

> On October 6, 1995, I was on one of my trips to present a paper at the Council for Children with Behavior Disorders International Convention in Dallas, Texas. Because I detest driving, I took a Greyhound bus from Emporia, Kansas to Wichita, Kansas, where my flight was scheduled to take off at around 6 a.m. My bus left Emporia around 2:30 a.m. en route to Wichita. Around 3 a.m., the bus driver stopped at El Dorado for some rest time. I went briefly to use the restroom, and by the time I came out, the bus had left me in El Dorado. I was stranded and frustrated in the strange hours of the morning. My frustration rose because I did not want to miss my flight in Wichita. I began to talk to anyone who would listen at this rest area. I knew the dangers involved, but I had to take the risk. I asked the people (I mean people of all races and cultures) that I saw for a ride to Wichita. Even the African Americans I asked did not respond – they ignored me. I lost hope until I asked a White man (Mr. C.W. Sisemore), who surprised me – he agreed. Remember, it was around 3:40 a.m. in the morning! This White man looked like a construction worker – he wore some mud-ridden "cowboy" clothes. I was dumbfounded that he consented to give me (a Black man) a ride this early in the morning. I thought the well dressed people, especially the African Americans, would consent to give me a ride, but I was wrong. Anyway, my new found friend began to speed to catch the bus. We did not catch the bus, but we got there not long after the bus arrived in Wichita. Luckily, my luggage was still on the bus. Mr. C. W. Sisemore waited for me to get my luggage, and he gave me a ride to the Wichita airport, where I took my flight to Dallas. I tried to give him some money to repay his kindness, but he refused.

Again, the above case may appear a bit far-fetched; however, many of today's general and special education teachers can learn from Mr. Sisemore. Even though I took a risk to ask for a ride in the early hours of the morning, he took a greater risk to give me a ride. Not only do such risks reduce stereotypes and generalizations, they also make long-term positive impression on people. How many of us would demonstrate such courage when people are down? Who would have imagined in these days of racial mistrust that a White man would give a ride to a Black man in the early hours of the morning? I am reminded of the biblical parable of the "Good Samaritan," in which the supposedly "good" people left a man stranded and the unsuspected stranger saved him. As it appears, Mr. Sisemore had nothing to gain by giving me a ride; yet, he took his time and risk to give me a ride. General and special education teachers can learn a lot from him! In a truly, multicultural program or school, general and special education teachers will take risks like Mr. Sisemore and be rewarded for taking them. Mr. Sisemore might not have looked like a true multiculturalist, but in my book, he was based on of the risk involved in his decision.

As indicated, when infused properly, multicultural education has the power to change attitude and enhance quality general and special education, especially when it exposes students to maximum learning and new dimensions of problem-solving. It acquaints individuals with divergent viewpoints and multiple voices to societal discourse, and it removes limits set on how learners are defined, understood, and valued. To a larger measure, multicultural education capitalizes on the resources and endowments of all individuals and fosters pragmatic efforts in discovering what has made the United States the greatest democracy in the world. About two decades ago, Gollnick and Chinn (1990, p. iii) explained that

> An overall goal of multicultural education is to help all students develop their potential for academic, social, and vocational success. Educational and vocational options should not be limited by sex, age, ethnicity, native language, religion, class, or exceptionality. Educators are given the responsibility to help students contribute to, and benefit from, our democratic society. Within our pluralistic society, multicultural education values the existing diversity, positively portrays that diversity and uses that diversity in the development of effective instructional categories for students in the classroom. In addition, multicultural education should help students think critically about institutionalized racism, classism, and sexism.

To properly infuse multicultural education, we must let our life speak. In his book, *Let Your Life Speak*, Parker (2000) challenged educators and service providers to be more dedicated than ever to achieve their life mission even when confronted by predicable and unforeseen drawbacks. He urged them to find their "sacred center" in their journey of life and concluded that

> Most of us arrive at a sense of self and vocation only after a long journey through alien lands. But this journey bears no resemblance to the trouble-free "travel packages" sold by the tourism industry. It is more akin to the ancient tradition of "pilgrimage" – "a transformative journey to a sacred center" of hardships, darkness, and peril ... In the tradition of a pilgrimage, those hardships are seen not as accidentals but as integral to the journey itself. Treacherous terrain, bad weather, taking a fall, getting lost – challenges of that sort, largely beyond our control, can strip the ego of the illusion that it is in charge and make space for true self to emerge. If that happens, the pilgrim has a better chance to find the sacred center he or she seeks. Disabused of our illusions by much travel and travail, we awaken one day to find that the sacred center is here and now–in every moment of the journey, everywhere in the world around us, and deep within our own hearts. (Parker, 2000, pp. 17–18)

Parker's (2000) statement was reiterated by Ford (2002) in her final comments as the first editor of *Multiple Voices*, the journal of the Division for Ethnically Diverse Exceptional Learners (DDEL), the Council for Exceptional Children. In her comments, she recounted the story of four people named everybody, somebody, anybody, and nobody. As the story goes,

> An important job needed to be done, everybody was sure that somebody would do it. Anybody could have done it, but nobody did. Somebody became angry because it was everybody's job and everybody thought that anybody could do it. It ended up that everybody blamed somebody when nobody did what anybody could have done! (Ford, 2002, p. vii)

A logical extension is that all of us must "let our work speak" as we work collaboratively and consultatively with others for the common good. We cannot afford to fake it! The critical question is, Did we do all we needed to do to solve problems of others different from us or did we betray our souls to achieve a phony sense of satisfaction? Yes, some of us have tried to solve problems; due to one reason or another, however, some of us have tried to create problems even when they do not exist. The fact remains that "our deepest calling is to grow into our own authentic selfhood, whether or not it conforms to some image of who we ought to be. As we do so, we will not only find the joy that every human being seeks – we will also find our path of authentic service in the world" (Parker, 2000, p. 16). It is not too late for us to wonder how posterity will remember us. At this juncture, our personal multicultural question should be, "Did I barely survive to boost my ego envenomed by the 'me, myself, and I' syndrome or did I make some positive contributions to the lives of others different from me?" Following are lingering multicultural questions that we must continue to ask in general and special education:

- Do race and culture influence the identification of CLD learners?
- Do assessment tools measure the construct that they purport to measure for CLD learners?
- Do categorical labels of CLD learners reflect their capability?
- Do placement options used for CLD learners restrict their abilities to maximize their fullest potential?
- Do instructional/intervention techniques take into consideration the rich backgrounds of CLD learners? (Obiakor & Utley, 2003, pp. v–vi)

The above multicultural questions will continue to haunt general and special educators, especially if they are interested in taking risks to make positive changes in their chosen profession. Surely, they cannot be answered by our self-hating or "player-hating" behaviors and by our mismeasurement and bastardization of multicultural education. In addition, they cannot be answered by falsely masquerading ourselves as multiculturalists while we practice, for example, fraudulent multiculturalism. Indeed, these questions can be answered when we understand their critical nature in relation to our sacred existence not just as multicultural general and special educators but also as positive human beings. In addition, these questions can be answered when we understand that race truly matters (West, 1993) and when we carefully put our "Anglo-cized" education into proper multicultural perspectives as Woodson (1933) suggested in his classical book, *The Mis-Education of the Negro*. Clearly, we must look at the "enemy within" (i.e., engage in personal reflections) and the "enemy without" (i.e., knowledge of external commitments) to inspire the spirits of hard-working individuals dedicated to making a difference in our profession. In the end, our nagging multicultural questions will be answered when we get out of the box and take productive risk in

- Acknowledging our personal pride and prejudice.
- Valuing integrity, loyalty, and commitment.
- Being open-minded in spite of our trials and tribulation.
- Respecting all voices even if they seem heretical.
- Reviewing our definition of goodness.
- Being pragmatic as we challenge old ideas and create new ones.
- Becoming realistic mentors to help our growing scholars, educators, and students.
- Valuing "quality with a heart."

- Continuing to learn, our experiences notwithstanding.
- Becoming the change that we want.

CONCLUSION

In this chapter, I have presented multicultural education as a powerful force in our lives, schools, communities, and government. I acknowledge that multiculturalism is here to stay; however, I also acknowledge that it has generated skeptical and opposing viewpoints because of its abuse, bastardization, and mismeasurement. While I believe multicultural education complements other theories of learning, and to a large extent, needs to be studied, learned, taught, and practiced, I also believe it creates divisions, balkanization, tribalization, and disunity when improperly infused in general and special education. Some people and institutions have played games with multicultural education, and they have tried to masquerade their bigotry as they dealt with it. Consequently, multicultural education has created more problems than it is supposed to solve. Does this mean that this makes it meaningless to our lives, schools, communities, nation, and world? Using Dewey's (1958) introductory quote, this means that we must make multicultural education to be more frantic, meaningful, and productive than ever before in our practice.

Finally, we must strive for measurable change and go beyond the rhetoric of multiculturalism to improve the quality of our humanity. To foster measurable multicultural changes in general and special education, we must reduce our blindness on human differences without defining our relationships based on our narrow differences. Not long ago, President Obama (2009) stated that "so long as our relationship is defined, by our differences, we will empower those who sow hatred rather than peace, and who promote conflict rather than the cooperation that can help all of our people achieve justice and prosperity. This cycle of suspicion and discord must end" (p. 1). As he concluded, "Recognizing our common humanity is only the beginning of our task. Words alone cannot meet the needs of our people. These needs will be met only if we act boldly in the years ahead; and if we understand that the challenges we face are shared, and our failure to meet them will hurt us all" (p. 3).

REFERENCES

Algozzine, B., & Obiakor, F. E. (1995). African American quandaries in school programs. *Scholar and Educator: The Journal of the Society of Educators and Scholars, 17*, 75–88.

Artiles, A., & Trent, S. (1994). Overrepresentation of minority students in special education: A continuing debate. *The Journal of Special Education, 27*(4), 410–437.

Banks, J. A. (1998). The lives and values of researchers: Implications for educating citizens in a multicultural society. *Educational Researcher, 27*, 4–17.

Banks, J. A. (1999). *An introduction to multicultural education* (2nd ed.). Boston: Allyn & Bacon.

Banks, J. A. (2002). Race, knowledge construction, and education in the USA: Lessons from history. *Race, Ethnicity and Education, 5*, 8–27.

Banks, J. A., & Banks, C. A. M. (2007). *Multicultural education: Issues and perspectives* (6th ed.). Hoboken, NJ: Wiley.

Bell, D. (1985). *And we are not saved: The elusive quest for racial justice.* New York: Basic Books.

Bell, D. (1992). *Faces at the bottom of the well: The permanence of racism.* New York: Basic Books.

Brooks, R. B. (2004). To touch the hearts and minds of students with learning disabilities: The power of mindsets and expectations. *Learning Disabilities: A Contemporary Journal, 2*(21), 1–8.

Ceaser, J. (1998). Multiculturalism and the American liberal democracy. In: A. M. Melzer, J. Weinberger & M. R. Zinman (Eds), *Multiculturalism and the American democracy* (pp. 139–156). Lawrence, KS: University Press of Kansas.

Chavez, L. (1998). Civic education in a changing society. In: A. M. Melzer, J. Weinberger & M. R. Zinman (Eds), *Multiculturalism and the American democracy* (pp. 165–172). Lawrence, KS: University Press of Kansas.

Chittister, J. (1999). *There is a season* (3rd ed.). MaryKnoll, NY: Orbis Books.

Chomsky, N. (2000). *Chomsky on miseducation.* Lanham, MD: Rowman & Littlefield.

Civil Rights Acts. (1964). Pub. L. 88–352.

Clark, K. B. (1963). *Prejudice and your child* (2nd ed.). Boston: Beacon Press.

Comer, J. P. (1997). *Waiting for a miracle: Why schools can't solve our problems – And how we can.* New York: Plume.

Cortes, C. E. (2000). *The children are watching: How the media teach about diversity.* New York: Teachers College Press.

Cullinan, D., & Kauffman, J. M. (2005). Do race of student and race of teacher influence ratings of emotional and behavioral problem characteristics of students with emotional disturbance? *Behavioral Disorders, 30*(August), 393–402.

D'Souza, D. (1991). *Illiberal education: The politics of race and sex on the campus.* New York: The Free Press.

Dember, W. (1961). *Psychology of perception.* New York: Holt, Rinehart & Winston.

Dewey, J. (1958). *Philosophy of education.* Ames, IA: Littlefield, Adams & Co.

Duvall, L. (1994). *Respecting our differences: A guide to getting along in a changing world.* Minneapolis, MN: The Free Spirit.

Ellison, R. (1972). *Invisible man.* New York: Vintage Books.

Ford, B. A. (2002). Final remarks. *Multiple Voices, 5*, vii.

Gollnick, D. M., & Chinn, P. C. (1990). *Multicultural education in a pluralistic society* (3rd ed.). New York: Merrill.

Gould, S. J. (1981). *The mismeasure of man.* New York: Norton.

Grier, W. H., & Cobbs, P. M. (1968). *Black rage.* New York: Bantam Books.

Grossman, H. (1995). *Teaching in a diverse society.* Needham Heights, MA: Allyn & Bacon.

Grossman, H. (1998). *Ending discrimination in special education.* Springfield, IL: Charles C Thomas.

Individuals with Disabilities Education Improvement Act. (2004). Pub. L. No. 108-446.
James, W. (1958). *Talk to teachers on psychology, and to students on some life's ideas*. New York: W. W. Norton.
Kauffman, J. M. (2002). *Education deform? Bright people sometimes say stupid things about education*. Lanham, MD: Scarecrow Education.
Kauffman, J. M. (2003a). Reflections on the field. *Behavioral Disorders, 28*, 206–208.
Kauffman, J. M. (2003b). Appearances, stigma, and prevention. *Remedial and Special Education, 24*, 195–198.
Kozol, J. (1991). *Savage inequalities: Children in American schools*. New York: Harper, Perennial.
Ladson-Billings, G. (1994). *The dreamkeepers: Successful teachers of African American children*. San Francisco: Jossey-Bass.
Lieberman, L. M. (2001). The death of special education. *Education Week, 5*, 39–41.
Melzer, A. M., Weinberger, J., & Zinman, M. R. (1998). *Multiculturalism and the American democracy*. Lawrence, KS: University Press of Kansas.
Minton, H. L., & Schneider, F. W. (1980). *Differential psychology*. Prospect Heights, IL: Waveland Press.
No Child Left Behind Act. (2001). Pub. L. No. 107-110.
Obama, B. (2009). President Barack Obama's speech at Cairo University, Egypt, North Africa, June. Available at http://yalibnan.com/site/archives/2009/06/text_of_preside_1.php
Obiakor, F. E. (1999). Teacher expectations of minority exceptional learners: Impact on "accuracy" of self concepts. *Exceptional Children, 66*, 39–53.
Obiakor, F. E. (2001a). *It even happens in "good" schools: Responding to cultural diversity in today's classrooms*. Thousand Oaks, CA: Corwin Press.
Obiakor, F. E. (2001b). Multicultural education: Powerful tool for preparing future general and special educators. *Teacher Education and Special Education, 24*, 241–255.
Obiakor, F. E. (2004). Impacts of changing demographics in public education for culturally diverse learners with behavior problems: Implications for teacher preparation. In: L. M. Bullock & R. A. Gable (Eds), *Quality personnel preparation in emotional/behavioral disorders: Current perspectives and future directions* (pp. 51–63). Denton, TX: Institute for Behavioral and Learning Differences, University of North Texas.
Obiakor, F. E. (2007). *Multicultural special education: Culturally responsive teaching*. Upper Saddle River, NJ: Pearson/Merrill Prentice Hall.
Obiakor, F. E. (2008). *The eight-step approach to multicultural learning and teaching* (3rd ed.). Dubuque, IA: Kendall/Hunt.
Obiakor, F. E. (2009). Demographic changes in public education for culturally diverse exceptional learners: Making teacher preparation programs accountable. *Multicultural Learning and Teaching, 4*(1), 90–110.
Obiakor, F. E., & Algozzine, B. (Eds). (2009). Executive editors' comments: The mismeasure of multiculturalism in teacher preparation programs*Multicultural Learning and Teaching, 4*(1), i–iv.
Obiakor, F. E., & Barker, N. C. (1993). The politics of higher education: Perspectives for African Americans in the 21st century. *The Western Journal of Black Studies, 17*, 219–226.
Obiakor, F. E., & Beachum, F. D. (2005). *Urban education for the 21st century: Research, issues, and perspectives*. Springfield, IL: Charles C Thomas.
Obiakor, F. E., Grant, P. A., & Dooley, E. A. (2002). *Educating all learners: Refocusing the comprehensive support model*. Springfield, IL: Charles C Thomas.

Obiakor, F. E., & Utley, C. A. (2003). Preview: Fraudulent multiculturalism reduces the goodness of general and special education. *Multiple Voices, 6*, v–vi.

Obiakor, F. E., & Utley, C. A. (2004). Educating culturally diverse learners with exceptionalities: A critical analysis of the Brown case. *Peabody Journal of Education, 79*, 141–156.

Ogbu, J. U., & Simon, H. D. (1998). Voluntary and involuntary minorities: A cultural-ecological theory of school performance with some implications for education. *Anthropology and Education, 29*, 155–189.

Parker, P. J. (2000). *Let your life speak: Listening for the voice of vocation.* San Francisco: Jossey-Bass.

Prater, L. P. (2006). Institutionalized terror: A social system's analysis of police brutality, October. Paper presented at the Annual Professional Development Conference of the National Social Sciences Association, San Francisco, CA.

Ravitch, D. (1991–1992). A culture in common. *Educational Leadership, 49*, 8–11.

Ravitch, D. (2000). *Left back: A century of failed school reforms.* New York: Simon & Schuster.

Sagal, P. T. (1983). *Introducing philosophy: A Socratic dialogue.* Las Cruces, NM: Dialogue Press.

Sasso, G. M. (2003). An examined life: A response to James Kauffman's reflections on the field. *Behavioral Disorders, 28*, 209–211.

Schlesinger, A. M. (1992). *The disuniting of America: Reflection on a multicultural society.* New York: Norton.

Sowell, T. (1993). *Inside American education: The decline, the deception, the dogmas.* New York: The Free Press.

Sue, D. W. (2004). Whiteness and ethnocentric monoculturalism: Making the "invisible" visible. *American Psychology, 22*, 761–769.

Utley, C. A., & Obiakor, F. E. (2001). *Special education, multicultural education, and school reform: Components of quality education for learners with mild disabilities.* Springfield, IL: Charles C Thomas.

Watkins, W. H., Lewis, J. H., & Chou, V. (2001). *Race and education: The roles of history and society in educating African Americans.* Boston: Allyn & Bacon.

West, C. (1993). *Race matters.* New York: Vintage books.

Woodson, C. G. (1933). *The mis-education of the Negro.* Washington, DC: The Association Publishers.

PART V
TRANSITION

CHAPTER 9

TRANSITION PLANNING, PREPARATION, AND IMPLEMENTATION: COLLABORATION AND CONSULTATION AT WORK

Kagendo Mutua and James Siders

OVERVIEW

The Oxford English Dictionary defines transition as "a passing or passage from one condition, action, or (rarely) place, to another; change." This definition captures the essence of the transition as experienced by youth and young adults with disabilities as they move from school to postschool settings. Additionally, the definition also raises the issue that transition encompasses the existential experience not only of passing from one condition (of being a student/child to becoming a graduate/an adult) but also of the physical movement/passage (from school services to adult services) and the change therein. This chapter begins by providing a brief historical framing of transition both from the standpoint of legal foundations of transition and the findings from early research on the postschool outcomes experienced by graduates of special education. In addition, the impact of those findings is discussed regarding the formulation and articulation of transition as a mandated element in the educational planning for students with disabilities at the secondary level. Next, the chapter reviews the initial models of transition that were developed and/or proposed as a way for meeting the needs of secondary age students with disabilities as identified in research. The essential elements of transition expressed in the transition definition provided by Individuals with Disabilities Education Act (IDEA) of 1990 and subsequent amendments are then described. A discussion of issues related to the best and promising practices in transition concludes the chapter.

HISTORICAL FRAMING OF TRANSITION

Early Research on Transition

Early research on the postschool/adult outcomes of youth and young adults with disabilities that was conducted a decade after the implementation of PL 94–142, The Education of All Handicapped Children Act of 1975, revealed very disturbing trends. The findings of that body of research on the postschool outcomes of special education graduates were overwhelmingly dismal. Specifically, research in special education conducted in the late 1970s to mid-1980s reported that few graduates of special education programs attained adult outcomes. Most special education graduates remained unemployed or entered the workforce underemployed (Wehman, 2006a). Community and social outcomes resulted in few contacts with nondisabled peers, no intimate relationships, little to no autonomy, and participation only in passive leisure activities rather than those that increased their community presence (Dykema-Engblade & Stawiski, 2008). Indeed, these disappointing outcomes experienced by graduates of special education continued to be evidenced in transition studies published in the mid-1980s and early 1990s. For instance, according to Harris (1986), youth with disabilities continued to live at home with parents four to five years after leaving school and had an 8% unemployment rate. The 1994 Harris Poll also found the following regarding persons with disabilities (Harris, 1994):

- Two-thirds of Americans with disabilities (16–64 years) were not working.
- 79% of those unemployed Americans with disabilities (16–64 years) wanted to work.
- 69% of willing adults with disabilities who wished to work did not need adaptive equipment; only about 26% required specialized equipment to work.

- Very few of those employed or able to work had any self-advocacy skill.
- Those employed rarely work in jobs that utilized their skills to the fullest; hence, many were underemployed.

These findings prompted the 1990 revisions of the IDEA to mandate *transition* as a component of secondary students' Individualized Educational Program (IEP). A requirement to prepare youth with disabilities, ages 14–21 years, for employment/work as a desired adult outcome was among the essential elements of a transition plan.

Curriculum plans in the area of life transition were articulated as early as 1970 when Kolstoe (1970) published his comprehensive vision of vocational and functional life skills for learners identified with mental retardation. Vocational placement was suggested in the controlled environment of the schools in janitorial, food service, and clerical support among other work experiences. Kolstoe suggested community placements during half the day as a measure to transition students successfully from school to work in the community. Comprehensive transitional achievement by many such youth required sustained and systematic instruction in work skills and attitudes as well as in the other essential elements that comprised the definition of transition, including recreation/leisure, community participation, postsecondary education, and independent living. The work of Brolin (1984), *Life Centered Career Education* (LCCE), a competency-based approach, complimented this call for comprehensive, life-long transitional instruction. This work and subsequent editions of Brolin's curriculum have served as the nucleus of programs throughout the United States and abroad. Soon after the decade of the 1990s saw the emergence of federal statutes and educational reform movements pointing to a renewed commitment to improving educational outcomes and to equip all high school graduates with skills necessary for achieving success in the global marketplace (Wehman, 2006b).

Legal Foundations of Transition

The centrality of work as a desirable adult outcome has been underscored in a number of federal education-related initiatives and legislation. Since the very beginning, public schools were charged with the primary responsibility of preparing graduates who are well-equipped with skills to work and to be productive citizens. Current public school goals focus on interventions and educational practices that lead to the achievement of valued educational outcomes for all students. However, over the years since the inception of transition as a strand of secondary programming for students with disabilities, experts have argued about what should constitute the critical elements of transition. Nowhere else is debate more self-evident than in the models of transition that were proposed before the articulation and definition of transition that emerged in the federal law, IDEA (1990), and subsequent amendments.

Work–study programs existed in the 1930s but were not supported by federal monies. They developed out of this need for a more functional curriculum that could potentially serve more students and promote their movement to postschool settings, particularly students with mild intellectual disabilities. Over the decades of the 1950s, 1960s, and 1970s, work–study programs continued to grow. Table 1 illustrates the growth and development of work–study programs over the decades. Those programs served youth with mild disabilities and provided integrated academic, social, and vocational curriculum and community work experience. Work–study programs started in the late 1950s as collaboration between public schools and local offices of state rehabilitation agencies. Federally funded work–study programs lasted for approximately 10 years. In the 1970s, the Rehabilitation Act Amendments in 1973 and the Education of Handicapped Children's Act (EHA) in 1975 were enacted, which, unfortunately, contained within those statutes, specific requirements that led to the demise of work–study programs.

During the decade of the 1970s, the work–study model died as a result of the "similar benefits" funding mechanism requirements in the 1973 Rehab Act Amendments. Within this "similar benefits" logic, with the passage of the EHA in 1975, the responsibility of work–study was considered to be a responsibility of schools in providing free appropriate public education (FAPE). Programs disappeared due to the way the law was interpreted, leading to the public schools becoming responsible for work–study experiences as part of the FAPE. State rehabilitation agencies could not justify the continuation of work–study programs because the services were considered the school's responsibility. Additionally, there was a requirement in the Rehabilitation Act that teachers who worked as program coordinators had to be supervised by certified rehabilitation professionals, and the schools were not willing to pay additional money for this supervision.

Specifically, the programs considered as constituting the work–study model included programs emanating from Vocational Rehabilitation Amendments of 1954, the Rehabilitation Act of 1973, and the EHA of 1975. Those work–study programs served students with mild disabilities, in part because research found a correlation between work experiences in high school and better outcomes after graduation. The components of the work–study model

Table 1. Development of Work-Study Programs.

Era	Character of Program	Target Population
1930s	Work–study more functional curriculum integrating academic, social, and vocational curricula and community work experience enhancing movement to postschool settings	Youth with mild disabilities
1950s	Work–study started anew as collaboration between public schools and local offices of state rehabilitation agencies. Federally funded work–study programs lasted for about 10 years	Youth with mild disabilities
1960s	Transition with related studies necessary to develop work aptitude and skill development promoted more functional curriculum	Youth with mild disabilities
1970s	Rehabilitation Act Amendments in 1973 ("similar benefits") and the Education of Handicapped Children's Act in 1975 (Free Appropriate Education – FAPE), unfortunately, led to the demise of work–study programs. Program coordinators required to be supervised by certified rehabilitation professionals created a funding demand the schools were unwilling to pay	Youth with mild disabilities
1980s	The Career Implementation Incentive Act (PL 95–207, 1977–1982) expanded previous work–study models, served all ages and types of students. Through this Incentive Act, work–study programs were much broader in scope focusing on life skills, as well as work skills. The scope was more comprehensive and considered residential, social outcomes, and employment. Programs were built upon elementary and middle school students receiving career awareness and exploration. Students with severe disabilities, as a result of FAPE, participated in community based instructional programs. However, the legislation expired in 1982 as projected at time of composition	Youth with severe and mild disabilities

included part-time work experiences for credit combined with part-time classes; a focus on students with mild intellectual disabilities; integrated academic, social, and vocational curriculum coupled with community work experiences to prepare youth for productive community adjustment. Within the work–study model, classroom teachers functioned as a work coordinator. Teacher salaries were used as in-kind matches to receive federal dollars to fund work–study programs. Within this model, collaborative interagency agreements existed between vocational rehabilitation agencies and schools.

This interagency cooperation between schools and rehab agencies constitutes the first example of collaborative agreements between agencies in service of students with disabilities. As stated previously, these work–study programs were discontinued, in part, because of similar benefit requirements of vocational rehabilitation and a shift of responsibility for appropriate education (including work study) to schools as part of EHA of 1975.

Similarly, Section 504 of the Rehabilitation Act of 1973 and the Americans with Disabilities Act (ADA) of 1990 assured access to and benefits of a federally funded program and prohibited discrimination of persons with a disability by a such-funded programs. Furthermore, similar to Section 504, ADA extended access to private programs in hiring, discharge, pay, and promotion; provided reasonable accommodations without causing undue hardship; and assured equal access in public transportation, telecommunications, and public accommodation.

The Career Implementation Incentive Act (PL 95–207, 1977–1982), which was an expansion of previous work–study models, served all ages and types of students. The programs under this Incentive Act, unlike previous work–study programs, were much broader in scope in that they focused on life skills, not merely work skills. Additionally, the scope was more comprehensive in that they considered residential, social outcomes and employment building upon elementary and middle school students targeted for career awareness and exploration. Students with severe disabilities, then protected by the law and FAPE, experienced the opportunity to participate in community-based instructional programs. However, the legislation expired in 1982 as projected at time of composition.

EARLY MODELS OF TRANSITION

Upon the realization that many special education graduates were experiencing negligible postschool outcomes; several models of transition were proposed in the 1980s as attempts to close the gap toward desirable postschool outcomes for this population. The Will's Bridges Model (1984) is perhaps one of the earliest and most well-known examples. The Will's model was established by Madeline Will who was the Director of the Federal Office of Special Education Programs under President Reagan. Will's model emphasized "bridges" or linkages between school and postschool environments and focused entirely on employment. The three "bridges" to employment that the model proposed included (a) transition without special services in which the individual pursued postsecondary education that ultimately led to employment, (b) transition with time-limited services in which the individual received time-limited support by vocational rehabilitation services, and (c) transition with ongoing support, in which the individual received ongoing support in accord with supported employment models. The Will's model was criticized because its sole emphasis on employment minimized the importance of quality of life outcomes in the residential and interpersonal domains (Halpern, 1985).

In 1985, Halpern proposed an alternative transition model that came to be known as Halpern's 3 Pillars model. Halpern asserted that Will's three transition services should focus not just on work, but on community adjustment in the areas of employment, residential environment, and social and interpersonal networks. The model argued that transition should build on three "pillars" of community adjustment and impact the overall quality of life and community adjustment of the student, not merely their employment outcome.

In addition to transition models, work preparation models also emerged. Vocational special needs education models emerged whereby occupational specific programs with supplemental services were adapted and modified. In these models, students with disabilities were placed in permanent jobs before graduation with adult services assuming work responsibility after graduation. One such model was Wehman's 3-Step Work Preparation Model (Wehman, Kregel, & Barcus, 1985). This model focused on instruction, planning process, and placement before graduation. In the initial step, the emphasis was on functional curriculum, experiences provided in an integrated environment, and instruction within community-based activities. The second step of Wehman's model was the planning process. This step placed students and family at the core of planning, called for the involvement of more than the public school, and mandated individualization. Step 3 involved placement before graduation. This step required that students be placed in competitive employment, supported employment, or specialized sheltered work.

There were several other models of transition that emerged in the 1990s, the most notable was Siegel's Career Pathway Model (Siegel, 1998). In this model, Siegel (1998) proposed an infusion career pathways model of transition with heavy emphasis on integrating transition with school to work programs. The career pathways model focused heavily on developing general courses of study (or career paths), while focusing on students needs, interests, and preferences for postschool goals and the most effective path for reaching those goals. In Siegel's Model, five levels of services were proposed. Level 5 services, the most intense pathway, provided for youth at greatest risk for underemployment and marginal entry into the community. Services at

Level 4 addressed youth at moderate risk for underemployment, working only a portion of the week or for substandard wages, or unemployment. Pathway at Level 3 services provided exploration for students in need of state-of-the-art education for careers. Career opportunities were emphasized for youth at Level 2 services who were in need of career opportunities. The most general pathway at Level 1 provided services for all students, including high-achieving, high-income youth. In this model, the levels are organized by decreasing degrees of intrusiveness of the range of supports that a specific student would need to achieve outcomes specified in each level.

ESSENTIAL ELEMENTS OF TRANSITION PER IDEA

The Individuals with Disabilities Education Improvement Act of 2004 provided a comprehensive definition of transition. Table 2 provides the essential elements included in IDEA's definition.

Furthermore, IDEA 2004 requires the implementation of transition assessment to develop postsecondary goals. Specifically, IDEA 2004 states that transition planning begins not later than the first IEP to be in effect when the child turns 16, or younger if determined appropriate by the IEP Team, and updated annually thereafter, the IEP must include (a) appropriate measurable postsecondary goals based on age-appropriate transition assessments related

Table 2. Transition Elements ([34 CFR 300.43 (a)] [20 U.S.C. 1401(34)]).

Activity	Outcome
Program a result-oriented process	Improving the academic and functional achievement
Facilitate postsecondary education, vocational education, integrated employment (including supported employment), continuing and adult education, adult services, independent living, or community participation	Learner realizes movement from school to post-school activities, including community and residence in addition to work
Program to individual learner's needs	Builds awareness of strengths, preferences, and interests
Deliver instruction, related services, and community experiences, based on a functional vocational evaluation	Acquisition of daily living skills and the development of employment and other postschool adult living objectives

to training, education, employment and, where appropriate, independent living skills; (b) transition services (including courses of study) needed to assist the child in reaching those goals; and (c) beginning not later than one year before the child reaches the age of majority under State law, a statement that the child has been informed of the child's rights under part B, if any, that will transfer to the child on reaching the age of majority [34 CFR 300.320(b) and (c)] [20 U.S.C. 1414 (d)(1)(A)(i)(VIII)].

This definition of transition services underscores four essential elements of transition. First, transition is an outcome-oriented process. Second, good instruction should lead to positive transition outcomes for students. Third, transition calls for a coordinated set of activities. Finally, instruction and transition needs are to be well organized, sequential, and with sufficient repetition and practice for learning to occur. Transition should have promoted movement to postschool activities, and instruction should develop the knowledge, skills, attitudes, and behaviors students needed to become responsible and successful adults. Transition should be based on student needs, preferences, and interests, and it should be noted that instruction, transition planning, and other educational activities are more likely to be successful when based on student interests.

Current Issues in Transition of Youth with Disabilities

A concern throughout the country with respect to all youth exiting school and entering the workforce is the use and abuse of alcohol, tobacco, and drugs. Association with substance abuse oftentimes leads to additional, negative conduct in society, particularly with regard to drug activity. Yu, Huang, and Newman (2008) analyzed the literature, data from the National Institute of Transition Study (NLTS) and the National Longitudinal Transition Study 2 (NLTS2) (Wagner, Cameto, & Newman, 2003) and concluded that young adults with disabilities did not engage in the use of these target substances in any degree different from the general population, with the exception of lesser involvement with drug use. One can speculate that different degrees of substance use may occur for differing disability types of youths depending on the substance in question. For instance, young adults identified in schools with a learning disability reported the greatest use of cigarettes, compared to youth previously identified with an emotional disturbance reporting higher degrees of alcohol use. Does the use parallel attempts to achieve social acceptance (e.g., learning disabilities and cigarette smoking) or would one conclude that a given individual may strive for some degree of therapeutic reprieve (e.g., emotional disturbance and alcohol)?

Evaluating survey data reveal some significant discrepancies among groups of people with disabling conditions and the degree of use of a given substance. Drug use was reported to be less of an occurrence for the total population of young adults with disabilities than the general population of young adults. Within the various categories of disability, however, persons identified with emotional disturbance (33%) were twice as likely as the next group, with learning disabilities (16%) to engage in marijuana use (Yu et al., 2008). Other forms of illegal drug use were consistent with the use of marijuana as persons with disabilities were less likely to be users when compared to the general population. Within the populations with disabilities, persons with emotional disturbance reported more frequent use followed by persons with learning disabilities trailing off to a much lower use reported by persons with cognitive impairments and multiple disabilities.

Continued attention to these social ills is incumbent on a positive, comprehensive service delivery to transition special needs populations. Subsequent to dealing with exposure to tobacco, alcohol, and drugs is the individual decision-making process itself. Job coaches (Wehman, 1996) have entered into the employment landscape to transition persons with disabilities initially into the workplace. These coaches provide intensive, specialized, and structured intervention necessary for the employee to immediately learn and perform job tasks to the employer's specifications. Social and interpersonal skills often times stand as barriers to employment and job coaching applies to that dimension of work as well as production and effort.

Numerous studies emerged in the literature that advocated processes to improve the decision-making capacity of young adults striving for work and community placements (Rusch, Morgan, Martin, Riva, & Agran, 1985; Wehmeyer, Agran, & Hughes 1998; Wehmeyer & Schwartz, 1997). Earlier efforts to improve self-regulation were built around routines and environmental prompts to instigate assessment of the immediate environment and encourage decisions by the individual. Building success around an individual's decision can be an empowering event and may lead to stronger generalization of action into novel settings.

A tendency continues to marginalize habilitation and community integration of persons with disabilities due to a preference for work and job placement. West, Wehman, and Wehman (1998) advanced the coach concept from job coach to personal coach through the Best Buddies system becoming prevalent on many college campuses. This practice pairs one young adult college student with a person with special needs of approximate same age. Pairing age peers in this manner promotes friendships and introduces the individual with disabling conditions into community activities that may not occur independently. Following the introduction by the Best Buddy, persons with special needs can begin to make decisions about self-interests and practice the all important skill of making choices.

BEST AND PROMISING PRACTICES IN TRANSITION

Within transition research, best or promising practice refers to a number of research-validated specific recommendations for facilitating successful movement from school to adult life for youth with disabilities. However, scholars in special education have remained keenly aware of the challenges that exist in transferring research-based strategies in actual instructional contexts. Despite this problem of identifying and applying best practices in transition without empirical validation, transition experts have identified several promising practices in transition that are generally supported in research. Those practices include self-determination, ecological assessment, backward planning, systems change, service coordination, community experiences, access and accommodation, and family involvement (Flexer, Simmons, Luft, & Baer, 2005; Wehmeyer et al., 1998).

Self-Determination

As a best practice, self-determination is the exercise of a combination of self-awareness and self-advocacy skills in goal expression and selection and decision making (Bakken & Parette, 2008; Wehmeyer et al., 1998). Self-determination increases one's control over personal life through the exercise of direct consent in making decisions. Additionally, self-determination entails informed choice making. For students with disabilities, the involvement of families is critical in the decisions about postschool outcome and the realization of those outcomes. Therefore family involvement is part and parcel to the process. In fact, parents find jobs for 25–30% of their children and families also provide ongoing support.

Ecological Assessment

With ecological approaches, the issue is one of focusing transition curriculum, developing formal and natural supports, providing experiences in varied environments, and instilling consistency across environments. Ecological assessment procedures, critical in transition planning, determine skills necessary for optimal functioning in a student's current and future environments made across four ecological domains (domestic, leisure, community, and vocational). Halpern's (1992) three ecological domains (residential, employment, and social) also hinges on ecological assessment. Such assessment and the resulting instruction will consider the student's cultural background and an extensive knowledge of the community, services, and service providers within the community.

Backward Planning

To help students focus on their future, the implementation of individualized backward planning techniques have been found to be highly effective (Flexer et al., 2005). Backward planning is implemented to assure that a student's years of transition programming reflect their desired adult outcomes. Flexer et al. (2005) have identified five pivotal steps in backward planning. Specifically, those steps involve determining (1) where the student wants to be after graduation, (2) where the student should be the year before graduation, two years before, and so on, (3) where the student needs to be at the end of each transition year, (4) what transition services are needed to support the student in reaching his/her desired postschool outcomes, and (e) how IEP goals support the student's transition.

Community Experiences

Rescarch shows a strong correlation between community experiences and positive postschool employment outcomes (Dykema-Engblade & Stawiski, 2008). Students with disabilities need more community experiences to overcome a tendency of limited experience and opportunity. Community experiences are also critical to the development of social maturity and work adjustment skills.

Service Coordination

The centrality of service coordination in transition cannot be overemphasized. Policy differences continue to exist among agencies that provide transition services. School-level interagency transition teams can help iron out agency policy distinctions. Business–education partnerships can enhance coordination with work sites. The IEP/transition plan needs to orient all school and agency plans developed for a student. Regular communication needs to be maintained with all members of the student's transition team.

Assistive and Self-Monitoring Technologies

Specific practices targeting the learner as an individual functioning with more autonomy are also beginning to occur. Video self-modeling is one such practice (Bidwell & Rehfeldt, 2004; Mitchell, Schuster, Collins, & Gassaway, 2000; Post, Storey, & Karabin, 2002) that provides videorecorded effort for an individual to self-evaluate and actualize personal decisions about work, living, and domestic responsibilities. Benefits of video include consistency of activity reviewed and relating to a strong role model – self. Work and/or habilitation performance can be recorded, edited, and replayed to allow an individual the opportunity to see themselves as a role model, which is very motivating.

Another example of technology promoting a stronger self-concept, which is becoming increasingly more practical with miniaturization, is implementation of iPods to deliver performance prompts. Youth attempting to develop a work or domestic routine can now be provided a prerecorded checklist, prompt, or rehearsal strategy independent of a job or personal coach. Because iPods and MP3 devices are not as bulky as older recording and playback devices; listening and even viewing work routine models can occur without significantly altering the authenticity of the work environment. Skill acquisition may actually be improved, due to the consistency of the prompt heard or video model displayed, but without dependence on the job coach.

Social networking (e.g., Facebook, Twitter, and MySpace) structures are in the early stages of use by persons with disabilities to build friendships and open new community options. These social platforms allow individuals to interact over greater distances and in some occasions with less attention to physical or sensory differences. Individuals free of disabilities may be more receptive to building a relationship with someone with a unique condition, which could be a barrier in a face to face encounter. Remote interactions allows both parties an opportunity to warm to the relationship and gain comfort and confidence communicating with a novel acquaintance thereby setting the stage for a face to face encounter later in the relationship. Caution needs to be maintained in order to deter relationships with others who may have ulterior motives. Individuals with cognitive impairments and circumstances that may inhibit good judgment about someone may need to work with a mentor or advocate (Nkabinde, 2008). As the instructor introducing social networking online, a major responsibility may also be the identification of an Internet filter and guidelines for the user with cognitive impairments to walk through with each interaction. A parent or advocate may be enlisted periodically, possibly weekly, to review social networking activities and build a capacity to self-evaluate safety in these environments.

Individuals with disabilities must combat a significant set of life circumstances. Owing to limits in employment opportunities, these citizens have a greater part of their day and life free for recreation and vocational pursuits. Ironically, they have not historically had as many options to fill that opportunity. In the absence of productive recreational outlets, many members of society coping with a disability have become dependent on media such as television and other passive, sedentary activities to fill their day. Poor hygiene characterized by obesity and limited mobility has become a common physical trait. More and more youth with disabilities arrive in schools and activity centers with game consoles to occupy their day, which are more engaging than television, but still physically passive events. Electronic games, with increased physical interaction required to participate, are emerging in homes and activity centers to move youth and young adults from passive to active recreational participants. Social benefits are also beginning to accompany such participation with teams and participation leagues formed to foster team effort and increased enjoyment.

Findings from the NTLS2 (Cameto, Newman, & Wagner, 2006) confirm that membership in society and the workforce are beginning to be realized. Greater numbers of persons with disabilities are beginning to become visible on community and senior college campuses. Advocacy groups, advances in interventions, and availability of offices for disability accommodations on university campuses have combined to open up new doors for persons with disabilities. Attitudes also appear to be shifting toward greater acceptance from the general population in public schools which assists in self-concept development of individuals with special needs.

CONCLUSION

Relying on the NTLS2 (Newman, Wagner, Cameto, & Knokey, 2009) report, it is easy to see that progress is occurring in the field of transition of persons with special needs from school to the workplace and community. The authors remain wary of the distinction from Study 1 and Study 2 with regard to positive outcomes reported as the timeframe and databases are also subject to the effect of No Child Left Behind (NCLB) (2002). On some fronts, the NCLB Act appears to have benefited students with exceptionalities as more learners report progressing deeper into school supports. One has to question, however, if the self-reported progress by schools and states, which shows gains in benefits compared to the gains in the general student population, is as transparent as data would suggest. First, the longitudinal data are self-report with some parent confirmation, and the reports vary. Second, do the populations from study 1 and study 2 compare? Has the impact of NCLB changed the demographics of the special needs population by virtue of the number of dropouts from the special needs sector in our schools? These are questions the profession may never be able to fully analyze due to the difficult nature of tracking these individuals residing outside the education agencies among all communities.

Advances in the treatment of youth and adults with disabilities in work and community life are encouraging. Individual and systems advocacy need to continue to (a) assess the systems involved in service provision, (b) press the life and vocational concerns that continue to infringe on the populations with special needs, and (c) advocate for inclusive life experiences that may positively influence persons with and without special needs. Distinguishing among people in communities and the unfortunate discrimination directed toward persons with disabilities appears to be less an issue than it was a decade or two ago. Philosophical foundations traced to various models of transition from Will (1984) to Halpern (1985) to Wehman (Wehman et al., 1985) are becoming more apparent in the lives of persons with disabilities. Continued dependence on family beyond the school years continues to serve as a distinction between persons with identified special needs and persons not identified. As we write, the country is experiencing an economic downturn that is influencing and changing lives in a negative manner, regardless of ability and/or disability. Subsequent studies will no doubt have to untangle the impact of an economic downturn on the benefits and limitations of transitional service and employability of individuals dealing with disabling conditions.

One demographic reported as a positive development was an overall downward shift in the number of learners with African-American makeup served in special education. A history of disproportionality among various races of students served in special education appears to be improving. Again, untangling the nuances of community composition, changes in categories of disability, and the pressures brought by NCLB all warrant close examination to assure that these shifts are, indeed, what they appear to be; improvement and not a shell game. Transitional services have proven to benefit persons with special needs across a continuum. A renewed commitment to school-based transition services and the relationship with vocational rehabilitation services deserves significant attention in order to realize better lives for all citizens.

REFERENCES

Bakken, J. P., & Parette, H. P. (2008). Self-determination and persons with developmental disabilities. In: A. F. Rotatori, F. E. Obiakor & S. Burkhardt (Eds), *Autism and developmental disabilities: Current practices and issues* (pp. 221–234). Bingley, UK: Emerald Group Publishing Limited.

Bidwell, M. A., & Rehfeldt, R. A. (2004). Using video modeling to teach a domestic skill with an embedded social skill to adults with severe mental retardation. *Behavioral Interventions, 19*, 263–274.

Brolin, D. (1984). *LCCE: Life centered career education: A competency based approach.* Reston, VA: Council for Exceptional Children.

Cameto, R., Newman, L., & Wagner, M. (2006). The national longitudinal transition study-2 (NLTS2) project update: Self-perceptions of youth with disabilities. Institute of Education Sciences, Washington, DC.

Dykema-Engblade, A., & Stawiski, S. (2008). Employment and retirement concerns for persons with developmental disabilities. In: A. F. Rotatori, F. E. Obiakor & S. Burkhardt (Eds), *Autism and developmental disabilities: Current practices and issues* (pp. 273–285). Bingley, UK: Emerald Group Publishing Limited.

Flexer, R. W., Simmons, T. J., Luft, P., & Baer, R. M. (2005). *Transition planning for secondary students with disabilities* (2nd ed.). Columbus, OH: Pearson, Merrill, Prentice Hall.

Halpern, A. S. (1985). Transition: A look at foundations. *Exceptional Children, 51*(6), 479–486.

Halpern, A. S. (1992). Transition: Old wine in new bottles. *Exceptional Children, 58*(3), 202–211.

Harris, L. (1986). Lou Harris Poll on disability: A national survey of disabled people. Available at www.aboutdisability.com/Resources/harrispoll.html

Harris, L. (1994). Lou Harris Poll on disability: A national survey of disabled people. Available at www.aboutdisability.comResources/harrispoll.html

Kolstoe, O. (1970). *Teaching educable mentally retarded children.* New York: Holt, Rinehart & Winston.

Mitchell, R. J., Schuster, J. W., Collins, B. C., & Gassaway, L. J. (2000). Teaching vocational skills with a faded auditory prompting system. *Education and Training in Mental Retardation and Developmental Disabilities, 35*, 415–427.

Newman, L., Wagner, M., Cameto, R., Knokey, A. M. (2009). The post-high school outcomes of youth with disabilities up to 4 years after high school. A report of findings from the national longitudinal transition study-2 (NLTS2) (NCSER 2009-3017), SRI International, Menlo Park, CA. Available at www.nlts2.org/reports/2009_04/nlts2_report_2009_04_complete.pdf

Nkabinde, Z. (2008). Using assistive technology to educate students with developmental disabilities. In: A. F. Rotatori, F. E. Obiakor & S. Burkhardt (Eds), *Autism and developmental disabilities: Current practices and issues* (pp. 273–285). Bingley, UK: Emerald Group Publishing Limited.

No Child Left Behind Act (PL 107-110). (2002). *Reauthorization of the Elementary and Secondary Education Act*. Washington, DC: U.S. Department of Education.

Post, M., Storey, K., & Karabin, M. (2002). Supporting students and adults in work and community environments. *Teaching Exceptional Children, 34*(3), 60–65.

Rusch, F. R., Morgan, T. K., Martin, J. E., Riva, M., & Agran, M. (1985). Competitive employment: Teaching mentally retarded adults self-instructional strategies. *Applied Research in Mental Retardation, 6*, 389–407.

Siegel, S. (1998). Foundations for a school-to-work system that serves all students. In: F. R. Rusch & J. G. Chadsey (Eds), *Beyond high school: Transition from school to work* (pp. 146–178). New York: Wordsworth.

Wagner, M., Cameto, R., & Newman, L. (2003). *Youth with disabilities: A changing population. A report of findings from the national longitudinal transition study (NLTS) and the national longitudinal transition study-2 (NLTS2)*. Menlo Park, CA: SRI International. Available at www.nlts2.org/reports/2003_04-1/nlts2_report_2003_04-1_complete.pdf

Wehman, P. (1996). *Life beyond the classroom: Transition strategies for young people with disabilities* (2nd ed.). Baltimore, MD: Paul H. Brookes.

Wehman, P. (2006a). *Life beyond the classroom: Transition strategies for young people with disabilities* (4th ed.). Baltimore, MD: Paul H. Brookes.

Wehman, P. (2006b). Integrated employment: If not now, when? If not us, who? *Research and Practice for Persons with Severe Disability, 31*(2), 122–126.

Wehman, P., Kregel, J., & Barcus, J. M. (1985). From school to work: A vocational transition model for handicapped students. *Exceptional Children, 52*(1), 25–37.

Wehmeyer, M. L., Agran, M., & Hughes, C. (1998). *Teaching self-determination in students with disabilities: Basic skills for successful transition*. Baltimore, MD: Paul H. Brookes.

Wehmeyer, M. L., & Schwartz, M. (1997). Self-determination and positive adult outcomes: A follow-up study of youth with mental retardation or learning disabilities. *Exceptional Children, 63*(2), 245–255.

West, M., Wehman, P. B., & Wehman, P. (1998). Competitive employment outcomes for persons with intellectual and developmental disabilities: The national impact of the best buddies jobs program. *Journal of Vocational Rehabilitation, 23*, 51–63.

Will, M. (1984). *OSERS programming for the transition of youth with disabilities: Bridges from school to working life*. Washington, DC: Office of Special Education and Rehabilitation Services, U.S. Office of Education.

Yu, J., Huang, T., & Newman, L. (2008). *Facts from NLTS2: Substance use among young adults with disabilities*. Menlo Park, CA: SRI International. Available at www.nlts2.org/fact_sheets/nlts2_fact_sheet_2008_03.pdf

CHAPTER 10

TRANSITION: WHY IT DOES NOT WORK

Michelle J. McCollin and Festus E. Obiakor

The transition from birth to childhood, through adolescence, and then to adulthood is a turbulent and sometimes unconventional evolution all people experience with varying degrees of achievement, challenge, and actualization. This transition involves several correlated actions, role changes, and socioemotional behavioral adjustments. These actions, changes, and adjustments are linked with many of the person-centered life occurrences (e.g., beginning school, puberty, search for independence, search for autonomy, graduating from secondary school, employment, family, recreation and leisure, social relationships, and growing older) that occur throughout adult life. Transition to the complexities of adulthood can be challenging for most young adults.

Many students with disabilities have difficulty in successfully making the transition from adolescence to adulthood and then from school to work. In fact, many students with disabilities do not graduate; encounter great difficulty in finding and maintaining suited employment; exhibit high levels of unemployment or underemployment; are socioeconomically unstable; have limited access to community resources; are involved with the justice system; do not receive postsecondary training; or become dependent on their families or government programs (Hallahan & Kauffman, 2003; Halpern, 1994; Rusch & Chadsey, 1998; Sands & Wehmeyer, 1996; Wehman, 2001). Overall postschool outcomes for students with disabilities are mediocre. Research has found that students with severe and multiple disabilities and those with emotional behavioral disorders typically have the poorer outcomes compared to those with specific learning disabilities or speech and language impairments (Rampey, Dion, & Donahue, 2009). Therefore, in preparing students with disabilities for continued education, adult responsibilities, independence, and employment, transition planning must also include strategies (e.g., self-determination, self-advocacy), for successfully negotiating the challenges, concerns, and uncertainties of adulthood. To ensure successful functioning in adulthood, these strategies should be acknowledged, considered, and addressed within the context of the transition plan so that students with disabilities are able to competently deal with the challenges of life (Patton & Dunn, 1998; Smith, Polloway, Patton, & Dowdy, 2006; Wehmeyer, Agran, & Hughes, 1998).

TRANSITIONING FROM SCHOOL TO ADULT LIFE

The concept of transition and preparation for adult life has been an important yet controversial governmental initiative since the early 1980s. This governmental focus prompted special educators to develop and implement curricula to better prepare students with disabilities for adult life (Price, Gerber, & Mulligan, 2007). The curricula process involves forming linkages among local educational agencies and other human service agencies, including employment and training, adult services, leisure and recreation, and health and rehabilitation. Educators and policy makers continue to encounter great challenges to building capacity and sustained implementation of the transition curricula process at both the local school and the community levels.

HISTORICAL OVERVIEW OF FEDERAL TRANSITION SERVICES LEGISLATION

The Rehabilitation Act (1973) – Section 504 established and extended civil rights to individuals with disabilities. Section 504 defines the rights of individuals with disabilities to participate in, and have access to, benefit and service programs. In 1976, the Vocational Education Amendments (P.L. 94-482) established the need for collaboration among vocational education and other job training programs as well as increased funding for vocational education programs and youth with disabilities. During the mid-1980s, the Carl D. Perkins Vocational and Technical Education Act (1998, P.L. 98-524) further provided resources for young people with disabilities to successfully prepare for transition from secondary education to the world of adulthood. The act was passed with the following intent:

> assure that individuals who are inadequately served under vocational education programs are assured access to quality vocational educational programs, especially individuals who are disadvantaged, who are handicapped, men and women who are entering non-traditional occupations, adults who are in need of training and retraining, individuals who are single parents or homemakers, individuals with limited English proficiency, and individuals who are incarcerated in correctional institutions. (P.L. 98-524)

Since 1983, there has been a legislative prioritization regarding *transition* services for students with disabilities. Individuals with Disabilities Education Act (IDEA, P.L. 94-142) was amended with a new Section 626, entitled "Secondary Education and Transition Services for Handicapped Youth." This amendment authorized federal grants to support the coordination of educational and adult transitional service programs for youth with disabilities. The 1990 amendments of IDEA continued federal support for *transition*-related activities, refined *transition* services, and mandated that student interests, preferences, and needs be considered when developing transition plans. Moreover, IDEA required that the Individualized *Education* Program (IEP) for students ages 16 years and older take into consideration specific *transition* components (i.e., *transition* services, interagency collaborations). The 1997 amendment of IDEA produced the most significant mandates related to *special education legislation* – (a) the expansion of the *transition* requirements regarding age at which services were to be introduced on the IEP, and more importantly, (b) the significance of postschool outcomes for students with IEPs. The most recent reauthorized Individuals with Disabilities Education Improvement Act (IDEIA) (2004) further defines transition services as a coordinated set of activities for a student with disability that

(a) is designed to be within an outcome-oriented process, which promotes both academic and functional achievement in an effort to facilitate the movement from school to postschool activities, including postsecondary education, vocational education, integrated employment (including supported employment), continuing and adult education, adult services, independent living, or community participation;
(b) is based on the individual student's needs, taking into account the student's capacity, access to support and resources, preferences, and interests; and

(c) includes instruction, related services, community experiences, the development of employment and other postschool adult living objectives, and when appropriate, acquisition of daily living skills and functional vocational evaluation (H.R. 1350, Sec 602[34]).

As a result of the prioritization of *transition* services for students with IEPs, there has been some improvement of postschool outcomes and student skill development; yet, educators still grapple with the effective implementation of individualized transition plans for students with disabilities (Lehman, Clark, Bullis, Rinkin, & Castellanos, 2002; Wehmeyer, 1998).

TRANSITION PLANNING

Preparation for the sometimes arduous transition from school to adult life involves a transformation and examination of a person's concept of self, their environment, and others; for youth with disabilities who require additional support systems and resources, the passage into adult life presents even greater challenge (German, Martin, Marshall, & Sale, 2000). The preparation for the transition to adult life may include the development of skills needed to overcome multiple socioemotional, academic, and environmental constraints that may present roadblocks to meeting society's expectations that include the ability to (a) live independently, (b) determine a career path, (c) find and maintain meaningful employment or postsecondary education, (d) establish fulfilling relationships with family and friends, and (e) choose leisure and recreation activities (Lehman et al., 2002). Therefore, the system and process for providing postschool transition support must be deliberate and individualized to effectively empower youth with disabilities.

The skill set needed to successfully navigate adulthood in the 21st century is much more complex and comprehensive than those skills required by previous generations. Today's young adults must not only contend with challenges of employment, family life, leisure and recreation, health, and quality of life but also with access to technology and community resources, interagency collaboration, and self-determination. Adulthood means being an active, contributing, and independent member of the community and greater society. Independence for an adult includes the ability to participate in society, work, have a home, autonomy, self-respect, raise a family, and share the joys and responsibilities of community life (Neubert, 2003). Adults with disabilities face numerous obstacles within the context of their daily living that affect not only their ability to access and use community resources but also limit the opportunities they have for social interaction and self-fulfillment (Heward, 2008). Therefore, transition planning is a critical aspect for successful navigation of adult life. Paramount to transition planning are the concepts of collaboration and interagency communication. These concepts are important and comparatively new to special education service providers (Heward, 2008). Transition planning is conceptualized as the coordination, delivery, and transfer of services from the secondary school program to receiving agencies (e.g., employers, postsecondary education and vocational training programs, and residential service providers).

Effective transition planning must have a student focus, involve parents and families, and foster interagency and interdisciplinary collaboration. Within the context of student-focused planning, students have an opportunity to strengthen and develop self-determination and self-advocacy skills through practice and implementation. Paramount to student-focused planning is the development of a student's self-awareness. The development of student self-awareness will have a direct impact on educational decisions because self-aware students will be able to take into consideration their own goals, vision, and interests when making educational decisions (Kohler & Field, 2003). An important strategy to help students identify their interests and preferences is to provide them with interdisciplinary curricular experiences so that they are able to (a) reflect on their experiences, (b) derive meaning particular to their context, and (c) use that information for future decision-making (Kohler & Field, 2003).

Parental and family involvement is a critical aspect of successful transition planning. It involves the development of participation and role, empowerment, and training of family members, hence allowing families the ability to actively participate in the decision-making processes for their family members. Family involvement has been shown to improve school attendance, improve student's self-esteem and confidence, reduce dropout rates, and improve student autonomy – a critical aspect of self-determination (Sands & Wehmeyer, 1996). Student-focused planning is extended and supported through parent and family involvement.

Collaboration and communication between and among professionals and families are keys to effective transition planning. In special education, teaming and collaboration are important in the planning and delivery of transition services for secondary students with disabilities. Although interagency cooperation is critical to the success of transition, the amendments to IDEA made it clear that the initial and most significant transition responsibilities lie with schools (Heward, 2008). Although every state has a history of federally maintained work study and vocational training programs, the systematic coordination of and communication between schools and community-based adult services have not regularly occurred (Sands & Wehmeyer, 1996). As a result of the limited collaboration, many young adults in transition are not able to access the necessary community supports and resources.

Interagency and interdisciplinary collaboration is fostered by agreements that clearly articulate goals, roles, communication strategies, and other collaborative actions that enhance the curriculum and service delivery. Interagency collaboration includes activities between family, special educators, and adult service providers such as working as a team, sharing information, attending transition planning meetings, accessing community resources, and establishing and utilizing effective lines of communication to benefit students with disabilities as they transition from high school to the adult world. The purpose of these collaborative activities is to implement an integrated system that addresses lifelong learning and supports the needs of a community's members. Addressing barriers to effective collaboration such as ineffective use of transition meetings, intimidating language, and complex agency procedures may be an important goal of the interagency collaboration thereby affording students with disabilities the opportunity to have successful entry into adult life (Oertle & Trach, 2007). To be successful in adult life, young people urgently need an interdisciplinary high school curriculum that has a strong focus on their transitional needs (Dowdy, Carter, & Smith, 1990).

SIGNIFICANCE OF SELF-DETERMINATION AND SELF-ADVOCACY

Self-determination is a set of skills or competencies that assist students in determining their wants and needs, making appropriate life choices, deciding on the best actions to take, taking the action, evaluating and improving on the outcome, and becoming empowered through the process (Reppetto, 2003; Wehmeyer, 1992). The ability to be self-determined is a highly critical skill to successful navigation of adult life; without this skill, others will be responsible for making decisions in the lives of individuals with disabilities (Carter, Lane, Pierson, & Glaeser, 2006). Specific skills in self-determination include decision-making, coping with failure, self-assessment, action planning, and option exploration

(Carter, Lane, Pierson, & Stang, 2008; Reppetto, 2003; Wehmeyer & Palmer, 2003). Engaging in self-determination skill strategies during the formal transition planning process and throughout adult life requires students to complete tasks they may find challenging. These skills may include the ability to actively participate in transition meetings, self-disclose strengths and weaknesses, and request services and accommodations (Reppetto, 2003; Wehmeyer, 1992; Wehmeyer & Palmer, 2003).

POSTSCHOOL OUTCOMES FOR INDIVIDUALS WITH DISABILITIES

The National Council on Disability has indicated that the implementation of legislative transition policy has been slow and inconsistent across states, thereby causing individuals with disabilities to lag far behind individuals without disabilities in the areas of employment and other aspects of community engagement (Kohler & Field, 2003; National Council on Disability, 2004).

Limited Opportunities for Planning

Researchers have found that youth with disabilities were generally unfamiliar with the formal transition planning process (Trainor, 2007; Sitlington, 2008). For example, Sitlington (2008) found that transition outcomes do not work because there is sometimes a failure to operationalize the transition theories. Furthermore, lack of preparation in research and personnel preparation make it difficult for professionals to know what is expected of them and what to do (Sitlington, 2008). The impact of limited student participation in transition planning and decision-making as well as little to no student control over the curriculum, student directed work on self-awareness, leadership, and self-advocacy all pose as challenges to transition (Wehmeyer & Schwartz, 1997). Another shortcoming of transition implementation within special education practice (e.g., classroom settings, simulated labs, isolated environments) is the limited "real life" available options for transition from school to adult life within the community. Skills taught out of context make it difficult for students to use and integrate when posed with community-based experiences. Generally, as needs increase and more specialization of services is required, the student becomes further removed from the integrated school and postschool environment.

The most recent standards-based reform movement and the reauthorization of the No Child Left Behind Act, 2004, has strategically shifted the focus attention of the educational system from school to work preparation to higher academic performance outcomes for all students. As a result of this paradigm shift, educational leaders have insisted on programmatic changes and systemic redesign of secondary education and transition planning for all youth, especially those with disabilities (Carter et al., 2008; Reppetto, 2003). One such redesign strategy is that the transition component of the IEP put emphasis on the supports that students need to live independently, establish social lives, become lifelong learners, and sustain employment (Jorgenson, 1998).

Studies (Carter et al., 2006; German et al., 2000) also highlight that there is a general lack of appropriate education, vocational training, and related services combined with socioeconomic realities that place youth at risk for successful transition to adult life. Additional concerns such as high rates of unemployment and underemployment as well as limited access to postsecondary programs, inability to live independently, and a lack of continuity and coordination between the educational and the adult service systems are contributing factors to why transition does not work (Sitlington, 2008). As a result, progress in implementing transition in many states has not resulted in significant improvement in postschool outcomes for youth with disabilities (National Council on Disability, 2004).

Additional Barriers to Successful Transition

Researchers (Kohler & Field, 2003; Sitlington, 2008) have also found that there are several contributing factors that may be barriers to successful transition for youth with disabilities. The factors include (a) the degree of student understanding of the nature of their disability; (b) student's ability to be proactive (e.g., self-advocacy, goal setting, knowledge of disability law, selection of an appropriate college, self-identification, organizing for living and learning); (c) the access to support systems; (d) the severity of the disability; (e) student's motivation level; (f) how willing he or she is to persevere in the face of adversity; (g) low expectations that students with significant disabilities such as mental retardation will go on to college; (h) adult service agencies with limited resources and long waiting lists; (i) problems in linking students with postsecondary education and workforce opportunities; and (j) limited access to transportation for students with disabilities. All are compelling barriers to the successful transition of students, and all encompass great challenge to appropriate resolution (Skinner & Lindstrom, 2003). To begin to move the continuum from barrier to transition success, educators will have to change their perceptions of transition education. Many educators view transition education as a curriculum add-on; researches view transition-focused education as a fundamental basis of education that provides developmentally appropriate educational programs (Kohler & Field, 2003). Moreover, student cultural identities, family characteristics, economic conditions, community contexts, and the availability of services also have a direct impact on transition outcomes. When educators fail to take these variables into postschool consideration and planning for adult life, significant challenges arise for all stakeholders. In a review of extant special education literature, Skinner and Lindstrom (2003) identified the following critical areas where students with disabilities are at a disadvantage compared to nondisabled students with regard to postschool outcomes: (a) limited study and organizational skills, (b) limited social skills, (c) academic deficiencies, (d) low self-esteem, and (e) disproportionately higher secondary school dropout rates. Researchers asserted that for transition to adult life to work, it would take "more than a special education teacher or a transition specialist to implement these practices—it takes the entire school community" (National Council on Disability, 2004).

Postschool Outcomes for Youth with Disabilities

The number of children and youth served under the IDEA has increased to about 6,000,000 students. Approximately 45 percent are in secondary school programs, and the number is expected to continue to increase until the year 2010 (National Council on Disability, 2004). Unfortunately, parents and educators continue to report that there is an ongoing lack of appropriate services, supports, and post–high school assistance to meet the educational and career training needs of teenagers and young adults – thus creating a pool of youth who are marginalized, unemployed, underemployed, and unable to obtain jobs that use their accessible skills. There is an estimated 15 million youths aged 16–24 years who are out of school. Of those 15 million, approximately 70 percent have a high school diploma or less. Other postschool assessments suggested that youth with disabilities (a) had difficulty adjusting to life after graduation from high school, (b) remained reliant on IEP teams to make decisions and assessments, and (c) rarely advocated for their own interests (Chadsky-Rusch, Rusch, & O'Reilly, 1991; Mithaug, Martin, Agran, & Rusch, 1998). The continuing unemployment, undereducation, substantial dependence on parents and families; social isolation; and lack of involvement in community activities are characteristic of the continued failure of transition planning for many individuals with disabilities. These results point out that, even with the legislative efforts, educators may not have the skill set nor support systems needed to help youth with disabilities succeed as adults in mainstream society.

CONCLUSION

Often students with disabilities experience even greater challenges when transitioning from school to the adult world. For the purposes of this chapter, the developmental imperative of transitioning from school to adulthood (e.g., choosing a career; moving out of one's parents' home; establishing social networks, transportation, and recreational activities independent of one's parents) is a challenge for most adolescents, but for students with disabilities, this transition may be considerably more difficult if adequate planning, support, and training are not provided. Successful participation in adulthood requires active long-range planning by students, their parents or families, school staff, and adult service providers. It is essential that students have a thorough understanding of the consequences and options for their transition plans. The attainment of positive postschool outcomes for adolescents and adults with disabilities is dependent on professionals becoming more knowledgeable about the changing demands of education. Creative solutions will be essential to helping this population gain access to tools and information so that they can add to the world knowledge and economy, thereby increasing their own potential worth.

REFERENCES

Carl D. Perkins Vocational and Technical Education Act. (1998). 20 U. S. C. 2301 et seq.

Carter, E., Lane, K., Pierson, M., & Glaeser, B. (2006). Self-determination skills and opportunities of transition-age youth with emotional disturbance and learning disabilities. *Exceptional Children, 72*, 333–346.

Carter, E., Lane, K., Pierson, M., & Stang, K. K. (2008). Promoting self-determination for transition-age youth: Views of high school general and special educators. *Exceptional Children, 75*, 55–70.

Chadsky-Rusch, J., Rusch, F., & O'Reilly, M. F. (1991). Transition from school to integrated communities. *Remedial and Special Education, 12*, 23–33.

Dowdy, C., Carter, T., & Smith, T. (1990). Differences in transitional needs of high school students with and without learning disabilities. *Journal of Learning Disabilities, 23,* 343–348.

German, S., Martin, J., Marshall, L., & Sale, R. (2000). Promoting self-determination: Using take action to teach goal attainment. *Career Development for Exceptional Individuals, 23,* 27–38.

Hallahan, D., & Kauffman, J. (2003). *Exceptional learners: Introduction to special education.* Boston: Allyn & Bacon.

Halpern, A. (1994). The transition to youth with disabilities to adult life: A position statement of the Division on Career Development and Transition. *Career Development for Exceptional Individuals, 21,* 113–128.

Heward, W. (2008). *Exceptional children: An introduction to special education.* Upper Saddle River, NJ: Prentice Hall.

Individuals with Disabilities Education Improvement Act. (2004). Amendments, 20 U. S. C. 1400 et seq. H.R. 1350, Sec 602[34].

Jorgenson, C. (Ed.) (1998). *Restructuring high schools for all students: Taking inclusion to the next level.* Baltimore: Paul H. Brookes.

Kohler, P., & Field, S. (2003). Transition focused education: Foundation for the future. *The Journal of Special Education, 37,* 175–183.

Lehman, C., Clark, H., Bullis, M., Rinkin, J., & Castellanos, L. (2002). Transition from school to adult life: Empowering youth through community ownership and accountability. *Journal of Child and Family Studies, 11,* 127–141.

Mithaug, D., Martin, J., Agran, M., & Rusch, F. (1998). *Why special education graduates fail: How to teach them to succeed.* Colorado Springs, CO: Ascent.

National Council on Disability. (2004). *Transition and post school outcomes for youth with disabilities: Closing the gaps to postsecondary education and employment.* Washington, DC: National Council on Disability.

Neubert, D. (2003). The role of assessment in the transition to adult life process for students with disabilities. *Exceptionality, 11,* 3–75.

Oertle, K., & Trach, J. (2007). Interagency collaboration: The importance of rehabilitation professionals' involvement in transition. *The Journal of Rehabilitation, 73,* 36–44.

Patton, J., & Dunn, C. (1998). *Transition from school to young adulthood: Basic concepts and recommended practices.* Austin, TX: PRO-ED.

Price, L., Gerber, P., & Mulligan, R. (2007). Adults with learning disabilities and the underutilization of the Americans with Disabilities Act. *Remedial and Special Education, 28,* 340–344.

Rampey, B., Dion, G., & Donahue, P. (2009). *NAEP 2008 Trends in academic progress (NCES 2009-479).* Washington, DC: National Center for Education Statistics, Institute of Education Sciences, U.S. Department of Education.

Reppetto, A. (2003). Transition to living. *Exceptionality, 11,* 77–87.

Rusch, F., & Chadsey, J. (1998). *Beyond high school: Transition from school to work.* NY: Wadsworth.

Sands, D., & Wehmeyer, M. (Eds). (1996). *Self-determination across the life span: Independence and choice for people with disabilities.* Baltimore: Paul H. Brookes.

Sitlington, P. L. (2008). Students with reading and writing challenges: Using informal assessment to assist in planning for transition to adult life. *Reading & Writing Quarterly, 24,* 77–100.

Skinner, M., & Lindstrom, B. (2003). Bridging the gap between high school and college: Strategies for the successful transition of students with learning disabilities. *Preventing School Failure, 47*, 132–137.

Smith, T., Polloway, E., Patton, J., & Dowdy, C. (2006). *Teaching children with special needs in inclusive settings* (4th ed.). Boston: Pearson.

The Rehabilitation Act. (1973). Amendments, 29 U. S. C. 794.

Trainor, A. (2007). Perceptions of adolescent girls with LD regarding self-determination and postsecondary transition planning. *Learning Disability Quarterly, 30*, 31–45.

Wehman, P. (2001). *Life beyond the classroom: Transition strategies for young people with disabilities.* Baltimore, MD: Paul H. Brookes.

Wehmeyer, M. (1992). Self-determination and the education of students with mental retardation. *Education and Training in Mental Retardation, 27*, 302–314.

Wehmeyer, M. (1998). Self-determination and individuals with significant disabilities: Examining meanings and misinterpretations. *Journal of the Association of Persons with Severe Handicaps, 23*, 5–16.

Wehmeyer, M., Agran, M., & Hughes, C. (1998). *Teaching self-determination to students with disabilities: Basic skills for successful transition.* Baltimore: Paul H. Brookes.

Wehmeyer, M., & Palmer, S. (2003). Adult outcomes for students with cognitive disabilities three years after high school: The impact of self-determination. *Education and Training in Developmental Disabilities, 38*, 131–144.

Wehmeyer, M., & Schwartz, M. (1997). Self-determination and positive adult outcomes: A follow-up study of youth with mental retardation or learning disabilities. *Exceptional Children, 63*, 245–255.

PART VI
HOW PREPARED ARE TEACHERS?

CHAPTER 11

INCREASING PROFESSIONALISM THROUGH TEACHER PREPARATION

Elizabeth Drame

Teacher education for general education and special education teachers has many detractors (Hansen, 2008). It is asserted that the basic skills necessary for being an effective educator (e.g., understanding how to work in a bureaucracy, knowing how to work with others, and general knowledge of various subjects) can be acquired through participation in good secondary and postsecondary education and life experience. Such a view assumes that teachers operate to maintain the current social, political, and economic structures and systems and that their successful socialization into these structures is sufficient. In many schools across the nation, teachers are working in educational systems strongly influenced and directed by societal pressures to maintain the status quo. Such views render teacher preparation meaningless and unnecessary.

Supporters of teacher education have a very different perspective on the value of formal teacher preparation. While acknowledging the functional, technical, and administrative roles that teachers must occupy in schools and classrooms, they view the aim of teaching as not to perpetuate the status quo but to encourage the regeneration of new ideas and realities. This is particularly important in the area of special education. To be a successful special education teacher, one must be able to (a) navigate the bureaucratic, legal, and political dimensions of special education; (b) successfully address the cultural, social, psychological, behavioral, and intellectual needs of diverse students; (c) collaborate with a myriad of individuals and organizations; and (d) master the content and pedagogy of multiple subjects. Formal teacher preparation is critical given the complexity of skills these special educators need to possess on day 1.

THE ROLE OF STANDARDS

Despite serious debates regarding different methods for preparing special education teachers (e.g., alternative routes, distance education, and programs with traditional student teaching), most supporters of teacher education agree on the importance of professional teaching standards as an underlying framework for defining professionalism in teacher preparation programs. For example, in a national survey of special education alternative route teacher preparation programs, Rosenberg, Boyer, Sindelar, and Misra (2007) found that the majority of respondents indicated their programs were designed around professional teaching standards, particularly standards developed by the Council for Exceptional Children (CEC), the Interstate New Teacher Assessment and Support Consortium, and the National Board for Professional Teaching Standards. The CEC, the leading professional organization for special educators, disseminates professional standards for beginning and advanced special educators that have been approved by the National Council for the Accreditation of Teacher Education (NCATE) (Council for Exceptional Children, 2004). Specific areas addressed by the CEC professional standards include (1) foundations of special education, (2) development and characteristics of learners, (3) individual learning differences, (4) instructional strategies, (5) learning environments and social interactions, (6) communication, (7) instructional planning, (8) assessment, (9) professional and ethical practice, and (10) collaboration. These standards include the core knowledge and skills essential for effective special educators and serve as guiding principles for professional programs and state licensing departments. They ensure that special educators are well prepared to enter the practice of teaching. Teacher preparation programs should be the vehicle through which professional standards are taught, understood, and translated into practice.

In addition to professional standards promulgated by professional organizations, federal policy also dictates the standards individuals must meet to be judged professionals in their special education discipline. The No

Child Left Behind (NCLB) act, passed in 2001, set a national policy mandate to address the quality of the teaching force, with a particular emphasis on the academic content preparation of teachers. NCLB provided broad parameters for what should be included in each of the 50 states' definitions of a highly qualified teacher. To be considered "highly qualified," teachers must hold at least a bachelor's degree, be fully certified or licensed by the state (not waived on an emergency, temporary or provisional basis), and demonstrate content knowledge in each of the core subjects they teach (i.e., English, reading or language arts, mathematics, science, foreign language, civics and government, economics, arts, history and geography) (ESEA Section 9101 (11) Blank, 2003).

When the NLCB act was first enacted, the application to special education teachers was vague. It was not until the 2004 reauthorization of the Individuals with Disabilities Education Act (IDEA) that the implications of these teacher quality provisions for special educators were clarified. The 2004 reauthorization aligned IDEA with NCLB guidelines (Council for Exceptional Children, 2006), resulting in the requirement that new and veteran special educators meet the same criteria for teacher quality as general educators. The core expectation is that special education teachers demonstrate that they are highly qualified in all the core academic subjects they teach.

However, only special education teachers who deliver content instruction to students in the core academic subjects are required to demonstrate subject-matter competency. If they provide only consultative services to general education teachers who themselves are highly qualified in the content area, special education teachers do not have to meet the content area requirement as long as they hold a bachelors degree and full special education certification. Such consultative support may include assistance in making curricular adaptations and providing behavioral supports and accommodations. The application of NCLB criteria to special education teachers placed new and veteran secondary special education teachers, particularly those who teach multiple core academic subjects to students who have learning and emotional disabilities in self-contained settings, in a serious quandary. Although they may be fully certified in special education, many are not, according to NCLB, highly qualified to deliver instruction in core content areas. Although content knowledge is not the sole criterion for good teaching and must be combined with knowledge of learners and their development, and knowledge of teaching (Darling-Hammond & Bransford, 2005), it is nevertheless an essential component of good teaching practice. Professional organizations such as CEC acknowledge the importance of subject matter proficiency, particularly for secondary special educators

(Council for Exceptional Children, 2004), while recognizing the critical role of pedagogy in a complex profession, such as special education teaching. Other studies have validated the importance of content knowledge combined with pedagogical knowledge to produce effective teaching (Education Commission of the States, 2003).

RESEARCH-BASED EVIDENCE FOR THE EFFICACY OF TEACHER PREPARATION

There is evidence suggesting that teacher preparation programs provide critical experiences necessary for the development of core knowledge and skills for teaching. Research shows that teacher preparation programs provide valuable pedagogical coursework focusing on core concepts such as student assessment, classroom management, and curriculum development (Education Commission of the States, 2003). In addition, general agreement exists as to the value of practical experience, although there is a lack of consensus over the viability of various types of field experiences (e.g., traditional student teaching, on-the-job experiences, and extensive vs. limited preservice training field experiences).

The efficacy of special education teacher preparation programs in the development of effective educators was evaluated by Nougaret, Scruggs, and Mastropieri (2005). These researchers evaluated the teaching efficacy of first year special educators who possessed licenses after a traditional teacher preparation program with those who possessed emergency licenses but had not completed a certification program. Participants in both groups were observed twice by trained observers unaware of the teachers' license status in various grade levels (early childhood through high school), teaching various subject areas to small groups of students with varying disabilities (e.g., learning disabilities, emotional disturbance, and mental retardation). Specific skills observed included planning and preparation, classroom environment and management, and instruction. In addition, teachers were asked to complete a self-assessment rating their performance in the same skill areas. Although the skills and dispositions required for success in teaching can vary somewhat by grade level, subject area taught, and disability, the findings clearly indicated that beginning special educators with formal preparation were rated to have higher levels of competence in all areas than those with little to no formal preparation. This study provides convincing evidence of the value of teacher education programs in promoting effective practices in special education teachers. Teacher preparation programs can be viewed as agents for the development of teachers who produce successful outcomes in their students with special needs (Goe & Coggshall, 2007).

Some of the debate around the importance of teacher preparation programs revolve around the conception of teaching as a *craft* – primarily learned through practical, on-the-job experiences – vs. teaching as a *profession* – where skills are acquired through substantive preparation prior to practical application (Alter & Coggshall, 2009). An effort to bridge these two schools of thought is through the conception of teaching as a *clinical practice profession*, which serves as a useful framework for understanding the nature of many special education teacher preparation programs. This reconceptualization characterizes the profession of teaching as including the following components: (a) direct and reciprocal work with clients, (b) acquisition of complex and specialized knowledge and skills, (c) use of professional judgment based on data and other evidence, (d) the creation of professional communities of practice responsible for accountability, quality monitoring, and knowledge dissemination, and (e) the completion of rigorous academic and practical preparation through the integration of pedagogical training in clinical settings into academic courses.

The Potential of Special Education Teacher Preparation to Promote Social Justice

Professionalism in teaching should extend beyond core knowledge and skills to addressing the social aspects and consequences of educational practices (Grant & Agosto, 2008). Teacher educators have integrated perspectives such as critical theory into their programs to frame discussions around practice. How injustice and subjugation shape people's experience and understanding of the world is the focus of critical theory. A critical theory perspective is concerned in particular with the issues of power and justice and the ways that matters of race, class, disability and gender, ideologies, discourses, education, religion, and other social institutions interact to construct a social system. Inquiry that is critical must be connected to an attempt to confront the injustices of society. What makes critical theory critical is that it seeks not only to study and understand society but also to critique and change it. No social arrangements are viewed as neutral but rather as artificial constructs structured to benefit one segment of society over another (Kellner, 2003).

Teacher preparation programs have the potential to prepare the next generation of special educators who are equipped to address strident calls for advocacy and social justice for many groups of children with disabilities. Given the current state of education for many students with disabilities, particularly urban and minority students, teacher education programs are moving beyond a focus on knowledge and skills to include an emphasis on professional and ethical responsibility within a framework of social justice. This is in response to the particularly negative outcomes for specific segments of the special education population.

For example, minority students often spend the largest part of their day away from their general education classroom receiving special instruction, resulting in a disconnected and fragmented school day (Capper, Frattura, & Keyes, 2000). Many minority students with disabilities, particularly those diagnosed with emotional behavior disabilities, are excluded at higher rates from general education and placed in more restrictive classroom settings separate from their nondisabled peers, going against their federally protected right to inclusion. Teachers who are socialized in their teacher preparation programs to be aware of such injustices can work in the prereferral and special education referral processes to reduce unnecessary and unwarranted referrals. In addition, they can learn skills to collaborate effectively with general educators to improve the quality of inclusive education, thus reducing the tendency to exclude these students from general education classrooms.

Moreover, these special programs have failed to result in high student achievement as measured by postschool outcomes or standardized scores. Students in urban public school settings, particularly African-American children with disabilities are at a greater risk of experiencing negative outcomes, such as poor academic achievement (e.g., Hogansen, Powers, Geenen, Gil-Kashiwabara, & Powers, 2008; Sinclair, Christenson, & Thurlow, 2005), higher dropout rates, and higher rates of entering the criminal justice system. For example, in the United States, despite extensive efforts at providing special education for more than 25 years since the implementation of federal disability law, 22% of students with disability labels fail to complete high school, compared to 9% of students without labels (National Council on Disability, 2004). For a more specific example, in Wisconsin, 13.8% of students with disability labels drop out, compared to 8.2% without labels (Wisconsin Department of Public Instruction, 2005). Of these students, 50% of those who are labeled with emotional disturbance dropout. Furthermore, 11.68% of students with disability labels are suspended, compared to 5.15% of students without labels (Wisconsin Department of Public Instruction, 2005). Quinn, Rutherford, and Leone (2001) found that minority students with disabilities are four times more likely than their white peers to end up in correctional facilities. Strategies that have been found to be effective for increasing the likelihood of a successful transition to postsecondary education or work include those which address students' functional academic, community living, personal–social, vocational, and self-determination skills (National Council on Disability, 2004). Many of these competencies are fostered by highly effective special educators. These educators must be equipped with effective instructional strategies proven to be effective with disempowered students with disabilities. For instance, research suggests that service learning has tremendous potential to increase engagement in school, attendance, grades, and reduce the exhibition of problem behaviors (Bridgeland, DiIulio, & Wulsin, 2008). Special education teacher preparation programs have an invaluable role to play in fostering the development of these competencies.

CONCLUSION

Although consensus is difficult to achieve regarding methods for achieving the broad goals around the purposes and methods of special education teacher preparation, agreement is clear regarding the role of teacher preparation in the development of future educators (American Association of Colleges for Teacher Education, 2002). Teacher preparation programs serve an invaluable role in the provision of critical experiences necessary for the development of effective special educators. These experiences include but are not limited to (a) varied practical teaching opportunities addressing the learning needs of different students with disabilities, (b) opportunities for critical, guided reflection on the development of core skills, knowledge, and dispositions, (c) opportunities for the development of valuable partnerships and collaborative relationships, (d) training in effective instructional strategies, (e) opportunities to observe modeling of professional behavior, (f) opportunities to discuss and reflect upon social agency and justice and a critical aspect of being an educator, and (g) connection of beginning special educators to professional organizations, resources, and networks critical for long-term professional growth.

The importance of developing reflective practices as a means of encouraging professional growth is undeniable. Special educators should have a disposition that makes them less likely to attribute academic failure or disruptive behavior solely to students with disabilities. Educators, including special educators, who are able to reflect upon the ways in which their instruction can impede or promote learning, are more likely to make changes to their practices to benefit students. It can be expected that reflective educators will engage in less blaming of students, colleagues, and families and will focus more on how specific strategies may need to be modified, revamped, or eliminated in favor of other approaches. Problem-solving is the emphasis for these educators, who also work to seek out their colleagues or other professional resources for ideas and strategies. Special education teacher education programs, which embed frequent and ongoing experiences with reflection on teaching practices through course discussions and assignments, portfolios, classroom observation and feedback, and peer dialogue and be instrumental developing reflective practices in novice special educators.

In addition to supporting the development of reflective practice, special education teacher education programs can be instrumental in providing students with the tools for building partnerships with families and community-based organizations. Building the capacity of our novice special educators to create meaningful yet challenging learning experiences for students with special needs in urban school communities through leveraging community and family resources should be a goal. Through these partnerships, older students with disabilities can have substantive opportunities to grow skills that will prove critical to their transition to postsecondary education or work. Special educators can also create partnerships with professional and university student organizations, which can serve as a support network, as well as an information resource. Special education teacher education faculty can assist students with accessing these supports in a number of ways, such as serving as a faculty advisor for a university-based student organization or identifying relevant professional organizations that meet specific teacher needs. Teacher education programs remains viable and vital in the field special education and their impact on developing the next generation of special educators is clear.

REFERENCES

Alter, J., & Coggshall, J. G. (2009). *Teaching as a clinical practice profession: Implications for teacher preparation and state policy*. New York: New York Comprehensive Teacher Center and National Comprehensive Center for Teacher Quality.

American Association of Colleges for Teacher Education. (2002). *Preparing teachers to work with students with disabilities: Possibilities and challenges for special and general teacher education: A white paper*. Washington, DC: American Association of Colleges for Teacher Education. (Available at www.aacte.org. Retrieved on May 29, 2009)

Blank, R. K. (2003). *Meeting NCLB goals for highly qualified teachers: Estimates by state from survey data*. Washington, DC: Council of Chief State School Officers.

Bridgeland, J. M., DiIulio, J. J., & Wulsin, S. C. (2008). *Engaged for success: Service-learning as a tool for high school dropout prevention*. Washington, DC: Civic Enterprises, LLC.

Capper, C., Frattura, E., & Keyes, M. (2000). *Meeting the needs of all learners*. Thousand Oaks, CA: Corwin Press.

Council for Exceptional Children. (2004). *Definition of a well-prepared special education teacher*. Arlington, VA: Council for Exceptional Children Board of Directors.

Council for Exceptional Children. (2006). *Understanding IDEA 2004 regulations: Side-by-side analysis comparison and analysis. Personnel qualifications*. Arlington, VA: Council for Exceptional Children, Policy and Advocacy Services.

Darling-Hammond, L., & Bransford, J. (Eds). (2005). *Preparing teachers for a changing world*. San Francisco: Jossey-Bass.

Education Commission of the States. (2003). *Eight questions on teacher preparation: What does the research say? A summary of the findings*. Denver, CO: Education Commission of the States.

Goe, L., & Coggshall, J. (2007). *The teacher preparation – teacher practices – student outcomes relationship in special education: Missing links and new connections*. Washington, DC: National Comprehensive Center for Teacher Quality.

Grant, C. A., & Agosto, V. (2008). Teacher capacity of social justice in teacher education. In: M. Cocharn-Smith, S. Feiman-Nemser, D. J. McIntyre & K. E. Demers (Eds), *Handbook of research in teacher education: Enduring questions in changing contexts* (3rd ed., pp. 175–200). Manassas, VA: Association of Teacher Educators.

Hansen, D. T. (2008). Values and purpose in teacher education. In: M. Cocharn-Smith, S. Feiman-Nemser, D. J. McIntyre & K. E. Demers (Eds), *Handbook of research in teacher education: Enduring questions in changing context* (3rd ed., pp. 10–26). Manassas, VA: Association of Teacher Educators.

Hogansen, J. M., Powers, K., Geenen, S., Gil-Kashiwabara, E., & Powers, L. (2008). Transition goals and experiences of females with disabilities: Youth, parents, and professionals. *Exceptional Children, 74*, 215–234.

Kellner, D. (2003). *Toward a critical theory of education*. Available at http://www.gseis.ucla.edu/faculty/kellner/papers/edCT2003.htm. Retrieved on October 31, 2003.

National Council on Disability. (2004). *Improving educational outcomes for students with disabilities*. Available at http://www.ncd.gov/. Retrieved on April 10, 2009.

Nougaret, A. A., Scruggs, T. E., & Mastropieri, M. A. (2005). Does teacher education produce better special education teachers? *Exceptional Children, 71*(3), 217–229.

Quinn, M. M, Rutherford, R. B., & Leone, P. E. (2001). *Students with disabilities in correctional facilities*. Available at http://www.eric.ed.gov/. Retrieved on May 21, 2009.

Rosenberg, M. S., Boyer, K. L., Sindelar, P. T., & Misra, S. K. (2007). Alternative route programs for certification in special education: Program infrastructure, instructional delivery, and participant characteristics. *Exceptional Children, 73*(2), 224–241.

Sinclair, M. F., Christenson, S. L., & Thurlow, M. L. (2005). Promoting school completion of urban secondary youth with emotional or behavioral disabilities. *Exceptional Children, 71*, 465–482.

Wisconsin Department of Public Education. (2005). *Annual Performance Report*. Madison, WI: Wisconsin Department of Public Education.

CHAPTER 12

TEACHING IS NOT A PROFESSION: HOW GENERAL AND SPECIAL EDUCATION TEACHER EDUCATION HAVE FAILED

Barbara J. Dray and Cathy Newman Thomas

In recent years, primarily as a result of the national mandate for a "highly qualified teacher in every classroom" (No Child Left Behind Act of 2001 [NCLB], 2002), traditional teacher education practices have come under fire from various sources (Cochran-Smith & Fries, 2001, 2005; Pullin, 2004). Those urging teacher education reforms advocate vastly divergent agendas that include professionalization, deregulation, regulation, social justice, and those focused on education as a science (Cochran-Smith & Fries, 2005). Interestingly enough, reformists seem to share a common goal (although not a common solution); standards and accountability, with improved students outcomes as the "holy grail of educational reform" (Cochran-Smith & Fries, 2001, p. 9). These reform efforts have been driven by the accumulated evidence of the significant limitations of teacher education to produce an effective and sustainable teaching workforce. These limitations include the nebulous connection between measures of preservice teacher preparedness and measures of teacher quality and student outcomes (Greenwood & Maheady, 1997; Hurwitz & Hurwitz, 2005; Zimpher & Howey, 2005), in-service teacher reports that college coursework left them unprepared for the rigors of teaching (George & George, 1995; Whitaker, 2001), and the well-documented research-to-practice gap between daily instruction in schools and evidence-based practices recommended by current research (Gersten, Vaughn, Deshler, & Schiller, 1997; McLeskey & Waldron, 2004).

Current reform efforts (Cochran-Smith, 2005; Imig & Imig, 2005; Putnam & Borko, 2000) and public mandates (Individuals with Disabilities Education Improvement Act [IDEIA], 2004; NCLB, 2002) have been designed to improve teacher quality to improve student outcomes, as the teacher has been identified as the single most powerful variable that impacts student performance (Cochran-Smith & Fries, 2001; Darling-Hammond, 2000; Imig & Imig, 2005). This chapter summarizes several key issues that have impacted the quality of teacher education programs such as the development of preservice teacher knowledge, dispositions and beliefs, and skills, the nature of field experiences, and teacher shortage and retention. In addition, it serves to provide recommendations to improve teacher education in special education through making a case for strong teacher induction and apprenticeships, developing national certification to increase the prestige of the field, and closing the research-to-practice gap.

FACTORS THAT INFLUENCE THE QUALITY OF TEACHER EDUCATION PROGRAMS

Development of Knowledge

Traditionally, preservice teacher education has been conducted in college and university classrooms and has relied heavily on what Shulman (1992) called "the twin demons of lecture and textbook" (p. 1). This educational model neglects the importance and strength of preservice teachers' beliefs about teaching and content (Nietfeld & Enders, 2003; Putnam & Borko, 2000) and has been termed a *transmission model* in which teaching is telling (McLeskey & Waldron, 2004; Russell, McPherson, & Martin, 2001). The type of knowledge conveyed is considered to be *declarative* (Sternberg, 1999) or *formal* (Lundeberg & Scheurman, 1997) and is derived from theory and comprised of facts, concepts, and rules. Whitehead (1929) and more recently Bransford, Brophy, and Williams (2000) reported that this type of knowledge tends to remain inert and is unlikely to be retrieved in the very circumstances that call for its use.

Many preservice and novice teachers struggle to understand the relationship between formal knowledge and expert practice. They are typically unable to recognize the pedagogical principles that underlie expert practice and fail to transfer declarative learning into effective practice during their beginning years in the classroom (Ball, 2000; Barron & Goldman, 1994; Russell et al., 2001). Historically, teacher education programs have grappled with the tension between what Cochran-Smith and Lytle (1999) term *knowledge-for-practice* and *knowledge-in-practice*, which highlight formal knowledge versus practical knowledge. Knowledge-for-practice assumes a core set of knowledge based on empirically based practices, and the more teachers know about theory, content, and instructional approaches, the better prepared they will be. In this view, "teachers are thus consumers of knowledge that is largely produced by others, and generally are not seen as generators of knowledge" (McLeskey & Waldron, 2004, p. 5). This promotes a top-down approach to preparing teachers. In the knowledge-in-practice approach, teachers' experiences and classroom practices contribute to the construction of knowledge. According to McLeskey & Waldron (2004), this approach emphasizes that knowledge-in-action is an effective practice of "what very good teachers know, and this knowledge is not formal knowledge that is 'out there' and readily available to all but rather is embedded in the practices of good teachers" (p. 8).

Contemporary perspectives in teacher education have moved toward *knowledge-of-practice* that pushes the boundaries of teacher knowledge to an inquiry-based stance whereby schools and communities collectively construct knowledge and engage in a problem-solving approach to develop best practices in education (Cochran-Smith & Lytle, 1999). Re-thinking how knowledge is constructed and allowing for multiple pathways to the construction of knowledge seem central in preparing teachers for the realities of the classroom. This means that teaching beliefs and practices centered on a single way of knowing can significantly hinder a teacher's ability to fully teach all learners, particularly if such knowledge excludes historically marginalized groups. Multiple pathways of knowing enable a teacher to recognize the long history of existing knowledge while using knowledge as a tool to construct new meanings (Bransford, Brown, & Cocking, 2000). In this constructivist model, learning and teaching are viewed as dynamic and not static.

Development of Dispositions and Beliefs

There is strong evidence to suggest that teachers' previous experiences influence how beliefs are constructed. Furthermore, a teacher's planning, instructional decisions, and classroom practices are strongly influenced by their educational beliefs (Pajares, 1992). However, teacher educators often fail to consider the influence of teacher beliefs on the adoption of practice (see Putnam & Borko, 2000; Simmons et al., 1999), paying little heed to the established and powerful convictions that preservice teachers carry with them into their programs about what it means to be a teacher and what good teachers do (Simmons et al., 1999). With this in mind, it is essential that teacher preparation programs address teacher beliefs and take measures to dialog about previous experience that influences what they believe and the paradigms that inform their understanding of knowledge construction and the practices they enact.

Since the 1960s, there has been a pervasive deficit perspective associated with diversity in education in which students from culturally, linguistically, and economically different (CLED) backgrounds are viewed as "at-risk" or "struggling learners" in need of "extra support" to succeed in school (Townsend, 2002). As a result, teachers equate student "underachievement" or "failure" to individual or environmental factors (Valencia, 1997) rather than understanding the underlying "culture of schooling" (Hollins, 1996) as promoting mainstream practices that reproduce cultural oppression and institutional racism in the school context (Gay, 2000; Wisneski & Dray, 2009). With the continued academic failure of students from poor and minority backgrounds, it has become essential to consider the role teacher beliefs play in this perpetuation and to equip teachers with the tools of reflection to undo such inequities. Trent and Artiles (1998) stated that teacher preparation programs "have tried to deal with the cultural differences without examining the complexities of schooling in our changing society" (p. 2). Such approaches look toward celebrating differences, which potentially serve to undermine the role of cultural contexts of teaching and learning. This means that schooling is a process of acculturation and that merely celebrating differences can further perpetuate stereotypes and the tokenizing of differences (Cochran-Smith, 1995). As a result, teachers lack awareness of systemic, societal, and institutional contributions for CLED students' perceived academic failure. Clearly if teacher education programs intend to serve to advance the notion of social justice in a democratic society, then teacher candidates need to be taught the tools of reflection to critically examine their knowledge, beliefs, attitudes, and assumptions about people who are different from them and about what good teachers know and should be able to do. Just as individual experiences affect what we do, professional preparation in teacher education programs also influence the views teachers hold about their prospective students, teaching contexts, and instructional approaches (Obiakor, 2009). "It is when the many factors that can affect students' learning are not fully understood that cultural, socioeconomic, and linguistic differences can come to be viewed as students' deficits in need of remediation" (Dray & Delgado, 2008, p. 783).

Development of Professional Skills

Preservice teachers acquire skills through limited and often inauthentic practice (Brown, Collins, & Duguid, 1989). According to Greenwood and Maheady (1997), preservice teachers are not required "to demonstrate an ability to produce meaningful changes in their pupils' academic performance to be certified to teach" (p. 266). Student teaching and field experience requirements vary widely, with performance standards differing across supervisors, settings, and duration (Conderman, Morin, & Stephens, 2005; Prater & Sileo, 1998). Mentor teachers, field experience supervisors, and teacher educators may disagree about what constitutes recommended practice, and mentor teachers may be those more readily available rather than the most exemplary models of evidence-based practice (Hess, 2001; Putnam & Borko, 2000). As a result, teacher candidates may feel conflicted or confused as they attempt to please and uphold three different sets of standards of practice because teacher educators may be teaching perspectives that are quite different from what the mentor teacher does and what the supervisor is assessing. To a large extent, teacher candidates may simply adopt practices based on their own beliefs versus what is the most effective approach. In addition, student teaching does not provide authentic practice for what the first-year teacher must do; invisible systems and supports developed by experienced teachers are already in place, along with rich understandings of children's thinking that are generally not perceived or understood by the novice practitioner (Barron & Goldman, 1994; Goor & Santos, 2002; Russell et al., 2001). Many novice teachers fail to notice many of the realities of teaching, such as the complexities of assessing children's thinking and misconceptions about a topic, gauging children's engagement and questioning levels, planning and structures that support classroom management, and the complexities of teacher decision-making on the fly (Barron & Goldman, 1994).

Cumulatively, the teacher education experience is more "knowing that" than "knowing how" (Sternberg, 1999, p. 364). Information is presented in discrete subject matter and methodology classes and reinforced during field practice. Together, they result in a fragmented experience that in turn contributes to (a) struggles novice teachers experience during their early teaching years and (b) the gap between research and practice (Ball, 2000).

Sternberg (1999) noted that "the expert first-year graduate ... is still a far cry from the expert professional" (p. 165) and that expertise is developed through deliberate practice within a domain, requiring "purposeful engagement involving direct instruction, active participation, role modeling, and reward" (p. 162). Compounding the problem is that teaching can be viewed as an "unstaged" (Goor & Santos, 2002, p. 63) profession, where novice teachers begin their careers with the same responsibilities as their more experienced peers (Hurwitz & Hurwitz, 2005; Levine, 2006). In fact, in many cases, novice teachers are placed in the most challenging teaching positions while their more senior colleagues opt for less demanding teaching assignments, leaving the novice teacher in situations where their skill sets are inadequate to meet classroom demands (Russell et al., 2001; Whitaker, 2001). One consequence of this entrenched system is that students with the most significant needs, including students from culturally and linguistically diverse backgrounds, students living in poverty, and students with disabilities, are taught by those who are least prepared to meet their needs (Billingsley, 2003; Dove, 2004).

Overall, there are consequences for the poor preparation of teachers. Preservice teachers enter their preservice teacher education programs full of enthusiasm, and dedicated teacher educators work hard to prepare these promising and eager candidates for their future positions (Whitaker, 2001). In spite of the commitment of both parties, preservice teacher education is fraught with limitations and challenges that historically have had a significant and negative impact on fledgling teaching practice (Imig & Imig, 2005). The transition from preservice teaching into a novice position is rarely smooth, with indicators of acute difficulties such as high attrition rates (Dove, 2004; McLeskey, Tyler, & Flippin, 2004), the research-to-practice gap (Gersten et al., 1997; McLeskey & Waldron, 2004), and unsatisfactory outcomes for students (Greenwood & Maheady, 1997; Hurwitz & Hurwitz, 2005; Zimpher & Howey, 2005). Teacher education so frequently has fallen short of its goals for many reasons. First, the characteristics of decontexualized college classrooms bear little resemblance to the dynamic, interactive environments of school classrooms in which future teachers will practice (Shulman, 1992; Whitehead, 1929). Research has shown that this disparity will impede the transfer of knowledge from the college classroom into effective, evidence-based teaching practice (Bransford, Brown, & Cocking, 2000; Whitehead, 1929). Furthermore, the value of field experience may be hindered by its short duration, the possibility of assignment to a mentor teacher who is a less than ideal model, and the lack of a developmental progression from observation to participation in multiple classrooms with exposure to diverse models of practice and alternative perspectives (Conderman et al., 2005; Foote & Cook-Cottone, 2004; Hollins & Guzman, 2005).

To a large measure, preservice teachers in field experience are typically unaware of hidden supports; they enter classrooms where critical features such as a working curriculum and effective classroom and behavior management systems are already in place (Barron & Goldman, 1994; Goor & Santos, 2002). Moreover, unlike other performance-based professions such as medicine and law that include an extended apprenticeship period before assuming a professional role with full responsibilities, preservice teachers frequently begin their teaching careers in the most arduous classroom assignment they will ever face (Zimpher & Howey, 2005). Furthermore, they are expected to provide their students with the same quality of service as the highly experienced and expert teachers in the neighboring classrooms (Goor & Santos, 2002; Hurwitz & Hurwitz, 2005). Not surprisingly, novice teachers who have reported feeling unprepared and incompetent also reported becoming discouraged (Russell et al., 2001; Whitaker, 2001). Complaining of a lack of administrative support and insufficient opportunities to be mentored by their more experienced colleagues (Kilgore & Griffin, 1998), it is no surprise that nearly 10% of all teachers leave the field before they complete their first year in the classroom (Dove, 2004). For teachers in special education, attrition rates are particularly grim, depleting the workforce faster than it can be replenished with newly trained recruits. According to analysis of attrition data by McLeskey et al. (2004), approximately 13% of special education teachers leave their classrooms each year, either to transition to general education positions or to leave the teaching field entirely. Therefore, cumulatively, over a 4-year period, more than half of all special education teachers likely will leave the field. Irrefutably, those in teacher education have an ethical responsibility to prepare novice teachers for the classrooms they will lead by promoting the development of the kinds of beliefs, knowledge, and skills that will ready them to enter and be sustained in the workforce.

HOW TO IMPROVE THE TEACHING PROFESSION

A cursory search on the requirements for becoming a teacher, an electrician, and a medical doctor using Google yielded significant differences in the certification process. To become a medical doctor or an electrician, one goes through a national process and then submits necessary paperwork to become certified in each state of practice, rather than having a different set of requirements and process for each state. On the contrary, teaching has a discrete set of standards and certification requirements for each state, which does not guarantee that credentials will be recognized by another state. Other performance-based professions, including medical doctors and electricians, are required to engage in multiyear apprenticeships (for doctors, it is 3–5 years, and for electricians, it is 4–5 years). In addition, they receive hands-on experience while being supervised and mentored before being able to practice as a fully licensed professional. Apprenticeships for electricians typically begin after a set of required courses in math, science, and electronics, and ongoing professional training occurs throughout the apprenticeship with a minimum of 144 hours of classroom instruction and 8,000 hours of on-the-job training (eHow Careers & Work Editor, n.d.). For medical doctors, apprenticeships called residencies do not begin until successful completion of a bachelor's, MCAT, and graduate studies at an accredited medical school and last anywhere from 3 to 5 years depending on type of medicine (Santiago, n.d.). In both career tracks, electricians and medical doctors are paid a reduced wage and receive a substantial amount of on-the-job training and mentoring from seasoned, established professionals. In fact, there are gate-keeping mechanisms to ensure successful completion. It seems as a profession, the teaching field could learn from these and other similar professions to structurally improve the process of becoming fully certified to professionalize the field and make it more marketable. How then can appropriate apprenticeships be instituted in teaching?

Instituting Apprenticeships

There is long-standing research that supports new teacher induction and strong mentoring programs within the first 3 years of a teachers' career (Billingsley, 2003; Darling-Hammond, 2000) as being a leading cause for retention. Yet, a key issue in the current system of teacher education is that it assumes once a teacher receives certification, he/she is fully prepared and highly qualified (Hess, 2001). However, we know that becoming a teacher is a process whereby the first few years are consumed with learning (a) to teach, (b) the culture of the school, (c) the culture and norms of the students and families (Hollins & Guzman, 2005), and (d) establishing one's identity as a teacher (Britzman, 2003). Becoming a teacher is much more than a core set of standard knowledge and skills, it is also about dispositions and one's ability to develop relationships with colleagues, students, and their families. Most importantly, becoming a teacher is a process that evolves over time much like other professions such as medicine, engineering, law, and some trades (e.g., electrician). We would not expect doctors to be fully qualified after taking coursework in medicine until after they have had their residency with years of supervised practice. Yet, often teachers with the least amount of experience are being placed in our highest need schools (e.g., high poverty and high concentrations of at-risk learners) where teacher knowledge, skills, and beliefs matter the most. These same schools are oftentimes understaffed, under-resourced, and provide minimal supports to new teachers and would be best served by highly qualified seasoned teachers (Whitaker, 2001). Our most experienced and skilled teachers are often "rewarded" with less responsibility and choose to work in schools with the most resources leaving our highest need schools behind. Unlike other professions, such as medicine where junior doctors are given less responsibility and less pay, novice teachers are given the most responsibility and the least amount of pay (Whitaker, 2001). It is no wonder then that (a) almost 30% of teachers leave teaching within the first 5 years of their career and (b) those in high poverty schools are 50% more likely to leave than those in low poverty schools (Dove, 2004). Similarly, new teachers in urban schools leave at higher rates than those in suburban schools. Ingersoll (2001) reported that special education teachers are more likely to leave the field than any other teaching group. All of these facts make a strong case for the need to re-structure the first years of teaching to include more systematic, in-depth mentoring with reduced responsibility as teachers learn the craft of teaching.

Hess (2001) proposed a competitive model to certification whereby teachers could be hired with only a college degree (not necessarily in education), successfully passing a test of essential skills and content knowledge by grade level and discipline, as well as clearing a criminal background check. He suggested that once hired, school districts should take primary responsibility for training the new hire through intensive in-service trainings and a strong mentoring program. Drawing on the argument that teachers need to be taught within the contexts of an authentic learning environment rather than in a decontextualized college classroom, it seems more realistic that schools/colleges of education provide the foundational knowledge and work toward developing key skills and dispositions, and that an apprenticeship model be instituted for teachers to gain the hands-on experiences so needed in mastery of teaching. There is no doubt that teacher education programs continue to grapple with being able to fully cover required foundational knowledge and develop core skills and dispositions while securing appropriate placements for field experiences (Conderman et al., 2005). Additionally, it has been well noted that teacher quality is strongly associated with the extent to which these programs link content knowledge with teaching and provide real-world opportunities for teacher candidates to practice what they learn in well-supervised settings (Darling-Hammond, 2000). With this in mind, it appears that field experiences provided in many higher education programs simply are insufficient to fully develop a highly qualified teacher.

Rather than novice teachers simply being hired under the assumption of highly qualified upon receiving certification (meaning that simply being certified equals highly qualified), a newly certified teacher would be considered initially or provisionally certified until successful completion of a 3- to 5-year apprenticeship. The idea is that teachers would enter a teacher education program and take courses in the foundational knowledge or knowledge-for-practice and be taught the skills to acquire and infuse other types of knowledge needed as a teacher (such as knowledge-in-practice and knowledge-of-practice (see Cochran-Smith & Lytle, 1999). In addition, new teachers ought to be hired as apprentices receiving strong mentorship from a seasoned teacher in their certification area, phasing in responsibilities, and continuing to engage in ongoing professional development that implements a reflection and renewal process to enhance effective practices and pedagogy. Once new hires have successfully completed their apprenticeship, they should become eligible to apply for full certification. However, another consideration that needs to be addressed is the preparation and qualifications of experienced, seasoned teachers who will serve as mentors. Teachers need to be held accountable for participating in and implementing state-of-the-art research-based practices. For example, commercial pilots in the United States are required to retrain a minimum of once a year and airplane captains twice a year. They are also required to prove their competence in the new practices and required to use them; otherwise, they are forced to retrain to proficiency before they can continue flying. Imagine the improvements that could be made in the outcomes of our students if we instituted such a practice with teachers! One caution is that with more stringent requirements, teachers need to be compensated. We cannot raise the bar, ask teachers to do more, and continue to underpay them.

Making the Profession More Competitive

In an analysis of the literature on special education teacher retention and attrition, Billingsley (2003) found that there are many variables that impact the extent to which teachers stay in teaching after the first few years. Some key elements include salary, age, induction and mentoring, and qualifications and preparedness. In the study, those teachers with higher salaries were more likely to remain in their teaching position versus those at low paying salaries. The trend of teachers who remain in the field versus those who leave was represented by a "U" shaped pattern; this meant that younger and older teachers were more likely to leave the field versus those in the mid-age range. New teachers who receive strong mentoring support early on are more likely to remain in their positions and similarly those who have strong pedagogy and content preparation are more likely to stay (Darling-Hammond, 2000). Interestingly, while teachers with stronger qualifications tend to stay in the field, those teachers with higher academic achievement and higher standardized test scores on teacher license exams were found to be more likely to leave the field than teachers with lower academic performance and test scores (Singer, 1992). The perception is that more education qualifications would yield better paying jobs and make them more marketable in other fields (American Federation of Teachers, 2007; The Education Trust, 2006). Which begs the question, if the teaching field was more competitive and professionally prestigious with higher salaries and benefits, would our well-educated and best prepared be more inclined to stay?

There is a great need to have a national certification process whereby teachers have reciprocity across states. Currently, a teacher certified in one state is not necessarily eligible for certification in another state. Typically, teachers moving to other states have to re-take courses, take additional courses, pass state-mandated certification tests, and reapply for certification. While contexts may vary from state to state, it is important to note that if we are to truly reduce the teacher shortage, we need inroads for certified teachers to have reciprocity in other states. Of equal concern are teachers who are certified in other countries – particularly those who have been professionally trained in a language other than English who desire to work with the same language groups in the United States. Because of the significant shortage of certified bilingual teachers, it seems counterintuitive that such teachers are denied reciprocity in the United States. Possibly, a set of exams and apprenticeship experiences could be created to enable teachers of other languages to be more readily certified. For example, teachers who are certified in Puerto Rico, a commonwealth of the United States, are forced to redo all of their coursework to become certified in the United States. As it stands, national certification with incentives that make certification and hiring more competitive should be instituted and should include higher salaries for fully certified teachers, with reduced salaries for apprenticeship teachers, and extra pay for seasoned mentor teachers. The system should support an infrastructure for professional development based on a hierarchy of need with respect to both experience and skill, and to ensure currency and effectiveness of practice. In some states, to combat/address teacher shortages, there has been a rise in alternative certification programs whereby teachers are hired on emergency or temporary certification while completing necessary coursework through districts to become certified. Many of these alternative programs are not accredited by national professional organizations or state education agencies. However, institutions of higher education must go through rigorous processes of accreditation both at the state and national levels. If national certification was instituted, initial teacher candidates should be required to successfully complete (a) an accredited teacher education program (which would ensure that alternative programs become accredited to prepare teachers for certification), (b) national teacher licensure exams (depending on content area and age level), and (c) a criminal background check before entering a 3- to 5-year apprenticeship. School districts should be given incentives for having adequate capacity to institute an apprenticeship program in which (a) highly qualified seasoned teachers would mentor and monitor ongoing professional development, (b) the infrastructure for ongoing professional development was established (e.g., resources, time allotment, funding, mechanism for selecting professional development, and staff), and (c) apprentice teachers and newly certified teachers were hired to complete a portion of their apprenticeships in high needs schools with incentives. For those coming from other countries, successful completion of an apprenticeship should be part of the process for certification reciprocity.

Closing the Research to Practice Gap

Education researchers have long debated and speculated about the research to practice gap (Gersten et al., 1997). Who is to blame for the gap in research to practice is arguable and defensible from multiple perspectives. However, it is important to consider the ways in which these arguments have been constructed so that we may consider how to ameliorate these potential barriers. McLeskey and Waldron (2004, p. 4) summarized some of the main arguments:

> Some blame researchers for failing to produce research-based practices that reflect the realities of the classrooms ... Others blame teachers, suggesting that some choose to ignore research-based methods, or use less effective methods because they are familiar with these methods. Still, others have suggested that the problem with translating research to practice may be traced back to the preparation of teachers. These critics thus blame teacher educators, and suggest that pre-service preparation programs do not

adequately provide future teachers with knowledge regarding effective practices and experiences where they learn to.

How then do teacher preparation programs respond to the above critiques? Teacher educators need to engage teacher candidates in the process of becoming consumers of research, healthy skeptics, and skilled practitioners who engage in research as part of their instructional practice with the understanding that research continues to evolve and teachers must ethically remain ethically informed. In other fields of study (e.g., psychology, communications, and business), it is common for undergraduate students to engage with advanced theoretical constructs and contemporary issues as well as peer-reviewed journal articles. In education, oftentimes, such literature is reserved for the graduate level candidate, which is highly problematic. Early in their careers, teacher candidates need to be exposed to and become consumers of research. Just like teaching is a process and a skill so is being able to understand research and application to the classroom. Greenwood and Maheady (2001) suggested ways that teacher preparation programs can better prepare teachers to become consumers of research. "Pre-service teachers should learn (a) what research is; (b) what the purposes of basic and applied research are; (c) how researchers and practitioners should communicate what they know; (d) how to evaluate research; and (e) how researchers and teachers can collaborate around evidence of student learning" (as cited in McLeskey & Waldron, 2004, p. 5).

It is critically important that teachers need to become healthy skeptics of research. A common belief is that scientific empirically based practices will promote equitable education for all students because research-based practices have been proven effective; thus they must work for *all* students (Obiakor, 2009). However, many of the practices that have been researched are mainstream constructions of effective teaching practices and have not been tested on populations for which they are now being used.

CONCLUSION

With the increasing demand of highly qualified, the continued attacks on the teaching profession, and threat of replacing teacher education with field-based alternative certification programs, teacher education programs across the nation need to come together to advocate for nationalizing the certification process to ratchet up the preparation of teachers and ensure that all teachers are consumers and practitioners of research. Similar to other professions, it is important that teachers gain a deep mastery and breadth of knowledge before entering the field as a practitioner to include knowledge-in-practice, knowledge-of-practice, and knowledge-for-practice (Cochran-Smith & Lytle, 1999). Preservice teachers must be provided not only with foundational knowledge, empirical understandings, and instructional practices during their coursework, but they also must be taught the art of inquiry so that they can continue to build and access different sources of knowledge in the classroom as a tool for learning. Equally important are the quality and depth of hands-on field-based experiences where preservice teachers have the opportunity to practice their craft and receive systematic feedback to develop mastery. It is no longer acceptable to equate certification with highly qualified because we know that becoming a highly qualified teacher takes many years of practice along with simultaneous reflection and ongoing professional development. With current legal mandates to implement evidenced-based practices, it is equally important that teacher education programs equip preservice teachers to become consumers, skeptics, and practitioners of research. And finally, to become more respected as a profession, the need to nationalize the certification process should take precedence. We can no longer afford to have separate and not equal certification standards across states. If we are to survive and improve as a profession, we must take steps to assert our stance that teaching *is* a profession!

REFERENCES

American Federation of Teachers. (2007). *Meeting the challenge: Recruiting and retaining teachers in hard-to-staff schools.* Washington, DC: Author.

Ball, D. L. (2000). Bridging practices: Intertwining content and pedagogy in teaching and learning to teach. *Journal of Teacher Education, 51*(3), 241–247.

Barron, L., & Goldman, E. (1994). Integrating technology with teacher preparation. In: B. Means (Ed.), *Technology and education reform* (pp. 81–110). San Francisco: Jossey-Bass.

Billingsley, B. S. (2003). *Special education teacher retention and attrition: A critical analysis of the literature.* Gainesville, FL: Center on Personnel Studies in Special Education.

Bransford, J. D., Brophy, S., & Williams, S. (2000). When computer technologies meet the learning sciences: Issues and opportunities. *Journal of Applied Developmental Psychology, 21*(1), 59–84.

Bransford, J. D., Brown, A. L., & Cocking, R. R. (2000). In: *How people learn: Brain, mind, experience, and school* (pp. 190–205). Washington, DC: National Academy Press.

Britzman, D. P. (2003). *Practice makes practice: A critical study of learning to teach.* Albany, NY: SUNY.

Brown, J. S., Collins, A., & Duguid, P. (1989). Situated cognition and the culture of learning. *Educational Researcher, 18*, 32–42.

Cochran-Smith, M. (1995). Color blindness and basket making are not the answers: Confronting the dilemmas of race, culture, and language diversity in teacher education. *American Educational Research Journal, 32*(3), 493–522.
Cochran-Smith, M. (2005). The politics of teacher education and the curse of complexity. *Journal of Teacher Education, 56*(3), 181–185.
Cochran-Smith, M., & Fries, M. K. (2001). Sticks, stones, and ideology: The discourse of reform in teacher education. *Educational Researcher, 30*(8), 3–15.
Cochran-Smith, M., & Fries, M. K. (2005). Researching teacher education in changing times: Politics and paradigms. In: M. Cochran-Smith & K. M. Zeichner (Eds), *Studying teacher education: The report of the AERA Panel on Research and Teacher Education* (pp. 69–110). Mahwah, NJ: Lawrence Erlbaum.
Cochran-Smith, M., & Lytle, S. (1999). Relationships of knowledge and practice: Teacher learning in community. *Review of Research in Education, 24*, 249–305. Washington, DC: American Educational Research Association.
Conderman, G., Morin, J., & Stephens, J. T. (2005). Special education student teaching practices. *Preventing School Failure, 49*(3), 5–10.
Darling-Hammond, L. (2000). Teacher quality and student achievement: A review of state policy evidence. *Educational Policy Analysis Archives, 8*(1).
Dove, M. K. (2004). Teacher attrition: A critical American and international education issue. *Delta Kappa Gamma Bulletin, 71*(1), 8–30.
Dray, B. J., & Delgado, R. (2008). Teacher beliefs about students. In: E. Provenzo (Ed.), *Encyclopedia for social and cultural foundations of education* (pp. 781–783). Thousand Oaks, CA: Sage.
eHow Careers & Work Editor. (n.d.). How to become an electrician. Available at http://www.ehow.com/how_8118_become-electrician.html. Retrieved on June 3, 2009.
Foote, C. J., & Cook-Cottone, C. P. (2004). Field experiences in high-need, urban settings: Analysis of current practice and insights for change. *The Urban Review, 36*(3), 189–210.
Gay, G. (2000). *Culturally responsive teaching: Theory, research, and practice.* New York: Teacher's College Press.
George, N. L., & George, M. P. (1995). An exploratory study of teachers of students with emotional and behavioral disorders: To leave or to stay. *Remedial and Special Education, 16*(4), 227–236.
Gersten, R., Vaughn, S., Deshler, D. D., & Schiller, E. (1997). What we know about using research findings: Implications for improving special education practice. *Journal of Learning Disabilities, 30*(5), 466–476.
Goor, M. B., & Santos, K. S. (2002). *To think like a teacher: Cases for special education interns and novice teachers.* Boston: Allyn & Bacon.
Greenwood, C. R., & Maheady, L. (2001). Are future teachers aware of the gap between research and practice and what they should know? *Teacher Education and Special Education, 24*, 333–347.
Greenwood, C. R., & Maheady, L. (1997). Measurable change in student performance: Forgotten standard in teacher preparation? *Teacher Education and Special Education, 20*(3), 265–275.
Hess, F. M. (2001). *Tear down this wall: The case for a radical overhaul of teacher certification* (21st Century School Project). Washington, DC: Progressive Policy Institute.
Hollins, E. (1996). *Culture in school learning: Revealing the deep meaning.* Mahwah, NJ: Lawrence Erlbaum Associates.

Hollins, E., & Guzman, M. T. (2005). Research on preparing teachers for diverse populations. In: M. C. Smith & K. Zeichner (Eds), *Studying teacher education: The report of the AERA Panel on Research and Teacher Education* (pp. 477–548). Mahwah, NJ: Lawrence Erlbaum.

Hurwitz, N., & Hurwitz, S. (2005). The challenge of teacher quality: High standards and expectations must apply to teachers as well as students. *American School Board Journal*, *194*(4), 38–41.

Imig, D., & Imig, S. (2005). The learned report on teacher education. *Change*, *37*(5), 58–65.

Individuals with Disabilities Education Improvement Act (IDEIA). (2004). Pub. L., No. 108–446.

Ingersoll, R. (2001). *Teacher turnover, teacher shortages, and the organization of schools*. Seattle: University of Washington, Center for the Study of Teaching and Policy.

Kilgore, K. L., & Griffin, C. C. (1998). Beginning special educators: Problems of practice and the influence of school context. *Teacher Education and Special Education*, *21*(3), 155–173.

Levine, A. (2006). Expectations for education schools are misplaced. *The Chronicle of Higher Education* (March 10), B53–B54.

Lundeberg, M. A., & Scheurman, G. (1997). Looking twice means seeing more: Developing pedagogical knowledge through case analysis. *Teaching and Teacher Education*, *13*(8), 783–797.

McLeskey, J., Tyler, N. C., & Flippin, S. S. (2004). The supply of and demand for special education teachers: A review of the research regarding the chronic shortage of special education teachers. *The Journal of Special Education*, *38*(1), 5–21.

McLeskey, J., & Waldron, N. L. (2004). Three conceptions of teacher learning: Exploring the relationship between knowledge and the practice of teaching. *Teacher Education and Special Education*, *27*(1), 3–14.

Nietfeld, J. L., & Enders, C. K. (2003). An examination of student teacher beliefs: Interrelationships between hope, self-efficacy, goal orientations, and beliefs about learning. *Current Issues in Education [online]*, *6*(5). Available at http://cie.ed.asu.edu/volume6/number5/

No Child Left Behind Act of 2001. (2002). 20 U.S.C. 70 & 6301 et seq.

Obiakor, F. E. (2009). Demographic changes on public education for culturally diverse exceptional learners: Making teacher preparation programs accountable. *Multicultural Learning and Teaching*, *4*(1), 90–110.

Pajares, F. M. (1992). Teachers' beliefs and educational research: Cleaning up a messy construct. *Review of Educational Research*, *62*(3), 307–332.

Prater, M. A., & Sileo, T. W. (1998). School-university partnerships in special education field experiences. *Remedial and Special Education*, *19*(6), 323–337.

Pullin, D. (2004). Accountability, autonomy, and academic freedom in educator preparation programs. *Journal of Teacher Education*, *55*(4), 300–312.

Putnam, R. T., & Borko, H. (2000). What do new views of knowledge and thinking have to say about research on teacher learning? *Educational Researcher*, *29*(1), 4–15.

Russell, T., McPherson, S., & Martin, A. K. (2001). Coherence and collaboration in teacher-education reform. *Canadian Journal of Education*, *26*, 7–55.

Santiago, A. (n.d.). How to become a medical doctor. Available at http://healthcareers.about.com/od/physiciancareers/ht/MedicalDoctor.htm. Retrieved June 3, 2009.

Shulman, L. S. (1992). Toward a pedagogy of cases teacher-written cases with commentaries: A teacher-researcher collaboration. In: J. H. Shulman (Ed.), *Case methods in teacher education* (pp. 1–33). New York: Teachers College Press.

Simmons, P. E., Emory, A., Carter, T., Coker, T., Finnegan, B., Crockett, D., Richardson, L., Yager, R., Craven, J., Tillotson, J., Brunkhort, H., Twiest, M., Hossain, K., Gallagher, J., Duggan-Hass, D., Parker, J., Cajas, F., Alshannag, Q., McGlamery, S., Krockover, J., Adams, P., Spector, B., LaPorta, T., James, B., Rearden, K., & Labuda, K. (1999). *Journal of Research in Science Teaching*, *36*(8), 930–954.

Singer, J. D. (1992). Are special educators' career paths special? Results from a 13-year longitudinal study. *Exceptional Children*, *59*, 262–279.

Sternberg, R. J. (1999). Intelligence as developing expertise. *Contemporary Educational Psychology*, *24*, 359–375.

The Education Trust. (2006). *Missing the mark: An education trust analysis of teacher-equity plans*. Washington, DC: Author.

Townsend, B. L. (2002). Leave no teacher behind: A bold proposal for teacher education. *International Journal of Qualitative Studies in Education*, *15*(6), 727–738.

Trent, S. C., & Artiles, A. J. (1998). Multicultural teacher education in special and bilingual education: Exploring multiple measurement strategies to assess teacher learning. *Remedial and Special Education*, *19*(1), 2–6.

Valencia, R. R. (1997). In: *The evolution of deficit thinking: Educational thought and practice* (pp. 20–35). Washington, DC: Falmer Press.

Whitaker, S. D. (2001). Supporting beginning special education teachers. *Focus on Exceptional Children*, *34*(4), 1–18.

Whitehead, A. N. (1929). *Aims of education*. New York: The Free Press.

Wisneski, D. B., & Dray, B. J. (2009). Examining diversity through mindful reflection and communication. *Focus in Teacher Education*, *9*(3), 2–4, 6.

Zimpher, N. L., & Howey, K. R. (2005). The politics of partnerships for teacher education redesign and school renewal. *Journal of Teacher Education*, *56*(3), 266–271.